MEDICAL TALK
AND MEDICAL WORK

This book is dedicated to John Stoeckle,
physician and social scientist

MEDICAL TALK
AND MEDICAL WORK

The Liturgy of the Clinic

Paul Atkinson

SAGE Publications
London · Thousand Oaks · New Delhi

First published 1995

All rights reserved. No part of this publication may be
reproduced, stored in a retrieval system, transmitted or
utilized in any form or by any means, electronic, mechanical,
photocopying, recording or otherwise, without permission in
writing from the Publishers.

 SAGE Publications Ltd
6 Bonhill Street
London EC2A 4PU

SAGE Publications Inc
2455 Teller Road
Thousand Oaks, California 91320

SAGE Publications India Pvt Ltd
32, M-Block Market
Greater Kailash - I
New Delhi 110 048

British Library Cataloguing in Publication data

A catalogue record for this book is available from the British
Library

ISBN 0 8039 7730 1
ISBN 0 8039 7731 X (pbk)

Library of Congress catalog card number 95-068384

Typeset by Type Study, Scarborough
Printed in Great Britain at the University Press, Cambridge

Contents

Acknowledgements

A great many people have contributed directly or indirectly to the work contained within this monograph. Unfortunately, the people who helped in the most direct manner – by allowing me to observe and record their work as haematologists – are precisely those who must remain anonymous. I am none the less in their debt. John Stoeckle encouraged me to develop some of the ideas I have presented here, and to undertake the fieldwork as I did. Sara Delamont has unfailingly supported me for over twenty years and continues to be the ideal companion, collaborator and critic. My past and present colleagues at Cardiff have helped me immeasurably over the years: I am especially grateful to Anne Murcott, Mick Bloor and Amanda Coffey. None of those friends and colleagues can be held responsible for the contents of this work: its shortcomings are mine alone.

The preparation of various drafts of this book has been helped by Liz Renton, Pauline Donovan and Jackie Swift. The fieldwork was undertaken during a period of sabbatical leave from University College Cardiff (as it was then called), and I worked on early analyses while I was a visiting scholar at Boston University, at the University of California, San Francisco, and at the University of California, Davis. I am grateful to those institutions for their generous support.

Introduction

I originally intended to call this book *Blood and Judgement* (deliberately misrepresenting *Hamlet*). Blood, because the book's empirical basis is a study of haematologists; and judgement because it evokes how doctors reason and discuss the evidence they assemble about their patients. It is not, however, just about a group of haematologists – a highly specialized segment of the medical profession who deal with disorders of the blood system, such as leukaemias, anaemias, haemophilia or thalassaemia. Frankly, I suspect that very few people would want to read a book that was exclusively about such specialists – unless perhaps it dealt with one of the more dramatic medical and social problems of our day such as AIDS. My intention, as I try to make clear throughout the book, is to raise more general issues in the sociology and anthropology of medicine through my detailed empirical work in that one specialty. Haematology was chosen specifically in order to provide the opportunity to explore those broader analytic interests.

The data were collected during a period of study leave from Cardiff. Their nature and my subsequent use of them reflect the fact that my time for data collection 'in the field' was fairly restricted. In sharp contrast to my experience of ethnographic work in a teaching hospital for my doctoral research, I could not conceive this project as long-term fieldwork. This book is not the fruit of a general ethnography. I did not immerse myself in my chosen research site for a protracted period of fieldwork. My main data collection was undertaken in the United States over a period of about ten weeks, and was supplemented by a similar period of work in a British setting.

As I explain in Chapter 1, my foreshadowed problems were well focused, therefore, before I embarked on the field research itself. None the less, even within such self-imposed limits, I gathered a fair amount of data, and developed a number of ideas and insights that I had not foreseen prior to the research itself. In this book I do not cover all the analytic themes thrown up by my time among the haematologists, nor do I present a great deal of the data themselves. Indeed, because I have sought to explore general themes through a highly selective use of those data, rather little of them actually appears in the book. For that reason, amongst, others, this is not a richly illustrated peek into the backrooms of medicine, even though I believe it raises and illuminates important issues about such settings. In that sense, my research interests were, from the outset, more formal than those associated with general ethnography and grounded theorizing.

It is necessary for me to say a little more about my use of the data at this early stage. It will be seen that I use data extracts – especially segments of transcript – to illustrate and develop my arguments. It will also become apparent that I do not normally rely on short snippets and quotes lifted out of the data. I prefer to use a smaller number of *extensive* sequences of data. I have explained that strategy in another publication (Atkinson, 1992a) and I do not recapitulate all of my argument here. Suffice it to say that my selective citation of lengthy data extracts is a deliberate strategy. I have been struck by the need to preserve the *form* of the talk and interaction I report. That form may unfold over protracted sequences of interaction: narratives and arguments are not captured adequately by the accumulation of short gobbets of talk. It is important, for instance, to trace how a particular patient's case is assembled, either by a single physician or collaboratively in a round or conference. That places something of a premium on the reader's patience in working her or his way through the selected data extracts. As I explain and justify in the first chapter, I have done my best to ease the reader's task.

My strategy in using and presenting such extracts means that I have not done full justice to some of the linguistic or discourse features that can be identified in the corpus of data. I have not even commented on all the possible features of the data reproduced in this book. My intention is to make available some rather more technical analyses in detailed papers in due course. For the purposes of this book, therefore, I have tried to keep the arguments accessible and their scope broad, despite the detail of the fieldwork itself.

I have now published a number of things about the writing of qualitative research (Atkinson, 1990, 1992b) and it might be thought as a consequence that this book would display some of the textual variety about which I have commented. It does not. Despite the interest displayed in this book about the ethnopoetics of medicine, its own textual forms are ordinary. I have made absolutely no attempt to experiment with my own narrative forms. I have never advocated gratuitous textual experimentation, and I found no analytic, sociological advantage in departing from academic convention in constructing this work. That decision, of course, does not preclude the construction of other texts in different forms, for different audiences elsewhere (cf. Richardson, 1990). In the meantime, this is a stubbornly conventional text, which attempts no experimental approaches to textual representation.

In many ways, however, representation in a more general sense is the guiding theme of the book as a whole. In paying detailed attention to the everyday work and talk of haematologists I seek to explore how they produce representations of haematological disorders. That is, how they produce and reproduce knowledge about particular medical conditions. I seek to convey how they see and describe the medical phenomena that are their stock in trade; how they describe and narrate their cases to their medical colleagues; how they seek to persuade one another about diagnoses and clinical management; how they justify and legitimate their knowledge and opinions. I try to give some insight into the visual and oral culture of haematology, and through that, to the frameworks of knowledge characteristic of much contemporary medicine.

In Chapter 1 I outline some features of the research itself, and comment more fully on the foreshadowed problems that informed the work. I set the scene and link this work with other contributions to the sociology of medical knowledge, with special reference to the ways in which medical knowledge is reproduced. In Chapters 2 and 3 I map out some of the sociological agenda for this work. In particular, I comment on the representation of medical work and medical knowledge in contemporary sociology and anthropology of medicine. In grounding my own contribution in the relevant disciplinary literatures I try to map out some of the absences that I detect in their treatment of medical work and medical discourse. I suggest that the field displays some notable biases and weaknesses, not least with regard to the everyday production of disease and pathology. My own perspective is constructivist, in that I seek to emphasize the *work* that goes into the social production of medical knowledge. I seek to justify such a position through a commentary on some of the issues surrounding constructivism. I also suggest that the sociological and anthropological constructions of medical work have been unduly biased, as a consequence of their repeated examination of doctor–patient encounters. I explain how I seek to redress that bias by concentrating here on doctor–doctor interaction. Indeed, the patients who are talked *about* by the physicians whose work I report are virtually absent as social actors in this book. I realize that such a treatment will irk some readers and commentators. It is, for all that, a deliberate choice on my part. I do so in order to point up some of the ways in which patients are constructed and reconstructed as objects of a medical discourse that is enacted away from the patients themselves.

In doing so I go on in the remaining chapters to discuss some of the processes of work and talk that go into the production of medical knowledge about patients and about their conditions. In Chapter 4 I concentrate on how aspects of patients' bodies are rendered visible and legible through medical work and medical talk. There I comment generally on how clinical practices and the technical division of labour in the modern clinic render the body amenable to the varieties of gaze available to the medical specialist. I then develop that approach with a more detailed treatment of how seeing and talking are articulated. The gaze is mediated and shaped by the discursive resources – of describing and classifying – that are socially shared and socially transmitted in the course of instruction and collegial discourse.

In Chapters 5, 6 and 7 I develop further my discussion of forms of medical discourse. In Chapter 5 I try to bring out how clinical cases are constructed through the narratives that clinicians construct about patients, and that they share with their colleagues on numerous occasions. Here therefore I start to develop my analysis of the talk that is produced in the course of clinical rounds and conferences. Many authors have now written about the narrative form of patients' experience of illness. Here I seek to reverse that emphasis by concentrating on physicians' narratives. In Chapter 6 I develop that argument further. There I propose that in the construction of such case-talk clinicians encode the credibility of their own and others' work. Here I address the recurrent issue of *uncertainty* in clinical work, and again pick up on some of my own earlier preoccupations. I try to exemplify how case narratives can, with considerable delicacy, convey the degree of certainty or uncertainty that is to be placed upon the evidence that is recounted. The narratives of case-talk do not merely chronicle the events of the patient's past history and current hospital admission: they contain evaluations of prior and current medical work and implicitly construct the trust that is to be placed on it. In a similar vein I go on in Chapter 7 to examine how knowledge and opinion are warranted through forms of talk. I pick up on the idea of *voices*. I suggest that medicine is expressed in several voices that may conflict with and interrupt one another. In particular, I illustrate how the voice of medical science contrasts with the voice of experience. I suggest how personal knowledge is conveyed through the forms of anecdotes and maxims.

My goal throughout is to show how medical work and medical knowledge are enacted through the rhetorical forms of the clinic. I refer metaphorically to the liturgy of the clinic in order to allude to the special quality of medicine's forms of talk. Like sacred liturgies the recurrent, even ritualized, occasions of talk about medical cases are potent methods for the affirmation of participants' membership in the professional culture. While I do not endorse the idea of a unified culture of biomedicine, I do believe that the forms of medical knowledge and discourse provide durable and symbolically powerful means for the socialization of practitioners and for the daily legitimation of their work. In one sense, medicine changes rapidly. Its knowledge-base undergoes constant transformation, and its structures change as a consequence of shifts in national policies, organizational arrangements and constraints of resourcing. On the other hand, many of the cultural forms I address have shown remarkable stability. Their origins are to be found in the earliest periods of modern medicine and before. The ceremonials and liturgies of the clinic express not just contemporary knowledge and practice. They also recapitulate long-standing and deeply embedded idioms of medical thought and practice.

1

Work among the Haematologists

Foreshadowed problems

This book is based primarily on fieldwork among haematologists – medical practitioners who specialize in problems of the blood system – in the United States and Britain. It is not, however, intended to be a work that is just 'about' haematology. Blood is undoubtedly important. Indirectly, through such contemporary concerns as AIDS and hepatitis, and the tragic irony of the treatment of haemophiliacs, blood and its management have become part of the general discourse of social problems. That is more or less coincidental to the present work. Equally, blood has powerful mythological and symbolic significance. The literature of social anthropology, for instance, is replete with descriptions of blood as a natural symbol (Douglas, 1970). My interests here, however, are not with blood *per se*. In essence, the empirical focus could be on any of a number of medical specialties. My intention is to produce a *micro-sociology of medical knowledge*. By that I mean a sociological account of the organized ways in which medical knowledge is produced and reproduced. I am interested in how that is accomplished as the everyday work of medical and other workers in clinical and laboratory settings.

To that end, therefore, fragments of data from fieldwork in haematology will be used throughout the book to illustrate and develop more general arguments concerning medical work and medical knowledge. Throughout the following chapters I shall address a series of issues in the contemporary sociology and anthropology of medicine. The *specific* data on haematology will thus be used to develop *general* arguments.

My work in haematology was not accidental or random, however. It derived from a very particular set of interests and commitments. Having worked in and taught the sociology of medicine for some time, I became very aware of its *partial* nature. The literature betrayed a very patchy coverage of medical settings and medical activities. As I shall discuss in more detail subsequently, it was thoroughly clear that social scientists had devoted a good deal of attention to medical consultations between practitioners and their patients. It was equally clear, however, that there were many aspects and areas of medical work that regularly escaped the notice of sociologists and anthropologists. One such area that I was particularly concerned about was the work of the laboratory and its associated regions. A great deal of modern medical work goes on away from the patient and the consultation. There are many specialists who are not necessarily consulted by the client or patient, but rather are consulted by fellow medical practitioners. Those specialists have important roles to play in the socially organized production of 'disease' in the modern clinic. They are crucial in the contemporary social and technical division of health care. They may occupy key positions in processes of diagnosis and other adjudications of medical work.

I became aware of the research potential of such medical specialties when conducting my first fieldwork in the Edinburgh medical school in the 1970s (Atkinson, 1976, 1981a). From time to time the medical students (and I, therefore) would attend presentations at which the clinicians who normally taught us were joined by others, including clinical pathologists. During my fieldwork in general surgery, for instance, pathologists would present and comment on frozen sections or other evidence gathered in the course of surgical treatment or exploration. What struck me at the time was a strong impression (I could not document it more strongly than that) that there was a marked difference in the evidence and oral testimony presented by the clinicians and the pathologists.

It appeared to be the case that the presentation of, say, microscopic evidence permitted the pathologists to adjudicate what disease process was in fact detectable. While the clinicians assembled their case from the diverse sources of evidence available to them (history, clinical examination, X-rays, tests, endoscopy), the pathologists' evidence gave every appearance of somehow being more definitive. In the discussions I observed the pathologists seemed to be granted the last word. They could adjudicate for instance whether a lesion was malignant or not, and how it should be described. At the time of the original fieldwork it was not possible to amplify on that theme, or even to explore further whether it was based on a well-founded hunch on my part. In any event it was clear that any exploration of such an analytic theme would require better data than I had at that time. More intensively focused fieldwork was called for, and it would be necessary to gather audio-tapes of the spoken presentations and interactions in order to capture their distinctive forms and contents.

When the opportunity presented itself for further fieldwork in medicine, therefore, I aimed to undertake ethnographic fieldwork in a specialty such as clinical pathology. It was also my intention to undertake fieldwork in the United States as well as in Britain. This would not take the form of a general ethnography of one or more medical settings. On the contrary, the fieldwork would be very precisely focused. It would be concerned with two related processes: how the specialists defined and adjudicated the presence of disease; how they discussed, negotiated and transmitted their expert opinions in company with other medical practitioners.

In the event, the research took a slightly different turn, but remained focused on the same underlying issues. The fieldwork was conducted not among clinical pathologists, but among haematologists. The reasons were primarily a series of happy accidents. Some of the details cannot be discussed, as they would breach the confidentiality of the research. In short, a colleague from the United States chanced to ask me at an international conference what my research plans were. I outlined to him my interests in pathological disciplines, and the interface between the clinic and the clinical laboratory. He expressed interest, but we discussed the matter no further, and I thought little more about the conversation. I was therefore surprised and delighted when my sponsor and gatekeeper (as he had become) wrote to me to report he had negotiated preliminary access to rounds in clinical pathology and haematology in a major teaching hospital, a major local university would probably give me status as a visiting scholar, and I could also have an honorary appointment at the hospital itself. I hastily revised the preliminary plans I had drawn up to spend part of my sabbatical year at another American university, and responded with enthusiasm. I also wrote to the two Chiefs of Service my sponsor had mentioned.

I arranged to pass through the university city in which the teaching hospital is located on my way to another international conference and was thus able to negotiate my access there before I embarked on my precious fieldwork. In the interim I had also begun to negotiate access with equivalent medical services in a British teaching hospital. Having had the possibilities of work in both Haematology and Pathology services opened up in the United States, I approached the equivalent departments in a British setting.

My experiences with both specialties, in Britain and the USA, were similar, and determined the precise outcome of the research. The pathologists I approached were, at best, lukewarm and at worst chose not to respond to any overtures I made. Even the senior pathologist in the American hospital – who had apparently agreed to my research in general terms – proved unwilling or unable to go so far as to set up any practical access to his colleagues. The reception offered by the haematologists, on the other hand, was entirely accommodating. Not only were the respective Chiefs of Service sympathetic to my proposed research, but they were able to indicate just how I could establish a practical presence with some of their colleagues, and so observe their everyday work.

It transpired, therefore, that I collected my data in two departments of haematology. As I have indicated, the research was not intended to produce a comprehensive ethnography of haematological work. The work was more restricted and more narrowly focused than that. It was restricted in time. Practical constraints and competing demands meant that my fieldwork in the United States occupied ten weeks. The complementary work in Britain was never intended to be very substantial; I wanted to generate some data for comparative purposes. For the purpose of this monograph, the American data produced the main illustrations.

The haematological settings more than adequately met my empirical and theoretical needs. The American context in particular provided precisely the data needed to address the foreshadowed problems I had formulated for the research. Indeed, haematology is an especially appropriate specialty in which to explore such issues, precisely because its practice typically encompasses aspects of general medicine and clinical oncology on the one hand, and clinical pathology on the other. In their everyday work haematologists singly and collectively enact those aspects of medicine I wanted to follow. Their work takes them from the bedside to the laboratory. In a following section I shall briefly outline the settings in which the data were gathered, and will provide a brief characterization of the routines and realities that prevailed there.

In the interim, a further foreshadowed problem needs to be addressed. While I was concerned with the nature of laboratory medicine (broadly defined) and its relationships with clinical practice I was also interested in the use of rhetoric and narrative in medical settings. Again, these commitments will be elaborated on in due course. At this juncture, however, it is worth noting that this too derived directly from reflections on my fieldwork among medical students.

I had for some time become interested in re-reading and re-analysing the field data I had collected in the Edinburgh medical school. There were substantial chunks of data that had never led to any of my published analyses. After the passage of some fifteen years, they no longer had credibility as data *per se*. (Although I feel sure that in fact affairs had changed little in the intervening years: the ceremonies of teaching rounds seem remarkably impervious to change, as can be gauged from such historical data as are available to us, see Atkinson, 1989 and Davenport, 1987.) I therefore subjected the data (those derived from ethnographic fieldwork in Surgery in particular) to a re-analysis. The results of that retrospective exercise have been published elsewhere, and are not recapitulated in detail here (see Atkinson, 1992a). One general feature of the exercise is pertinent to the present work, however.

In re-working my data from Surgery, I became preoccupied with aspects of the *rhetoric* of medical work and medical instruction. Implicit in the early published accounts, but made explicit in the re-analysis, were the rhetorical devices used to construct and convey the cases that provided the basis for so much medical discussion. On re-reading my own field data I was forcibly struck – as I had not been when I first analysed them – by the presence of various narrative and descriptive methods that had been used by clinicians to generate and reproduce medical knowledge. I was aware of instances where surgeons artfully created *stories* about patients and their conditions. These narratives could take various forms and serve different functions. Sometimes they would be akin to mysteries or cliff-hangers, sometimes atrocity stories, sometimes morality tales of success and failure. A great deal of medical work and instruction was couched in spoken performances. One could think of medical work in terms of rhetorical skills. One could start to think in terms of an *ethnopoetics* of medical work (Atkinson, 1992a).

In foreshadowing the research reported and drawn on here, therefore, I hoped to be able to undertake systematic investigation of at least some aspects of rhetoric and narrative performance. In negotiating the research sites in haematology I hoped to be able to combine ethnographic fieldwork of a conventional (albeit very focused and selective) variety with tape-recordings of selected episodes of medical interaction. As I have indicated already, my focus in this latter area was primarily on talk between physicians. While there was no irrational desire to avoid doctor–patient interactions, there was no intention to recapitulate the considerable volume of research that has already been published on the latter topic. It was, therefore, the intention to concentrate on talk and work that would take place *within* the team of clinicians, or between them and other hospital personnel. In foreshadowing the research, therefore, I did so in the following terms.

I wanted to examine how the facts of medically defined disease are produced and shared between medical practitioners and others; how they persuade one another of the facts of the case; equally, how they construct the case itself; how senior clinicians coach and instruct students and junior colleagues and so reproduce the orthodoxies of medical thought, knowledge and talk. I hoped in addition to be able to develop some insight into how clinicians coach colleagues and juniors to *see* those facts. Confronted with the normal visual evidence and arrays – from the microscope, the X-ray film, or whatever – the clinician needs to learn how to observe those phenomena that correspond with the normal features of anatomy, physiology and pathology. Again, these issues were not to be approached as a matter of individual perception. My earlier research on medical students had alerted me to the extent to which such perception – literally, the clinical gaze – is socially organized, and is shaped by language. My medical school fieldwork had not yielded sufficiently detailed data to enable close analysis of the issue, however. (Although intensive participant observation of bedside instruction was possible, I had not collected tape-recordings of spoken interaction.)

What *had* been abundantly clear in the earlier fieldwork was the volume and diversity of occupational talk that is performed in a modern medical setting. Even a fairly broad characterization of the teaching hospital reveals that there is a range of professional encounters in which spoken performances are constitutive of the work that is accomplished in particular contexts. In the course of my medical school fieldwork, for instance, I attended and made notes on different kinds of rounds, during which senior and junior staff and students presented and discussed cases; the students and I attended clinical lectures at which consultant physicians and surgeons presented a series of patients (some invited in from outside the hospital to make the equivalent of a guest appearance). We observed the conduct of operations in surgical theatres that were accompanied by a running commentary on the part of the surgeon. The students and I were passive members at weekly unit meetings at which cases were presented and reviewed by the clinical firm and other specialists, such as pathologists. In all of these professional encounters there are various types of verbal performance. Students, house staff and senior colleagues narrate the patient's presenting problem and rehearse the patient's history; they recount the events of the hospital stay, the investigations and treatments; they argue or express agreement over appropriate courses of action; they express their views on prevailing opinion concerning, say, the treatment of choice; they voice and endorse professional morality concerning the success or failure of their diagnoses. They find words and pictures to describe noteworthy features.

In other words, my early ethnography of the medical school had alerted me to the dense repertoire of spoken performances that characterize the modern clinic. With full seriousness I felt one could make the case that the patient is merely the pretext for a very great deal of *talk* – much of it at one remove from the patient. Indeed, the case which is discussed is constructed through these various spoken activities. (It is also, of course, assembled out of various shards of *written* text in the folder of case notes or chart, laboratory reports or discharge notes.) Sociologists of health and illness have occasionally commented unfavourably on the bureaucratic and dehumanizing processes whereby the person is transformed into a patient, and the patient in turn into a case. When I embarked on this research, however, I felt that a normative orientation to that process had led sociologists to neglect *how* that organizational work was actually accomplished.

It should be apparent that this research was not intended to be a general, open-ended ethnography. The foreshadowed problems – though sufficiently broad to allow for a flexible and strategic approach in the field – were fairly clear. They were firmly grounded in the sociological study of medical work, the sociology of medical knowledge and the sociology of medical talk. The trinity of background interests helped to demarcate the terrain for this micro-sociology of medical knowledge. As I have suggested, the contents of this book attempt to do more than just report the outcomes of a single fragment of field research. The data from haematological settings are used to address more general themes and issues. Nevertheless, those data are central to the arguments presented in the chapters that follow. It is therefore appropriate to include an account of the data and their collection, as well as a characterization of the fieldwork setting.

The research and its setting

The main collection of data was undertaken in a major teaching hospital in the Eastern United States. It was associated with the medical school of a major university. I call it Beacon Hospital. (There will be little need to refer to it by name anyway.) The fieldwork itself was focused on the work of a group of haematologists who worked in a Haematology–Oncology service. With the help of the chief of that service, my day-to-day fieldwork in Beacon Hospital was centred on the activities of three clinical fellows. Those three young physicians were at an advanced stage of specialist training. They were responsible for a good deal of the everyday work of the service, especially the consulting work – to be amplified below. By following the clinical fellows I automatically came into contact with a wide range of clinical and other personnel, and found myself in various kinds of meetings. The fellows led me into every part of the hospital, and brought me into contact with a diverse collection of patients. A good deal of our work was peripatetic. The reason for our movement through the physical and clinical space of the hospital was the nature of haematology as a consulting service.

A good deal of the work of the service was devoted to the provision of expert advice to the teams of physicians, surgeons and other specialists throughout the hospital. As part of their work and training, the fellows each took turns to take on the *consults* that were requested by hospital doctors from elsewhere. The reasons for consultations may be various, and many will be encountered implicitly in the case presentations reproduced and reported on later in this monograph. The day-to-day work of the clinical fellow was supervised by an 'attending' physician, that is, one of the senior physicians attached to the service (with a status equivalent to that of consultant in a British teaching hospital). The attendings also rotated among them the responsibility for the service consults. Their rotations were staggered *vis-à-vis* those of the fellows. Consequently, each fellow would find him or herself supervised by different attendings, while each attending's period of responsibility would normally include working with two of the fellows in tandem.

The attending and the fellow were thus jointly responsible for whatever haematological consultations came the way of the service. During my own fieldwork, this dyad was almost always turned into a triad by the addition of a medical student. Several students rotated through the haematology service (not all of them from the local university – several were visiting from elsewhere, one of them from Europe). For much of the routine work of consults, therefore, there was a small three-generational team: an attending, a fellow, and one or two medical students. On a few occasions, that team was joined by a resident physician who was taking the opportunity to work up his acquaintance with haematology.

It is immediately apparent that the position of haematology at Beacon Hospital reflects the complex division of labour in contemporary medicine. As an occupation, medicine – especially American medicine – is hyper-segmented. It is composed of a large number of specialties and subspecialties (cf. Bucher and Strauss, 1961). By the same token, the modern hospital is an extremely complex organization. The work of medicine is distributed among a vast number of different personnel, located in a bewildering array of divisions, services, floors, wards, laboratories and other settings. The consulting activities of the haematologists took them, and me, through many parts of the vast teaching hospital: from Eyes and Ears, to Burns, from Intensive Care to Thoracic Surgery, from Cardiology to Neurology. Together we saw many patients, from those whose problems were regarded as fairly straightforward to those with complex and unusual conditions. There were cases when the haematologists' involvement was a relatively fleeting one: there were others for whom the haematologists became the central players in the management of their disease.

By attaching myself to the clinical fellows, then, I came into contact with a wide range of places and persons in the hospital. I did not, however, attempt to 'shadow' the fellows for all their everyday work. There were several reasons. First and foremost, I was not interested in producing a general ethnography of haematology *per se*. My intentions were always more limited and more focused than that. Secondly, given how small was the number of doctors involved, a close involvement with all aspects of their work could have proved unduly intrusive. Thirdly, I was particularly interested in specific kinds of professional encounters in the hospital: my main substantive interest lay in those occasions when patients are discussed as 'cases' and when specialists attempt to adjudicate on the nature of the disease and on the facts of the case. It was, therefore, in the light of that interest, and in accordance with the 'natural' timetable of the hospital setting that I concentrated on various more or less formal occasions when patients were discussed or presented. As I have remarked elsewhere, in a major teaching hospital one is forgiven for believing that patients are there primarily in order to provide doctors with the opportunity to talk about them (cf. Pithouse and Atkinson, 1988). There are numerous opportunities for doctors to tell one another and to consult one another about individual cases.

A daily event that formed the basis for much of the data collection was the *round*, consisting of the fellow, the attending and the student(s). Typically meeting at about 9 o'clock each morning, the two main protagonists would discuss the patients about whom they had been consulted. The students participated in these rounds to varying degrees, depending on their own acquaintance with the case, and the extent to which the more senior members chose to make the occasion an explicitly instructional session. Of course, the term 'round' in such a clinical context conjures up the image of the traditional ward round or teaching round: the senior physician or surgeon, accompanied by an entourage of subordinates, visiting the patients, stopping in turn at each bedside or at the foot of the bed. It is like a royal progress, or a sacred procession (Atkinson, 1981a). There was, however, nothing remotely sacred or processional about the rounds in haematology each morning. They were rounds by name, but they rarely straggled into the wards. Rather, they were small, semi-formal meetings that took place around the table in the haematology seminar room. The fellow (sometimes the student) would present new consults – summarizing the history, recounting the patient's current hospital admission, addressing the problems and puzzles identified by the medical or surgical team, on the ward and so on. Likewise, old consults would be brought up to date on a daily basis. The physical resources brought to those meetings consisted typically of 3×5 file cards on which at least some of the participants kept jotted notes about the patient, laboratory values and the like. (The patient's chart remained on the ward.) Slides of blood smears or bone marrow aspirates might also be inspected under the microscope.

The room where the rounds typically took place was one of the social and work centres of the haematology service. The fellows went there when they began their day at 7.30 a.m. or thereabouts. There too the students would go when they began their day (typically a little later, at about 8.00 a.m.) to find out what was happening and what they were supposed to be doing. Chairs were arranged around a large table. The room was lined with library shelving. Three major textbooks or atlases of haematology were chained in place on the table. At one side of the room was a small table, with a microscope (with four pairs of eye-pieces) at which slides could be inspected by the haematologists and their students. This room was also the setting for various other regular meetings, including a weekly meeting at which the fellows and others took turns to present a particular topic (such as the current understanding of a particular disease, or a particular treatment). At these larger meetings, twelve to fifteen participants – fellows, students, attendings, researchers and others – would squeeze round the table and find chairs elsewhere in the room.

I began my work by identifying the attending physician's daily round as a key feature of the medical work and medical talk to be investigated. I therefore ensured that from the beginning of the fieldwork I attended the rounds on a daily basis. From the outset it was apparent that a good deal of important work was being accomplished in these encounters. They proceeded at a considerable pace, and were packed with technical information. Cases could be presented and summarized at breakneck speed, and couched in language (often abbreviations) that defeated me (for all that I had prior acquaintance with medical work and medical instruction). There was clearly no way in which such fundamentally important material could be captured using the pencil-and-notebook methods of conventional fieldwork. I therefore obtained permission from the participants to record the rounds, using a small portable recorder, placed unobtrusively on the table. It was also possible to record those sections of the round when we moved over to the microscope. The recorder could be placed directly next to the microscope, and the participants' spoken interaction captured. (Recordings were often imperfect for reasons given below.)

The attending's morning rounds were only one part of the weekly meetings at which I found myself present. The most important of the others was the weekly Haematology–Oncology conference. This took place at a lunch-time, one day a week. It was located in a small lecture theatre. Lunch was provided, in the form of bread, cold cuts, cheese and soft drinks. This was a more formal occasion than the daily rounds. Patients were presented by the clinical fellows and the students to an audience of colleagues and superiors. The case presentations of new patients were formal, following well-established rhetorical formats. Each presentation was immediately followed by an exchange of questions and answers between the presenter and members of the audience. I taped several such presentations, although the arrangement of the conference itself meant that the questions from the floor were rarely as audible as the presentation itself and the presenter's answers to the questioning. Each of these conferences would typically last for about one hour. During that time several cases would be presented and discussed.

In addition, the fellows, students and I would find ourselves part of the audience at the weekly Mortality and Morbidity Review in the Division of Medicine. This was a large meeting, also held at lunch-time: many people brought their brown-bag lunch with them. Latecomers found themselves sitting on the floor, peering at the proceedings through the legs of chairs and colleagues. At these meetings the residents in medicine provided a weekly review of cases. The immediate audience consisted of the senior physicians, including the Chief of the Service. The cases were presented at great speed, with little or no concession to the general audience. The conference provided a formal occasion at which the work of the resident staff was subject to formal scrutiny by the most senior members of the profession. For the groundlings in the main body of the audience, there was perhaps more of an element of entertainment. They could relish the occasional ritual humiliation of a resident at the hands of a senior colleague or peer. They do not form part of the data drawn on in this book, but the M and M meetings are significant. They were part of a wider round of meetings and conferences at which medical work was reported and accomplished through the more or less formal presentation and exchange of talk about patients. (The character and function of such work will be considered rather more fully at a later point.)

The total amount of collegial talk recorded in Beacon Hospital was not vast. In total, the corpus of data amounts to about forty hours of rounds and similar presentations. While not absolutely large, this amount of talk provides ample scope for the exploration of key aspects of medical work. It certainly yields case presentations that permit a preliminary analysis of medical rhetoric. An informal comparison with the talk at the other meetings not recorded suggests that there was nothing out of the ordinary about the presentations and discussions that were recorded. Whether or not they are typical of contemporary (American) medicine is indeterminate. It is not clear, however, that their representativeness (however defined) would have been enhanced by the collection of 'more of the same' at Beacon Hospital, or indeed by the collection of similar data from other hospitals (the typicality of which would be equally moot). At face value there is nothing to suggest that the data drawn on and reproduced here are anything other than ordinary, unremarkable samples of medical collegial discourse. Although the field has been under-explored hitherto, it will be seen in subsequent chapters that the data compare very closely with those collected and subjected to similar analysis by Anspach (1988).

Needless to say, the collection of audio-recordings does not in itself yield data on medical work and talk. The tapes were transcribed. This was an especially arduous task. All transcription is time-consuming at best. These particular tapes were especially demanding. First, the *content* was difficult. Technical terms and abbreviations – such as initials or acronyms – are very difficult to catch and to disambiguate. This is especially so when they are delivered at very great pace, as these were. I have no doubt that in the transcribed materials that follow I have, despite my best endeavours, incorporated errors and created clinical nonsense by mishearing a disease, proprietary drug name or suchlike. (I have always referred to printed sources such as textbooks in order to check on spellings and abbreviations, but they do not always help, especially when one cannot be sure quite what is being heard in the first place.) Consequently, the content and the tempo of the speech create their own problems in the preparation of adequate transcripts. For the most part, the talk was delivered at a recognizably fast East Coast American tempo (cf. Tannen, 1984). Furthermore, there seemed to be a cultural requirement that cases should be presented at the fastest possible speed, with facts and figures fired at the recipients with little or no hesitation; indeed with very little variety of intonation, amplitude, stress etc. Some of the fellows (and residents at the M and M) were especially noteworthy for this trait in their spoken performances.

The tapes were also difficult to transcribe because of high levels of interruption and overlapping talk. While the more formal presentations were marked by relative audience silence, the daily rounds, normally consisting of two or three participants, were marked by quite high levels of simultaneous talk, mutual interruption and other perturbations. Unlike the formal conferences, where turn-taking was straightforward and the rules of politeness normally adhered to, the informal interactions were much less ordered. That is, of course, a constitutive feature of relative formality (J. M. Atkinson, 1982). For the moment I note it only to indicate some practical problems of transcribing tapes of naturally occurring talk in such occupational settings.

On the other hand, the collection of such data is imperative for an adequate understanding of the fine grain of everyday medical work. It is essential to recognize that a great deal of medical work is achieved not only through the content of collegial talk, but also through the form of that talk. The preservation of both form and content through permanent recordings is, therefore, a vital element in the documentation and analysis of such work. Equally, however, one must recognize a danger in the contemporary use of audio and video records. Because they can seem to yield 'the best' data – because most detailed and most 'faithful' – there is a danger of reducing the scope of qualitative research to those occasions suitable for recording, and of treating transcribed materials as the only source of data. I have argued elsewhere that this is an unnecessary restriction on what counts as 'the field' for sociological fieldwork (Atkinson, 1992b). Although I concentrated my attention on 'rounds' and 'conferences', I did not entirely overlook more general ethnographic fieldwork methods.

In addition to the collection of tape-recordings, I also treated my time at Beacon Hospital as an opportunity for more general participant observation. There are, of course, many occasions when it is neither appropriate nor feasible (let alone ethical) to tape-record. Moreover, there are many aspects of everyday social life that are in no way captured through the tape-recorder. During our peripatetic visits to patients on the various wards, and during much of the routine work of the day, I was a conventional ethnographer, observing and making what brief jottings I could on the spot or soon after. These were turned into daily processed fieldnotes – worked-up narratives of each day in the field. In the fieldnotes I was able to write detailed accounts of the social settings as well as the actors and action I had observed. In the analyses that follow I have drawn on both sources of data – fieldnotes and transcripts – although the extracts reproduced from the latter are much the more prominent. I believe, however, that my understanding of the tapes (whatever its merits) would be severely impoverished in the absence of my general ethnographic understanding of the relevant social settings. In addition to those data sources, I interviewed and talked informally with the three clinical fellows, the students and several of the attending physicians. Again, such interactions have played their part in informing the analyses that follow.

In total the tape-recordings amount to some forty hours of rounds, conferences and other discussions. They were transcribed initially using the established conventions for conversation analysis. Using the full range of keyboard characters, those conventions are used to capture many of the relevant features of talk. They do not preserve all the linguistic and paralinguistic features, nor are phonetic transcriptions normally used for such purposes. They are used to indicate features such as pauses and interruptions that reflect the main preoccupations of fine-grained sequential analysis. My transcribed data are preserved in that form. As a consequence the fully transcribed data are very hard to read. Indeed, in many cases they are virtually unreadable. On the other hand, my analyses do depend on a fairly close reading of medical discourse. A detailed exploration of discourse and knowledge production cannot altogether dispense with the details of spoken interaction. For those reasons, I have decided not to preserve all the possible features of the talk and to exercise a certain amount of editorial licence. As I have suggested elsewhere, the tension between readability and fidelity is a recurrent issue for ethnographic analysis and there is no pure or perfect mode of representation. There seems to be no point in the preservation of details in the transcripts if they detract from the analysis rather than informing it. Data extracts will, therefore, be presented in a form edited to remove the most distracting aspects, such as many of the timed short pauses, hesitations and the like. Detailed analyses of a technical nature and intended for a more specialized audience (e.g. Atkinson, 1994) will contain the more detailed transcriptions.

In producing the transcripts I used conventional orthography as often as I could. This is not a straightforward matter. Standard spellings and punctuation can make spontaneous speech look far too formal and precise. On the other hand, the liberal use of non-standard spellings and absence of punctuation can make the speakers look unnecessarily odd and render their speech unintelligible (even though it may have been quite clear in the original context). The over-enthusiastic use of 'eye spellings' has been criticized by Preston (1982, 1985), and I have tried to avoid giving the misleading impression that the physicians and students were speaking in noticeably non-standard dialects. Likewise, I have represented medical and scientific abbreviations *as* abbreviations and not as laboriously spelled out transliterations (hence *BT* not *bee tee* for 'bleeding time' abbreviated). I have therefore tried to remain faithful to the speakers and their speech in general rather than relying on the illusory fidelity of over-detailed and unreadable textual representations (cf. Atkinson, 1992b). I have, therefore, used the normal conventions for transcription selectively (see Appendix).

I have, of course, given pseudonyms to all the clinicians, students, scientists and patients. I have occasionally changed or omitted dates and other references that might by implication disclose personal identities and details. The pseudonyms (taken from American fiction) broadly reflect the original participants' names, in terms of ethnic or class connotations.

The fieldwork in Beacon Hospital spanned some ten weeks. Data collection was undertaken on most working days in that period. Although the work of the hospital continued throughout the twenty-four hours of the day, I concentrated most of my own fieldwork into a few hours each day. My fieldwork normally began at 8 or 9 o'clock in the morning (depending on what rounds or meetings were scheduled) and continued for several hours until the early afternoon (again, depending on the actual timetable for that day). The morning to lunch-time period gave me access to rounds, conferences, visits to patients and the like. During the afternoon, the fellows would frequently be seeing patients in the oncology clinic (where I also spent some time) and working on their own. Likewise, the students would be working alone. I avoided imposing myself on them during such periods of more private work.

For the most part the fieldwork at Beacon Hospital was smooth. My sponsor there had arranged for me to be granted the position of 'Honorary Consultant' in the Division of Medicine for the duration of my fieldwork. (I was also granted the status of Visiting Scholar in the Department of Sociology at the local university.) This gave me, *inter alia*, the authority to be present in the hospital settings, without rights or privileges of patient care, validated by my possession of an identity card. For the majority of the participants, there appeared to be no special difficulty about my presence, and most were indifferent to my note-taking and tape-recording. The fieldwork was not entirely without hitches, however. Early on in the fieldwork it became apparent that at least one of the fellows was becoming unhappy about my presence, and had drawn her reservations to the attention of the Chief of the Service. He in turn sent for me and – in a thoroughly pleasant way – drew the problem to my attention and suggested I do something to tackle it. It seemed to be the case that the fellow had become generally uneasy about my fieldwork. She tended to feel and to express a certain amount of stress and pressure in managing the various tasks imposed on her, and I suspect that she experienced my presence as rather threatening. Her general anxieties were, however, exacerbated and brought to a head by one particular incident I was witness to and which apparently caused her some distress. (She was much more affected by the event than I was, and I was quite unprepared for her response.)

The critical incident concerned one particular patient about whom the haematologists had been consulted. The patient in question was a man in his thirties, with aplastic anaemia. He was seen earlier in the day, by the fellow and two of the students, when my notes show:

> . . . At 8.52 we went into Mr Giacommetti's room. Heather [*a fellow*] asked how he was feeling today, and he launched into a complaint about the diet he was receiving. He said he wasn't getting enough of the right sort of protein. Heather said thcy are still investigating the possibility of a bone marrow transplant. Mr Giacommetti replied that he wasn't sure about whether he was interested in the possibility of a bone marrow transplant – he'll see how he feels in a couple of days.

On the way out of the patient's room, Heather, the fellow, said that the patient was the most anaemic she had ever seen. He looked, she said, the way that the textbooks describe – his lips, his hands were so pale. A little later, we returned to the haematology seminar room for the morning round with Dr de Kalb, the attending physician. In the course of that, Dr de Kalb's temper became rather frayed. He became especially annoyed when the fellow's bleeper kept interrupting the discussion, and she responded by using the telephone. At one point he snapped, 'Tell 'em you're busy. I mean it, you *are* busy . . .'. Irritably, he kept interrupting the presentation of cases by the fellow and the students.

Dr de Kalb's sour temper was reflected and amplified in the subsequent episode. When we finished the round in the seminar room, the doctor suggested that we should go up to see the patients who had just been discussed. He pottered back into his own room and picked up his stethoscope. We then went up to the wards. My notes recorded:

> As we went into Mr Giacommetti's room, Heather asked him if it was alright if we came to seem him. Mr Giacommetti complained about doctors coming to see him every minute. He said it was OK, if it was reasonable. Dr de Kalb replied 'What's reasonable? Who's to decide what's reasonable?' Mr Giacommetti said he didn't think he was getting reasonable care here in the hospital. He repeated his complaint about his diet, insisting that he must get sixty-four grams of the right protein. Dr de Kalb replied very sharply, 'We're here to decide what you need.' Mr Giacommetti said he thought he should see another doctor. 'Well, there's lots of doctors looking after you here.' 'No, I mean another opinion at another hospital . . .', and Mr Giacommetti again repeated that he's not satisfied with the treatment he's getting here. Dr de Kalb said in a slightly more conciliatory tone. 'You're very sick my friend', and reached down to touch his arm. But Mr Giacommetti continued to complain, and Dr de Kalb stomped out, saying in a loud angry voice, just as he passed through the doorway, 'He needs to see a psychiatrist!' 'You too!' Mr Giacommetti shouted at us as we all trooped out. Throughout this brief interlude in Mr Giacommetti's room, Heather looked very strained, while the students were making constant eye contact between each other and me.

We passed on to see other patients, but this ill-tempered episode clearly upset the fellow and the students. Indeed my fieldnotes for later that morning recorded:

> After the round, Jean-Paul [*student*], Lillian [*student*] and I sat in the library for a while discussing Mr Giacommetti, Dr de Kalb, and Mr Giacommetti's dietary

fixation. Lillian tended to see his food fixation as a coping mechanism for dealing with everyday problems. She suggested that he was using his diet and his complaints about nutrition as a way of handling his anxieties and fear in the hospital.

One of the most remarkable things about today . . . is the extent to which Dr de Kalb's handling of Mr Giacommetti was a recurrent topic of conversation between the students. The incident clearly made a deep impression on them – especially Lillian, I think. She implied that she had never before witnessed a physician talking to a patient in that way.

A day or two later it transpired that the clinical fellow had felt especially threatened by my presence during this episode, and had complained about my presence. Her anxiety was highlighted further by a dispute about a diagnosis of aplastic anaemia in Mr Giacommetti's case, at the clinical conference that week. One of the attending physicians, Dr Starkovich, complained vociferously that Mr Giacommetti had not been 'worked up' properly prior to her presentation of the case.

I was unaware of the problem until four days after the encounter with Mr Giacommetti. I went in to the hospital to find myself requested to contact Dr Kretschmer, the chief of the Haematology–Oncology service. I went to see him as soon as I could. Without preamble he told me what the problems was:

He said that he'd had an impromptu meeting with the fellows, to see if everything was OK with them. And the only problem they'd reported was me. They felt that I was not getting a sufficiently rounded picture of their work, and they also felt that they had not been given a sufficiently clear understanding of what my work involved. I said I was honestly shocked and surprised, as I had no sense of any such unhappiness or resentment.

I reiterated what I'd said to Dr Kretschmer before – that I had no interest in, or competence in evaluating the health care provided, or the fellowship programme, though of course I was interested in what the fellows might have to tell me about their views of such matters.

Dr Kretschmer said he understood that there had been one particular 'incident' between a doctor and a patient; Heather had said I'd asked her 'What did you make of that?' and hadn't known what to say. I said that, as Dr Kretschmer himself had known, that sort of thing was not really relevant to my interests, and I thoroughly wished that the incident had never happened. He said that people got understandably nervous, when their work was being discussed and criticized anyway – like Dr Starkovich screaming about a patient not having been worked up properly at the last conference. I said that I thought that was a good case in point, as what I had been interested in about that incident was to find out whether his intervention had made any difference to the diagnosis or management of that particular patient – for instance at the next day's round. Dr Kretschmer added that Heather's attending should have been there to defend her – but he wasn't . . .

Much later that morning I was sitting in the library, while the fellows and the students were busy elsewhere. Heather came through on her way to the lab. I asked her if she could spare me half a minute and said I wanted to thank her for putting up with me last week, and asking if it might be time for a talk. Her reply was, 'You'd better ask the other fellows. I'm, really busy right now, and I have to prepare two talks for this week.' She went on to say that after next Thursday would be better for her. But she said she could sit down and talk now if I liked. So we sat at the library table for a few minutes.

Heather said that she felt she hadn't been told enough about the nature of my research, and that even if it were to be 'secret', she'd still have appreciated having that explained. I said I certainly had no desire to make it secret, and if she had got that impression then it reflected ineptitude on my part rather than any deliberate secrecy, and I was sorry for it.

Heather said she felt that if she'd known what I was interested in she could have been more help, but she felt very pressured, what with having the students, and preparing for conference, and visiting all the patients. She said that it was really difficult in the mornings, running around checking to see if the patients are still alive (some of them barely are, she added). And a lot of the decision-making and sharing of information goes on after 5 o'clock when things are quieter. She said that she had asked more than once what I was interested in, but that I hadn't replied. (Although I didn't argue with this, I had no recollection of such requests for information having been made, or that I had evaded them: it is a salutary, if rather unfortunate lesson in the uncertainty of one's own perceptions and impressions.)

That incident, which occurred during the early days of my fieldwork at Beacon Hospital, precipitated the only overt problem in my working relations with the haematologists. It proved to be resolved in a fairly straightforward manner. I wrote a personal memorandum to each of the fellows, in which I explained that I had no intention of evaluating or criticizing their work, nor of intruding on it. I realized in retrospect that I had inadvertently fallen prey to a common enough fieldwork problem. I had conducted most of the initial negotiations from a distance, by letter, with one personal visit to the hospital on my way to an international conference several months previously. Access had been granted by the Chief of Service and a senior haematologist. I had not had the opportunity to meet and talk to all the other key personnel. Consequently, the fellows had every reason to feel that I had been dumped on them. Indeed, despite my previous correspondence, I suspect that the fellow who felt most put out had received little or no prior warning (let alone consultation) before I appeared in the hospital.

After this initial episode, the fieldwork was untroubled. I attempted to be sensitive to the actors at all times, of course. For instance, there was at least one occasion when one of the fellows was having a hard time, and was getting visibly and audibly flustered. He might well have asked me to leave the round altogether, though he did not actually do so. However, as we sat at the table to begin the morning 'round', he looked at my little tape-recorder, looked at me, and snapped, 'Do we have to have that thing on?' I was able to tell him that I had not even turned it on because I had sensed he would not want me to. On another occasion I offered to wipe the tape when one of the students had got flustered and performed poorly (she felt). She decided that it was not necessary, adding that it was the first time she had been a recording star.

On the other hand, my presence and my tape-recorder could sometimes prove to be useful – especially to the student participants. On more than one occasion a round had covered a great deal of information about a patient, and a number of further actions agreed on, including tasks for the student to undertake. It could prove too much to take in on the spot, and a rapid rewind and replay of the tape could refresh the student's memory and give him or her an *aide-mémoire*.

My everyday relationships were closer and more collegial with the medical students. Despite my greater age and academic seniority, my marginal status placed me much closer to them in Beacon Hospital. In fact I reflected on that issue in my field journal, while thinking about my field relations:

> In some ways it is strategic for me to align myself with the students: they are personally welcoming, and to some extent I and they share similar problems. Their working day is to some extent – actually, a large extent – determined by the busy-ness and scheduling of the relevant fellow. They have to sit around reading or pottering about waiting to see if there is a consult to see, or waiting to catch a fellow. And if I stick with them, then I can pick up on visits, trips, news, and so on. And it is then difficult for my presence to be seen as illegitimate.

It had not been my original intention to focus on the knowledge and experiences of medical students. Indeed, before I began the actual fieldwork I was not aware of the extent of the students' presence. As the fieldwork unfolded, however, I found myself paying attention to the students. Indeed, their participation was especially useful. When work and talk include some element of overt instruction, and when novices are present, then it is common for senior and more competent participants to make things more explicit than they might otherwise. The three-generational encounter between senior physician, clinical fellow and medical student was an ideal setting in which to study the transmission and reproduction of medical knowledge.

The following incident, recorded in my fieldnotes, gives another example of how my own recipe-knowledge could be useful to the students. I had been to the university's library with Lillian, who had to look up some of the journal evidence on the use of a particular drug. It was being used to treat Mr Campos, and she had been asked to give a talk about the drug at the next day's round:

> As we walked back from the library we talked about Mr Campos. Rather to my surprise, I found I was able to remember more of the background to the case than Lillian did. She had forgotten that the original reason for the haematology consult was the fact that Mr Campos had hairy cell leukaemia – and it was in that context that Charles [*clinical fellow*] had alerted them to the bleeding time issue.

Despite the occasional problem during the earliest days in the field, I became a taken-for-granted member of the team on most occasions. By virtue of my immersion in the field of haematology I was granted the status of a 'well-informed citizen', if not exactly an 'expert'. As I had already spent some time on the service, I knew more about haematology than the new students whose rotation began in the course of my fieldwork. For instance, one of the fellows asked Sophie Samuels, a student 'What is indicated by ristocetin-induced platelet aggregation?' and added, looking at me, 'Paul knows'. I did know because, unlike that particular student, I had recently sat through several presentations on von Willebrand's disease (a condition caused by an inherited Factor VIII defect). My knowledge, of course, was essentially 'recipe-knowledge', gleaned from the rounds, conferences and so on, backed up with a certain amount of background reading from basic textbooks on haematology. Equally, as I did not rotate, I sometimes knew more about the individual patients than a fellow or student who had only just begun. One of the transcripts includes the following sequence, for instance. Here the fellow and the attending were both discussing the patients that the previous fellow and attending had been consulted on:

F: It's an interesting case for sure
At: = And he's had disease now for six to eight weeks?
F: That's right, and I've already covered him a week, and they tell me he had
          a subacute presentation over a couple of months I *guess*, and he had dated
          this to. Didn't he have an exposure to er some, he's a
PAA: Yeah, he's a landscape gardener
F: That's right. He's a landscape gardener, so he's had lots of insecticide
          exposure
At: How old is he?
F: Thirtyish?
St: Early thirties
PAA: Thirty-two, I think
F: Thirty-two

I was able to chip in with such non-technical information about a patient I had met and had heard discussed on several previous occasions. I would have felt much less comfortable about offering technical clinical or pathological information – even had I felt confident about my recollection and understanding.

The incident is illustrative of a more general point. In attempting to understand a cultural domain such as medicine it is often necessary to attempt to acquire some degree of 'insider' knowledge. The detailed exploration and understanding of a domain such as medicine is virtually impossible in the absence of the will and capacity to make sense of the technical content of working knowledge.

In studying such occupational groups as medicine and similar learned professions or academic communities, there arises the problem of the extent to which the ethnographer needs to grasp esoteric knowledge in order to conduct research. By and large, with the exception of Collins (1984), the problem has been discussed inadequately by writers on fieldwork methods. There is no need for the ethnographer to become an 'expert' in medicine or whatever, but there may often be a need to become something of a 'well-informed citizen' (Schutz, 1964). In other words, there is no need, indeed every disadvantage, in 'going native' by means of the detailed acquisition of professional knowledge. The ethnographer does not seek to 'become' a surrogate haematologist, surgeon, physicist or accountant. On the other hand, as I have remarked elsewhere (Atkinson, 1984), we have a sociological literature in which we encounter doctors who seem to practise no medicine, lawyers who exercise no special legal expertise, teachers who teach no particular school subjects. There is a danger in much ethnographic work of reducing both the ethnographer *and* his or her host to a 'man or woman in the street', devoid of the special competence that constitutes their expert work. This danger is partly inherent in the preferred intellectual stance adopted by many ethnographers.

It is something of a commonplace in the methodological literature on ethnographic fieldwork that the ethnographer should adopt the position of the 'marginal' person, the 'acceptable incompetent', or the 'stranger'. It is easy to misunderstand that methodological commitment as implying a resolute determination to remain a complete ignoramus, and to resist the acquisition of expert knowledge in one's chosen research setting. But a neglect of specialist knowledge is certainly not entailed by a stance of ethnographic (or anthropological) estrangement. In that respect, I think that Collins misunderstands the basic position. He seems to accuse the majority of ethnographers of a wilful disregard of expert knowledge because they endorse a methodological stance based on the position of the outsider or stranger. But as I have indicated, a commitment to anthropological strangeness does not imply a refusal to *learn* specialist knowledge and to explore esoteric cultural domains. On the contrary, such learning should clearly be part of the ethnographer's cultural exploration. Equally, the ethnographic stance means that the content and legitimacy of esoteric knowledge should not be taken on trust by the ethnographer. He or she must be willing and able to ask *how* expert knowledge is produced, used and warranted in the setting under scrutiny.

In this book, the argument will be illustrated primarily with reference to the data collected in the United States. Some complementary fieldwork was also undertaken with haematologists in a British teaching hospital. The fieldwork itself was more sporadic, less intensive and less formal. It did, however, cover a range of settings and medical encounters similar to those documented in the American hospital. I undertook participant observation and participant recording, with consultant haematologists and house staff. I attended a number of ward rounds, case presentations and research seminars. I spent time observing in the laboratories: it was noticeable that in the British hospital setting there seemed to be a much closer relationship between clinicians and laboratory technicians than had been observable in Beacon Hospital. It was a perfectly 'natural' part of fieldwork in Britain that some degree of participation with the clinicians should bring me into direct contact with laboratory workers. It proved possible to undertake a certain amount of tape-recording in the British hospital. I was able to record some case presentations and some occasions when clinicians were examining bone marrow or peripheral blood smears under the microscope. As I have indicated, it was never my intention to produce a systematic comparative analysis of haematological work as between the two national settings. The small-scale, intensive fieldwork on which this book is based would not permit such an analysis. In any event, I am far more interested in features of work and knowledge that appear to be pervasive of modern medicine, rather than confining attention to the one medical specialty of haematology.

Nevertheless, there were some organizational differences between the

two settings that deserve brief comments. Like their American counterparts, the British haematologists were consulted by hospital staff in different
specialties. Surgeons, physicians, gerontologists and others had occasion to
seek specialist advice. On the other hand, the haematologists in the British
teaching hospital had their own wards. The patients with leukaemias,
clotting disorders, lymphomas and the like were admitted to the haematology consultants' beds, and the consultants and house staff had direct
responsibility for their hospital treatment. In that sense, therefore, the
British practitioners were much less restricted to the purely 'consulting' role
of their Beacon Hospital counterparts. A further, obvious, difference
(which has little direct bearing on the analyses and discussions that follow,
though it is largely important in other respects) concerned the *market*
position of haematologists as a consulting specialty. The 'consults' that were
the stock-in-trade of the Beacon department were part of a system of
exchange in the hospital that was translated directly into money terms. Each
consultation, each investigation or procedure had a cash value. The clinical
fellows' and attendings' time was billable. Each bone marrow aspirate, each
lymph node biopsy, each blood sample – they all had a price, which was
added to the hospital's bill for the patient's treatment.

There were other differences between the two settings – observable if less
easily described. In particular, Beacon Hospital had a more 'hyper-active'
atmosphere to it. The day started earlier, was packed with more occasions,
such as rounds, conferences and the like. The daily round of work was
conducted by the fellows at a breathless rush. There was a great deal of hurry
and a constant reference to the 'schedule'. Likewise, the pace of talk and
interaction was noticeably faster than in the British context. By these
contrasts I do not mean to imply that the British doctors were more lazy, or
less efficient in their work. On the contrary, I suspect – though I have no
evidence – that they accomplished just as much, with less fuss, than the
United States practitioners. It does, however, produce a rather different
quality to the work, talk and social interactions that is not conveyed in the
following discussions and data extracts. It deserves mention here, therefore,
as part of the general 'scene setting' of the haematology fieldwork that will
inform this book throughout.

2

The Sociological Construction of Medicine

Sociology: illness and disease

All academic disciplines actively create and construct their subject matter. The world – be it the natural or the social world – does not present itself to our academic gaze already packaged into the subject matter of research and theorizing. Indeed, the very processes, intellectual and practical, whereby we undertake our research serve to demarcate the proper subject matter for inquiry. Disciplines define themselves in relation to the objects of research. In so doing, they simultaneously define those objects themselves. Disciplines and their objects each co-exist, mutually defining one another.

This is well recognized. Indeed, it is something of a commonplace in contemporary sociology and philosophy of science. We now recognize that within those symbiotic relationships between scholars and their domains, the academic often defines the core characteristics of his or her chosen field. The boundaries so defined demarcate special, esoteric, even sacred spaces in the intellectual field. In performing those acts of definition and discrimination, members of the academic community define the essential 'otherness' of their subject matter.

Among the social sciences we have become acutely – even uncomfortably – aware that we construct 'the other'. In recent years social anthropologists have been forced to take note of how they conceptualize and define their own discipline. For decades the anthropologists have legitimated their work in terms of understanding 'other cultures' (to take the title of an introductory text). For many years it was taken as read that *cultures* was the problematic term. Nowadays, the anthropologists recognize that equally, if not more, problematic is how they recognize and produce the *other*.

Sociologists are just as implicated in the same intellectual traditions and problems. While their subject matter is less self-evidently exotic or alien than that of the anthropologists, they are just as fully involved in defining the otherness of the individuals and groups that they study. Whether constructing classes, races, communities, organizations or occupations, the sociologist differentiates and discriminates. In so doing, the sociologist sets off the social group, category or action as other: as different from other categories, similarly defined, and other than the social world inhabited by the social scientist.

All domains of sociological work partake of this process. It is not confined

to the intellectual construction of the obviously other. The other worlds of
the street gang, the prostitute or the religious cult may appear just as
self-evidently exotic as those studied by the social or cultural anthropologist.
But otherness is not confined to those areas of the deviant and the
flamboyantly distinctive. All aspects of the social world are transformed into
appropriate fields and topics by sociologists themselves. They are all
rendered 'other' in the process of scrutiny.

Sociologists and anthropologists of medicine are a case in point. Over the
past decades, sociologists of medicine (or of health and illness) have had
considerable success in the market-place of ideas and resources. The volume
of research and publishing in the field has been quite remarkable. Since the
late 1960s and early 1970s medical sociology has burgeoned in Britain, North
America, Europe and elsewhere. In the course of that intellectual development the discipline has consistently enjoyed an uneasy and ambivalent
relationship with its field of inquiry – medicine itself (see Strong, 1984). The
other that it defines, and so seeks to capture in its interrogatory gaze, is itself
a powerful source of knowledge and interrogation. Medicine is a vast array
of activities; its division of labour is dizzyingly complex; its knowledge-base
is vast and growing exponentially.

How, then, has sociology constructed the otherness of medicine? How in
doing so has it rendered tractable domains of medicine? How has the
sociology of medicine thus constructed its own boundaries and its own
identity in the process? Like many fields of sociological discourse, medical
sociology has over the years generated and employed a relatively small
number of discursive devices in order to produce and reproduce its own
proper and distinctive sphere of work. In doing so, it has repeatedly sought
to legitimate its own existence and medicine's essential otherness.

The first device – like all such devices – has proved both productive and
constraining. It is productive, in helping to set and warrant intellectual
agendas. It set out the discipline's territorial claims. In using it, the
sociologists were able to demonstrate the existence of a social or cultural
realm of medically related discourse that was clearly theirs. It was different
from medical discourse itself. Its construction and colonization represented
one of the earliest territorial successes for the emergent field of medical
sociology.

This first productive step was also profoundly restricting, however. For
just as it defined a legitimate area for sociological inspection, it did so at the
expense of demarcating vast areas of potentially relevant subject matter as
other – as beyond the appropriate territory of the medical sociologists. What
was this discursive device? It was the first step that separated out *illness* and
disease. In its earlier days – certainly in its own creation myths – medical
sociology found it necessary to discriminate between the realm of the *natural*
and the world of the *social*. The natural world was the realm of biological
processes – including those pathologies identified as disease. The social or
cultural world was the realm of cultural definitions and understandings of
social processes. The cultural world gave rise to illness.

There was, of course, nothing revolutionary in such a discrimination. The distinction at the heart of medical sociology was part of one of sociology's most well-entrenched epistemological and ontological positions. The interpretative tradition that owed at least part of its heritage to Weber, Dilthey and the German historiographic tradition, insisted upon the necessary difference between the natural and the cultural, and equally on the necessary difference in method between the natural and cultural disciplines. At first blush, therefore, the distinction at the heart of medical sociology's early programme appeared to mirror that time-honoured theoretical perspective. As we shall see, however, it was a half-way house in implementing the full implications of such a sociological paradigm.

It was, therefore, one of the most successful, but potentially limiting, ideas in the collective orthodoxy of medical sociology – the identification of illness and illness behaviour. In its classic formulation, the latter is defined as the way in which symptoms are perceived, evaluated, acted upon or not acted upon by social actors of different cultures, and under different social circumstances. This elementary notion, and its developments, have done much to draw attention to the diversity of beliefs and actions that are conventionally available to social actors concerning their perceived state of physical and mental well-being.

In the most general application the formulation of illness behaviour partakes of a series of implicit and explicit binary oppositions. These undergird much of the taken-for-granted intellectual culture of medical sociology itself. Not all sociologists are equally constrained by an uncritical adherence to such ideas, of course. Nevertheless, the very endurance of the ideas is testimony to the influence they have exerted. In so far as they embody and reproduce received ideas then they can act to limit or to restrain the scope of thought and imagination.

The oppositions that constitute the conceptual armature of the discipline are: disease/illness; biology/culture; signs/symptoms; professional/lay; medical/sociological. To note, comment on and criticize such contrasts – and others like them – is not in itself novel. But my intention is to use this fairly familiar territory to ask what is needed to redress some of the implicit biases, and to escape the symbolic boundaries that constrain the sociological enterprise.

The contrast between disease and illness is a standard one in many courses and textbooks of medical sociology. To take as one example a fairly recent British textbook (Bond and Bond, 1986), the following is a representative example of this well-rehearsed formulation:

A simple distinction we need to make here is between *illness* and *disease*. Disease refers to a medical concept of pathology, which is indicated by a group of signs and symptoms. The presence or absence of a disease, as indicated by signs and symptoms, is clinically defined by the medical profession. The doctor or his substitute, using a common body of knowledge, makes the decision as to whether or not a person has a disease. In contrast, illness is defined by the person who had the signs and symptoms' experience of 'health' and 'ill-health' and is indicated by the person's reactions to the symptoms . . . (Bond and Bond, 1986: 200, emphasis in original)

In this and equivalent formulations, disease becomes equated with the realm of pathological processes: physical abnormalities, lesions, imbalances and so on, which are the stuff of pathophysiology. Illness, on the other hand, is identified as a social state or attribution. It is, therefore, essentially part of a province of meanings, definitions and understandings. One may exaggerate the basic definitions a little, perhaps, to suggest that in many such usages illness equals 'disease plus meaning', just as in the conventional Weberian contrast between behaviour and meaningful social action (cf. Dingwall, 1977). On that basis, therefore, the analysis of culture and of social action would be focused primarily on illness. The conceptualization of the fundamental distinction thus paves the way for the sociological analysis of social action (unhelpfully labelled illness behaviour) and the social processes of management and allocation (the sick role).

The dichotomy between disease and illness depends on the parallel contrast between biology and culture. Disease is portrayed as a function of the natural, while illness is a reflection of the cultural domain. The further implication is that the biological consists of a substratum of invariant natural phenomena, while the cultural is an epiphenomenal superstructure of interpretations – subject to historical, cultural and situational variation.

The traditional contrast between *signs* and *symptoms* depends upon similar underlying oppositions. While the terms are derived primarily from medical rather than sociological discourse, their deployment in both contexts is parallel. Symptom is conventionally taken to denote a manifestation of discomfort or disease, as experienced and reported by the sufferer. Sign, on the other hand, refers to a manifestation that may be perceived (seen, heard, or felt) by an observer – especially by a medical practitioner.

This contrast, then, reinforces and reflects the contrast between the lay and the professional. The oppositions of medical sociology recognize that the encounter between the lay client – a patient – and the professional practitioner may be thought of as an intersection or juxtaposition of different cultures. But all too often, those cultures are not analysed in truly symmetrical fashion.

While by no means all sociologists of medicine are guilty of it, there is a profound danger implicit in the conceptual frameworks already identified. The danger is this: that the world of nature (biology, anatomy, pathophysiology) is treated as *given*. The taken-for-granted contrast between the cultural and the natural too readily implies that the 'natural' is a realm that exists prior to and independently of cultural interpretation. Hence, the sociological focus is turned towards the field of culture. But since the latter is associated primarily with the lay or non-medical, the world of disease and pathology is implicitly granted a privileged status. While illness resides in social meaning and social action, disease resides in the natural world.

Studies of illness behaviour by no means exhaust the scope of the sociology of medicine, and some correctives to that bias will be discussed below. Nevertheless, the relative success of the idea of illness behaviour was possible by virtue of this implicit bias in sociology's treatment of medical knowledge. Indeed, as I have suggested above, that bias was productive in that it helped to demarcate the sociological domain itself. Within this model, however, illness behaviour clearly takes sociological precedence over the study of 'disease behaviour'. (I use this latter term ironically and have no desire to introduce it as a mirror-image.)

From within this conceptual framework (albeit often implicit) there is little or no place for the sociological study of professional medical knowledge. The medical and/or scientific definitions of natural states and conditions escape sociological inquiry. They are – by default – taken for granted within the sociological framework.

The sub-discipline of medical sociology, therefore, was not grounded originally in a systematic sociology of medical knowledge. In more recent years, there have been more sustained attempts to redress the balance, and it is to one of those that we now turn. There have been attempts to reveal the cultural basis of contemporary medical knowledge and practice. One of the central concepts in this frame of reference is the identification of modern *biomedicine*.

The anthropological construction of biomedicine

In recent years sociologists and anthropologists of medicine have attempted to characterize contemporary medicine as a *cultural* system. The analytic programme, which has been associated especially strongly with American anthropology of medicine, seeks to identify a characteristic collection of assumptions, values and practices. The search is not for the distinctive traits of a medical 'profession' (an earlier sociological preoccupation). Rather, analysts seek to identify a world-view or its equivalent.

Again the inspiration derives – in part – from the analytic imperatives of identifying medicine as other. There are various important dimensions of contrast that underly this framework. Biomedicine may be used to contrast with the variety of traditional, non-Western systems of belief and action that are the main intellectual province of the anthropologist of medicine. Biomedicine may also contrast with various non-orthodox medical systems that co-exist with it in contemporary Western societies. It may also be held to be characteristic of modern advanced industrial societies – and hence to contrast with the medical ways of other historical epochs. Finally, and related to all of those positions, biomedicine may be used to contrast with actual or potential alternatives to current practice. It may therefore be compared to various improved, or even utopian, values and practices.

The designation of biomedicine in contemporary social science is both descriptive and evaluative. The identification of its characteristic traits is always redolent of criticism and the search for alternatives. The modern anthropologist or sociologist is often ambivalent towards his or her chosen object of research. It is undeniable that modern medical knowledge and medical institutions are (in every sense) *powerful*. They clearly incorporate potential power for good. They are also powerful in that they can provide the means for social control and domination. While health and its promotion may be seen to be a universally valued end, it is widely recognized that medicine serves sectional interests (national, regional, class, racial or gender).

The sociological or anthropological construction of biomedicine, then, also carries multiple and complex connotations of otherness. Biomedicine is contrasted with what *is* (elsewhere), with what *could* be, and with what *ought* to be. Biomedicine is thus another way of formulating contrasts and discriminations. It is another term in the labelling of otherness. In the semantic games whereby the intellectual field is partitioned and annexed, the identification of biomedicine has served the sociologists and anthropologists tolerably well. It carves out a discursive domain that presents itself for exploration, commentary and critique.

What, then, are the criteria of this distinctive culture of biomedicine? The observations provided by Gaines and Hahn, in introducing a collection of anthropological essays, are a useful starting-point.

> Anthropologists and colleagues have entered a new territory in the heartland of their own society, the domain of Biomedicine. They have returned with accounts both strange and strangely familiar. Practitioners of Biomedicine assume as essentially and exclusively true their own theory and practice, their 'science' which professes the cellular, even biochemical basis of pathology. Anthropologists and medical critics have been struck by this reductionism which excludes alternatives and which asserts biological universalism and individualism (idiopathic etiologies) which ignore, if not deny, basic anthropological understandings which see cultural and social forces as wellsprings of human behavior, including healing and suffering. (Gaines and Hahn, 1985: 3)

As the authors go on to remark, even within the anthropological field, there has been a tendency to treat such biomedicine as the primary reference point. Anthropologists have paralleled the sociologists' interest in illness. They too have placed considerable stress on illness as cultural experience (Good, 1994). Likewise, they began by defining the scope of their interest as ethnomedicine – and originally excluded biomedicine from that categorization.

For the most recent anthropological studies, however, biomedicine is itself an ethnomedicine. It is 'the pre-eminent professional ethnomedicine of Western cultures' (Gaines and Hahn, 1985: 18, n. 1). Its main, defining characteristic for these and other authors is, as already indicated, its reductionist and materialist models. Its theories of biological structure and function are based on explanations that reduce pathology to universal, elementary laws. Biomedicine is fundamentally a triumph of positivist science. It explains the phenomena of health and ill-health in terms of cellular or molecular events.

The anthropological account of biomedicine sketched here (and developed by several authors in recent years) is itself shot through with ambiguity. On the one hand, there are statements that insist on the diversity of beliefs and practices of biomedicine in contemporary society. Gaines and Hahn, for instance, insist to their readers that 'Biomedicine is a *cultural system* comprised of numerous variations, the many medicines' (1985: 4). They go on to refer to studies showing how 'folk' theories may interpenetrate with those of biomedicine in various fields of practice. (In itself this formulation is problematic: on what basis are the 'folk' and the 'biomedical' separated out, if practice is so eclectic?) On the other hand, in many published accounts, it is apparently the cultural unity of biomedicine that is stressed. Indeed, even in the brief comment cited above, the phrase that is emphasized – *cultural system* – has strong connotations of unity and coherence, rather than an eclectic and pragmatic diversity. Within that very same introductory essay, for instance, the authors go on to say that contemporary anthropological research finds in biomedicine:

> a more or less coherent and self-consistent set of values and premises, including an ontology, an epistemology and rules of proper action/interaction embodied and mediated through significant symbols . . . (Gaines and Hahn, 1985: 10)

As Helman remarks, in a criticism of the conventional distinctions between illness and disease:

> One problem with this disease/illness dichotomy is that the biomedical model, that is, the medical perspective on ill-health, is often assumed to be a homogeneous, internally consistent, and rationally scientific body of knowledge. It is also assumed that the diseases which comprise this model are consistent, scientifically defined entities that are unchanged in whatever context they appear. (Helman, 1985: 293)

Helman suggests that this view is held not only by most clinicians, but by some anthropologists (for example, Kleinman, 1980) as well. In recent years, more anthropologists have addressed the production of biomedicine more directly (Lindenbaum and Lock, 1993; Lock and Gordon, 1988). Nevertheless, major statements such as the authoritative synopsis from Good (1994) continue to place greater stress on the cultural bases of illness rather than socially organized practices of disease construction. Helman himself analyses the variety of explanatory models held by different clinicians, and hence draws attention to the organizational distribution of knowledge. Biomedicine is far from homogeneous and the expression of its internal diversity may be accounted for in sociological terms.

Indeed, contemporary perspectives on biomedicine recognize and emphasize the socially constructed nature of diseases and diagnoses, although – as I shall indicate later when discussing narrative forms – there remains an imbalance within the anthropology of medicine, with far greater attention to the production of illness. Attention to the construction of disorders will be returned to in more detail in the following chapter. For now it is worth noting that medical anthropologists themselves have now extended the boundaries of culture-bound syndromes to include categories of orthodox biomedical knowledge, while recognizing the problematic character of culture-boundedness. Prince (1985), for instance, raises the problem by means of a careful appraisal of attributions of anorexia nervosa and brain-fag, while Hahn (1985) also raises fundamental questions about the ascription of the category culture-bound syndrome itself. (See also Arksey, 1994; Banks, 1992; Blumhagen, 1980; Gaines, 1992; Hall and Morrow, 1988; Helman, 1985, 1987; Hopkins, 1989; Karp, 1985; King, 1987; Low, 1985; McLean, 1990; Reynolds and Swartz, 1993.)

In general, it looks as though the anthropological investigation of health, illness and medicine in 'our own' societies has either discovered or constructed a very tightly framed, distinctive domain. This way of knowing is well-nigh universally taken for granted as the preferred way of understanding medical phenomena in Western societies. Other systems are constructed *as* other by being treated (by social scientists, biomedical practitioners and others) as 'folk', 'ethno-', 'alternative', 'unorthodox', 'quack' and so on. The anthropologist of medicine reverses the polarity. For now it is the conventional and dominant system of medicine that is treated as other. (One can detect from several of the comments already cited that one of the shortcomings of biomedicine is its apparent indifference, incomprehension or hostility towards the anthropologists' own insights.)

The anthropological version of medicine as other bears conceptual and analytic dangers. Not least is the danger of erecting and hypostatizing a strongly bounded, relatively homogeneous and coherent body of knowledge and action. The analysis can readily become a self-justifying exercise in circular reasoning. Anything that is said or done by a professional practitioner of contemporary orthodox medicine is assigned to the culture of 'biomedicine'. *Ipso facto* that culture is seen as dominant and all-encompassing.

The underlying model can readily become confused. On the one hand biomedicine is portrayed in terms of its adherence to the world-view of natural science. On the other hand, relevant anthropological studies show that non-scientific elements (folk-medicine, ritual, superstition etc.) are readily detectable in contemporary medical practice. Looking at the literature overall, therefore, it is hard to see whether biomedicine is unitary or diverse, rigid or flexible, exclusive or inclusive.

The problem – in so far as there is a serious problem here – stems from the particular disciplinary origins. Its roots in cultural anthropology have influenced the conceptualization of biomedicine. It has been defined, as we have seen, primarily as a *cultural* system. Equally, the emphasis of cultural anthropology lends the analyst to emphasize the cultural specificity of any given system – indeed, to stress its very *systematic* nature. Rather than attempting to characterize contemporary medicine in terms of its institutional elements, its organization and division of labour; rather than delineating its historical developments – the careers and trajectories of segments, and ideas, and practices; the anthropological paradigm prefers to represent a culturally bounded collectivity.

In many ways, therefore, contemporary biomedicine is a product of the boundary-work of *anthropological* definitions. It is a transformation of an orthodox and dominant occupation into a culturally defined collectivity. That academically produced category is misleading. It is biased in favour of an image of a relatively homogeneous cultural system. It is a device whereby anthropology constructs its object.

In other words, it can be argued that modern sociology and anthropology of medicine have used various argumentative or rhetorical devices to *construct* medicine and medical knowledge. Each makes the other in terms of its own discourse. Paradoxically, even while attempting to demystify medicine itself, the disciplines of social science have too often left the essential craft-mysteries of medicine inviolate. When the sociologists contrasted illness and disease they made illness into their domain. They carved out a field of meaningful social action. They constructed an ideal-typical social actor whose ill health could be represented in terms of rational action. The patient could be shown not as the passive victim or carrier of a disease, but as having a career. Illness therefore was not something suffered, but something actively accomplished. The scope for sociological understanding was thus established. But in the longer term, sociology's field of inquiry was bought at a price. The separation of illness and disease explicitly distinguishes the cultural from the natural, and implicitly diverts sociological attention away from the natural domain of biological disease categories and processes. The net effect is an awkward asymmetry in the classic sociological formulations: lay medical understanding is self-evidently appropriate subject matter for sociological analysis, while professional medical understanding somehow escapes equal scrutiny.

In much the same vein, the construction of biomedicine is paradoxical. Unlike the sociological treatment summarized above, the primarily anthropological treatment appears to tackle the content of medicine itself. To some extent it is successful. Yet its own version of medicine's otherness is limited and limiting. It is the cognitive equivalent of the doomed attempt to specify the core characteristics or traits of professions – an exercise that diverted too many sociologists for too long (Johnson, 1972; Roth, 1974). In like manner, the attempt is made to identify the core characteristics of the culture of contemporary cosmopolitan medicine. While medical knowledge is not privileged in this model, its otherness is guaranteed by its supposed *differentia specifica*. It is, moreover, treated as a distinctive culture in such a way as to exaggerate its homogeneity. Likewise, the emphasis on bio-medicine as a *culture* too readily implies that it provides an adequate explanation for medical action and medical knowledge. It is almost as reductionist as the medical understanding it seeks to interrogate. If biomedicine is the distinctive Gestalt of contemporary medical practice, then the latter can always in principle be understood and explained by reference to that cultural system. There is, therefore, little incentive for the social scientist to explore and document this 'culture' further. Once its lineaments have been sketched, then it remains to be illustrated and criticized. The accomplishment of 'biomedicine', or the production of its variegated knowledge-base, may be treated as relatively unproblematic.

It is worth noting that the anthropological rhetoric stands in partial contrast to that of sociology, but it recapitulates its limitations at various key points. For instance, part of the stock-in-trade of modern medical anthropology is the concept of the *culture-bound syndrome*. If taken seriously as an analytic contrast, this would appear to imply that some processes are culture-free. (Indeed, its distribution in the literature – virtually confined to relatively exotic phenomena – would implicitly define virtually all of medical phenomena as culture-free, and hence return them to the domain of nature unscathed by social analysis.)

On the other hand, biomedicine may be treated as just one, especially pervasive, ethnomedicine. Strictly speaking, therefore, from this standpoint any socially recognized entity of sickness should be regarded as a culture-bound syndrome. Viewed from a historical perspective, a condition such as *chlorosis* was recognized, defined and treated in ways specific to a particular period in modern Western societies, reflecting specific gender-related values, as was *fatigue*, *neurasthenia* and various other conditions. Viewed from an anthropological perspective, *susto* is specific to particular cultural contexts (Ruben et al., 1984). But viewed sociologically, and with due regard to principles of methodological symmetry, a condition such as von Willebrand disease (a condition defined in terms of an inherited coagulation defect, related specifically to Factor VIII) is identifiable precisely by virtue of the assumptions and frameworks of contemporary biomedicine. It is dependent on the technologies of investigation, the epistemological and ontological assumptions that drive biomedical research. It is dependent, in a rather more subtle way, on elementary features of medical thinking: not least those that guide the identification, classification and naming of disease entities. Indeed, the very nosography that rests on such clinical entities as 'von Willebrand' is a persistent feature of medical thought. It is deeply embedded in the mythological charters of medicine's own past as well as its contemporary typologies. It is, for all that, part of the culture of modern medicine. It is central to its thought-style as Fleck (1927, 1935) put it (Lowy, 1988). To that extent it is just as culture-bound as any other entity. In dealing with the discussion and management of von Willebrand's and other disorders of the blood system, then, I shall be assuming that they are culture-bound entities.

It is not clear what biomedicine is intended to contrast with. If it is to contrast only with ethnomedicine then – as we have seen – it reinforces rather than suspends the boundary surrounding contemporary medical practice. On the other hand there is the danger that it is used implicitly to contrast contemporary medicine with some utopian alternative. The latter would, presumably, be non-reductionist and would acknowledge the cultural as readily as the biological. But as a utopian model it provides a poor analytic perspective on the actual practices and beliefs of contemporary practitioners. It offers little perspective on the diversity of practices, or on their institutional settings.

The construction of the clinic

The social-scientific literature on medical work and medical encounters is characterized by a very marked bias in its coverage. It has been a feature of this intellectual domain since its emergence. A good deal of sociological analysis has been carried out on medical encounters. Social interaction in medical settings has become one of the most consistently studied topics in micro-sociology (ten Have, 1989). The reasons are not hard to find. The clinic provides a rich source of focused encounters, in which the exchange of information between the parties is of major importance. The medical encounter has been taken as a microcosm for the complex division of labour and its interactional consequences in modern society. It readily provides a localized manifestation of the differential distribution of knowledge within that division of labour.

An inspection of the relevant research literature reveals consistent biases in the microsociology of medical encounters. Again, they reflect some of medical sociology's taken-for-granted assumptions concerning what is self-evidently social. Interpersonal encounters in medical settings are overwhelmingly represented as 'doctor–patient' interactions. The social encounter in and of the clinic is, therefore the *consultation*. Over the past decades we have accumulated a substantial corpus of data and interpretation concerning doctor–patient interactions.

Doctor–patient interaction lends itself to contemporary investigation from a number of points of view. Sociologists, anthropologists and linguists have increasingly come to recognize the significance of spoken action. The analysis of talk by conversation analysts or discourse analysts has already proved one of the most important and fruitful areas for micro-sociological work. The accomplishment of the medical consultation is readily approached as the collaborative task of two parties – doctor and patient. In common with other focused encounters that have proved popular – such as school lessons (for example, Mehan, 1979) or courtrooms (for example, Atkinson and Drew, 1979) – the medical consultation has certain in-built advantages for the would-be analyst. First, the talk itself is focused and consequential. Whatever the merits and advantages of studying mundane discourse, there is a certain inherent interest in the form and content of medical consultations.

One reason for that is the *political* character with which it may be endowed. Again, like the classroom recitation, the medical encounter is essentially asymmetric. It may thus be addressed as the micro-social play of power. The doctor and his or her patient confront one another with different resources of cultural capital. Whatever the everyday status of the patient, he or she is – by definition – a lay participant in the medical consultation. Likewise, whatever his or her actual competence and skill (however defined and measured), the medical practitioner is by definition 'expert' within the consultation. It may therefore be assumed by many sociological analyses that the consultation encapsulates the wider social system or cultural cleavage that divides the professional from the lay. The micro-sociology or discourse analysis of the consultation all too readily recapitulates the construction of medicine as other. The encounter may be represented as the coming together not just of two social actors, but of two contrasting cultures – hence emphasizing not just the difference between the medical and the lay, but also implying a cultural unity for medicine itself. (The latter is more often assumed than demonstrated in practice.) The asymmetry of the encounter thus provides occasion for the sociological exploration (or at least *invocation*) of authority, control and power. (They are not always distinguished adequately or explored with sufficient sensitivity, however.) None the less, the medical encounter is seen as the occasion for the professional manipulation of talk and appearances. Often in ironic contrast with the claimed or imported ideals of medical practice, the consultation may be portrayed as controlled rather than collaborative, repressive rather than receptive, inhibiting rather than facilitating. The smooth accomplishment of medical consultations thus appears to be the outcome of the medical practitioner's coercive control over the form and content of talk. The lay client – powerless and dominated – is therefore excluded from the discourse. The medical problem ceases to be his or hers and is transformed into the object of the medical practitioner's own gaze. This asymmetric encounter may become the vehicle whereby existing inequalities are reproduced or amplified. The injuries of class, race and gender may be recapitulated in the consultation. The medical encounter thus becomes more a microcosm for the mechanisms of exclusion that characterize the wider cleavages of modern society.

The clinical consultation has exerted a special fascination not least because of this convergence of formal and political concerns. The analysis of interpersonal communication and negotiation has repeatedly been used to demonstrate mechanisms of domination and control in operation. The social distance between the doctor and his or her patient, and the asymmetrical distribution of expert knowledge and interactional resources, provide grist for the sociological mill. Sociologists and discourse analysts have therefore produced a substantial literature on the consultation. It includes analyses of encounters wherein social class and gender are shown to amplify social difference and in turn give rise to interactional processes of manipulation and exclusion. (This voluminous literature includes: M. Bloor, 1976a; Davis, 1988; Fisher, 1984; Fisher and Todd, 1983; Frankel, 1984; Hak, 1994; Mishler, 1984; Silverman, 1987; Waitzkin, 1989, 1991; Waitzkin and Stoeckle, 1978; West, 1984; Woolhandler and Himmelstein, 1989.)

In the course of these encounters the lay person is widely represented as losing his or her problem. It is appropriated by the practitioner and incorporated into his or her discourse of expert knowledge. This alienation of the client's own medical or health experience is mirrored in the micro-sociological literature by the medical transformation of his or her *identity*. The confrontation between the medical and the lay is reflected in the objectification of the person of the client. Just as the problem is appropriated, so too is the client.

The sociology of medical encounters is therefore replete with accounts of how the personhood of the patient is transformed into the case of the practitioner. This is the professional equivalent of the impersonal bureaucratic processing of cases. The organized routines of everyday practice transmute the unique, biographically constituted troubles of the person into the appropriate classes of diagnosis and management. The individual thus becomes fixed in a domain of typified actors, actions and outcomes. The consultation becomes one of a series of functionally equivalent encounters, and the patient one of a series of typified clients. That process of typification serves and legitimates the recipes of knowledge and action that are the stock-in-trade of the experienced practitioner. Medical sociology adopts an ambivalent perspective. It recognizes on the one hand the pervasive – even necessary – presence of practical reasoning in the most specialized and arcane of fields. It acknowledges that the practitioner must draw upon such devices as typification and recipe-knowledge in order to render his or her work manageable. The practicability and stability of the social world are ordered by such cognitive and interactional devices. There is no escape from them if the world is not to be recreated afresh at each and every social encounter. On the other hand, the sociological imagination recoils from the depersonalizing consequences of these *im*personal routines and recipes. Once more, the world of medicine is ironically contrasted with a (largely mythical) alternative in which patient and practitioner encounter one another as fully realized persons. The patient retains control not only of his or her 'problem' but also of his or her biography.

The consequences of typification are typically held to be especially shocking when they deprive the patient not only of the problem, not only of his or her identity, but even of dignity. The production and use of disparaging or stigmatizing typifications is an especial offence for micro-sociology. It seems to represent the utmost abuse of the professional's discursive power. The asymmetry of the relationship is exaggerated to the point that the lay client becomes not the beneficiary but the *victim* of the consultation. In so far as the sociological perspective readily aligns itself with that of the lay person (and of the underdog) then the analysis of the consultation affirms the otherness of the medicine.

This bias in the coverage of medical encounters has one immediate consequence. The sociological treatment of doctor–patient interaction, and the almost exclusive attention devoted to that dyadic relationship, has meant that other types of encounter, and other types of participant, are all but invisible. The implicit assumption of what counts as social has meant that sociologists have collectively misrepresented the variety of medical encounters and medical settings. There is a rich diversity of social action and interaction that escapes the obsessive focus on doctor–patient dyads. In contrast with the doctor–patient consultation, there is precious little analysis of how medical practitioners deal with one another. In other words, doctor–doctor interaction is poorly researched. Indeed, the entire range of possibilities is under-researched. With some notable exceptions we know little of how interaction is managed within clinical teams or firms – how superiors and inferiors in the medical profession engage with one another. Apart from some studies that focus primarily on educational work in such contexts, there is little specific attention to the discourse of medical teams. Likewise, there is little to guide the sociological understanding of how clinicians interact with non-clinical specialists – medically qualified and others. Within the complex division of labour of modern medicine, the clinician or clinical team may draw on the expertise and advice of many others – pathologists, geneticists, radiologists, haematologists and so on. Those consulting services themselves include medical practitioners, laboratory scientists and technicians. There are many occasions when consultation between practitioners takes place: sometimes in face-to-face interaction and sometimes by less direct means.

The net effect, however, is that too much sociological work treats virtually all medical settings and all medical work as synonymous with the consultation. The entire organization of medical institutions and the complex division of labour is imploded into this one microcosm. The naive observer, who had access only to mainstream sociological research, could all too readily assume that medical work was a predominantly solitary affair that occurred within the consulting rooms of family practitioners and their hospital counterparts.

By contrast, great tracts of work remain all but invisible. There is little or no sociological illumination of most of the back regions of medical institutions. We know next to nothing about the laboratories of modern hospitals; of the regular encounters between practitioners at case conferences, grand rounds, mortality and morbidity reviews. We know as little about the myriad interactions – some fleeting and informal, others more formally contrived – through which medical practitioners consult one another. We know depressingly little about how the work of the laboratory relates to the work of the clinic. There is far too little research on how medical practitioners from different specialties cooperate or compete in the management of particular conditions. The implicit assumption that the social is to be found with the patient, and his or her consultation, is therefore a limiting one. In consequence, much of contemporary medicine is left under-explored. Again, the danger is in assuming that the interesting sociological issues – of cultural variation, of belief, practical reasoning – are to be found only in the interaction of the patient's biography and the practitioner's expert knowledge. This bias therefore parallels the classic sociological preoccupation with illness behaviour. The 'purely' medical and technical knowledge of medical science goes by default. The sociological and anthropological literature tell us far too little about how medical science is produced and reproduced, how it is shared and transmitted, how it is legitimated in practice. The contemporary sociological literature all too often portrays a solitary craft worker, who makes no use of other experts, of scientific evidence or of published research.

The emphasis on the consultation has over-simplified the representation of medicine as a social domain. The dyadic doctor–patient interaction offers an elementary exemplar. Each individual may be held to stand for two respective cultures, or two elements in a social system. They furnish a simple model for culture-clash, for the play of power, for gender inequalities, for professional dominance (or whatever analytic axe the sociologist grinds). Moreover, this microcosm is readily grasped and documented because it is *bounded*. The doctor–patient consultation can be encapsulated within Aristotelian dramatic unities. (I return to this issues in the next chapter when I discuss representations of decision-making.) It is a commonplace of the sociological and psychological analyses of consultations that they are characteristically short. Though the length is demonstrably affected by the patient's social position and personal characteristics, the modal length of medical encounter is relatively brief. The consultation routinely occupies no more than a few minutes. It characteristically takes place in one physical location. Within the privacy of the consulting room, then, the interaction is bounded in time and space. This relatively brief, focused, dyadic interaction thus provides manageable strips of spoken and unspoken activity that are amenable to recording and analysis. The structure of the consultation provides the analyst with manageable episodes. A substantial corpus of such episodes can be assimilated fairly straightforwardly, and the results aggregated quite readily. Medical work is thus isolated in time and place, apprehended in convenient chunks. The dyad presents little complexity in analysing patterns of interaction. Again, therefore, we can see how the opportunity offered by the consultation is ultimately a limitation. The tendency is for medical work and medical interaction to be seen as bounded spatially and temporally. The analysis of doctor–patient interaction, conventionally conducted, cannot capture the more protracted and dispersed processes of work that are pervasive of modern medical organizations. The division of labour is lost: the lone practitioner stands for the whole occupation. The diverse settings for medical work are represented only by the consulting room. Protracted investigations and deliberations are reduced to a single episode. Multiple meetings and conferences are condensed into one fleeting interaction. As we shall see, this means that the one-to-one medical consultation is a kind of *synecdoche*: that is, it stands in a part-for-whole relationship with the whole field of medical work, interaction and discourse (Kuipers, 1989). This means, in turn, that the very character of medical work is condensed within this one episodic encounter. The process(es) of trouble formulation, history-taking, investigation, discussion, debate, judgement, management and so on become represented as single *acts*. Rather than diffuse and protracted, the cognitive and linguistic tasks of medicine are all too easily summarized as if they were virtually instantaneous events.

The implications of this restricted focus in medical sociology will become apparent later when we turn to consider parallel literatures on medical 'decision-making' by psychologists and cognitive sociologists. There it will be argued that the organized character of much medical work has been misrepresented in the vast majority of published studies. It will also be argued – and elaborated on subsequently – that the nature of medicine as *work* has not always been captured by contemporary analysis.

In this chapter I have tried to introduce some elementary issues in the contemporary sociology and anthropology of medicine. I have suggested that their conceptual schemas have too readily and too often constructed the subject matter of medicine in such a way as to limit its exploration. The radical separation of illness and disease invited an almost exclusive concentration on the former, while ignoring the production and repro-duction of technical medical work. The identification of biomedicine has tended to over-emphasize the presence of a single dominant culture of medicine; like the other dualities I referred to, it too readily presupposes a radical difference between the medical and the lay. Both sets of background assumptions have led social scientists to concentrate their efforts unduly on the doctor–patient consultation. Whether viewed as a clash between two contrasting cultures, or as the local play of political processes, the consultation or clinical interview has too readily become a microcosm for all aspects of medical work and practice.

It will be apparent that in erecting the arguments of this chapter I have exaggerated things somewhat. I have not paid systematic attention to those studies by sociologists and others that have documented processes whereby the culture-bound syndromes of contemporary biomedicine are produced; nor have I paid any attention yet to those parallel research programmes that are concerned with medical decision-making and cognate issues. In the next chapter, therefore, I shall turn my attention to themes and issues in the production and reproduction of medical knowledge.

3

The Production of Medical Knowledge

Construction and production

For many years the sociology of medicine paid surprisingly little attention to the production and use of medical knowledge. It treated medicine as the medium for other issues (gender, class, race and power) but rarely addressed the character of medicine itself. Secondly, the sociology of medicine developed more or less in isolation from the sociology of science, despite the fact that much of medical work and medical knowledge may be characterized as scientific, in the narrow sense of being grounded in biological and other natural or applied sciences (Wright and Treacher, 1982). By the same token, relatively few sociologists of science have turned primary attention to the form and content of medical knowledge. (There are several notable and important exceptions to those generalizations: they will be mentioned later in the argument.) As a consequence, the sociological treatment of medical knowledge by sociologists of medicine themselves for long remained a stunted affair. Sociologists have still not produced a comprehensive and systematic analysis of most domains of medical knowledge, and core activities in the accomplishment of medical work. On the contrary: too much of the sociology of medical knowledge has been conducted at a high level of generality and abstraction. There has been insufficient detailed, empirical analysis of concrete examples of medical knowledge in practice. There is now a small, but rather muddled, literature on the social character of medical knowledge. It is loosely grounded in contemporary sociologies of knowledge, but uncertainly so. It is all too frequently couched in terms of rather ill-focused appeals to constructivism, realism, materialism or whatever. There is need for careful appraisal of what is meant and what is possible within an adequate sociology of medical knowledge.

A recommendation for the sociology of medical knowledge is not an argument against other aspects of sociology. It is, however, a recognition that all too frequently in sociological studies of expert communities *everything but* esoteric and everyday knowledge is explored. This argument was elaborated for the sociology of education as early as 1971, when the so-called new sociology of education was promoted by its advocates (Young, 1971). They pointed out then that sociologists of education were typically preoccupied with the latent functions of educational institutions and systems. Education was seen as a vehicle for the reproduction of other social forces – inequalities of class, race and gender. Little attention was devoted to the content of education itself, or its manifest function: that is, the management and transmission of *knowledge* and skills.

By the same token, medical settings and institutions have all too frequently been treated as the occasion for commentary on 'other' themes. As I suggested in the last chapter, it is common for sociological commentary to portray the medical encounter as an arena for the play of class inequalities, gender differences, professional dominance and manipulative control. The medical practitioner is repeatedly implicated in patterns of social control, or in forms of social interaction characteristic of professional interests. The medical practitioner's routines of talk are also explored from similar perspectives. The spoken interaction that constitutes much of the medical consultation is characteristically inspected for evidence of professional hegemony. The search is made for models of the consultation that succeed in capturing its essence in the distinctive imbalance of power and resources as between practitioner and patient.

It is noticeable, for instance, that when sociologists have examined collegial interaction and have explored the backstage regions of the clinic, they have done so in order to examine issues such as professional failure and mistakes. Millman (1976) is a classic case in point. In a powerful and highly readable ethnographic account, Millman explicitly sets out her stall to document 'features of the everyday world of the hospital that adversely affect the quality of patient care' (p. 9). Hers is, therefore, a study of professional regulation and its failures. For instance, she includes an ethnographic account of medical mortality and morbidity reviews which helps to evoke some of its characteristic forms:

> The Mortality Review Conference has a special quality of high tension, and the meetings are better attended than are those of the other regular teaching conferences. At Lakeside Hospital, the Chief of Medicine stands on the stage and presides over the Mortality Review Conference as a master of ceremonies. As the case is reviewed in chronological order, starting with the time of the patient admission to the hospital, and proceeding to the autopsy report, the chief calls on the various doctors who were involved in the case, asks them to step to the front of the auditorium, and instructs them to recall and explain what they did and what they thought at each moment in time. He counsels them not to jump ahead of the chronological order, nor to divulge information gained at a later time, in order not to spoil the final diagnosis for the members of the audience. As one after another of the staff testifies about how they were led to the same mistaken diagnosis, a convincing case for the justifiability of the error is implicitly presented and the responsibility for the mistake is spread so that no one doctor is made to look guilty of a mistake that anyone else wouldn't have made, and in fact, didn't make. (Millman 1976: 97–8)

Millman's concern with medical failure and her exposé of the failure of regulation leads her to focus almost exclusively on possible latent functions of this piece of clinical ceremony. She sees it as a device for managing failure and masking guilt; and it undoubtedly can have such outcomes. On the other hand, she pays virtually no attention to any manifest functions or to its form. Indeed, she is almost dismissive of the overt reasons of the review: she manages to sound sceptical as to its overtly instructive and preventative purposes.

Now my own observations in Beacon Hospital included occasional attendance at the weekly Mortality and Morbidity Review in Medicine. Indeed, patients for whom the haematologists had been consulted were sometimes being presented, and the meetings could provide yet another arena for the rehearsal of a case. I did not record those meetings on tape: I had no permission to do so, and in any case such large, crowded meetings would have been difficult to capture on tape without elaborate recording arrangements. One can, however, confirm that they were of the same general type as described by Millman, but for my purposes it is that *type* itself which is significant. The form of this ceremony is important, not just its latent control function.

The Reviews I attended (wedged in with a large number of students and resident staff, many consuming their brown-bag lunch) certainly contained accounts of errors, including technical blunders. During the discussion of one of the haematology cases, one of the residents admitted botching a bone marrow aspirate (a painful procedure for the patient): the first time he tried he did not go in far enough and failed to obtain any marrow, and the second time he went too far, again failing to obtain a good specimen. This error was greeted with shared laughter. In many ways, however, this is less significant than the overall ceremonial of the occasion. Along with many other encounters, it constitutes part of the *spectacle of the clinic*. Millman's description of the chief of service as a master of ceremonies is telling in this context. After all, this is not a single one-off event designed specifically to accommodate and diffuse medical failure. It is one of a recurrent cycle of meetings and conferences through which cases are presented and work is scrutinized. The course of illness and medical management is repeatedly refracted through the discursive acts of medical specialists. It is, in other words, part of the round of rounds, in the course of which are affirmed the clinical division of labour and the legitimacy of medical knowledge (even when specific shortcomings are exposed). Millman, therefore, touches on those fundamental features when describing the prescribed order in which medical personnel contribute, and the narrative requirements that are enforced. Those conventions in effect impose particular rhetorical formats on the reconstruction of medical events. (It is noticeable that Millman's summary reconstructions of cases from the mortality review understandably rob them of their rhetorical force.)

My specific remarks here are not designed to deny the importance of Millman's general theme. The issues of collegial control, regulation and scrutiny are readily apparent through my own analysis. They have also been the themes of several of the most important ethnographies of medical work and interaction between professional colleagues (for example, Bosk, 1979; Freidson, 1976). Some elements of those analyses also reflect some of the ritualized features of medical work and discourse. Many of the encounters that form the empirical subject matter of this book are occasions for the mutual scrutiny of physicians, as well as for their instruction. They are also occasions for the sharing and transmission of knowledge and opinion. They provide opportunity for the self-presentation of junior doctors to their peers and superiors. Like the encounter summarized by Millman, they also impose similar narrative and rhetorical formats.

Throughout these recurrent sociological motifs, the theme of medical knowledge is understated. Undeniably, it is there. As will be indicated in due course, there is attention to the frames of reference for various specialists and other categories of actor. It is, however, noticeable that even here there is rather too much stress on the exotic, on the irrational and magical, on fringe unorthodoxy, on ideological biases or overlays. Equally, the sociology of medical knowledge has been unduly coloured by attempts to characterize it in the most general of terms. Sociologists have been too ready to appeal in rather vague ways to 'the clinical mentality', to the central role of 'uncertainty', to the supposed limitations of 'biomedical' reductionism and similar broad conceptual categories. They are themselves too easily deployed in a reductionist mode, such that the particularities of medical knowledge and medical work in specific social contexts are lost to view, hidden behind the global generalizations and catch-all terms. There is, therefore, an important task to be performed just in sorting out and clarifying some of the main conceptual issues in this now rather confused area. The intention here is not just to engage in sterile debate concerning alternative or competing 'paradigms' with regard to the character of medical and scientific knowledge. The task is, however, a necessary preliminary to an adequate sociology of medical knowledge that is empirically grounded in a sociology of medical *work*.

It needs to be established, indeed, that much of the recent debate, many of the positions adopted on one or other side in it, are based on a consistent failure to ground analysis in a careful ethnography of socially organized medical practice. There is little or nothing to be gained by *a priori* adoption of general (often vague) theoretical or epistemological positions. They are important, of course. But too many sociologists prefer to engage in 'paradigm wars' than to undertake the detailed sociological research that is necessary to illuminate the forms and processes of medical work. This is not a call for atheoretical empiricism. Theoretical and epistemological issues do indeed need to be taken seriously. They must be tackled at a suitably sophisticated level. Nevertheless, they do not substitute for painstaking sociological inquiry that is open to the everyday life of medical and other personnel. Appeals to constructivism, materialism or realism do little to resolve the sociological problems of how medical knowledge is produced and reproduced, shared, legitimated and used. They tend to obscure rather than illuminate how medical and laboratory staff actually set about manipulating physical equipment and human tissues; how they generate and interpret representations of anatomical features and pathological processes. It is, however, important to review the most recent contributions and debates in this area, if only to differentiate the present work from many of the more extreme positions.

In recent years, the sociology of medical knowledge has been especially coloured by the influence of Michel Foucault. The Foucauldian perspective has informed a variety of historical and ethnographic research. It has inspired (not always for the better) a growing literature on 'discourse' and 'power' in medical domains. It is not surprising that Foucault's work should have been so readily appropriated by sociologists and historians of medicine. The birth of modern medicine was itself the topic of one of Foucault's classic works (Foucault, 1973). While *Naissance de la Clinique* (*The Birth of the Clinic*) has not received a great deal of attention from general theorists and followers of Foucault, it has understandably inspired a number of major scholars whose interests are defined primarily or exclusively by medical knowledge and practice.

The precise details of Foucault's own treatment are not relevant to this discussion; the accuracy of his precise historical treatment is equally beyond its scope. There are good grounds for arguing that Foucault's treatment of French hospital medicine is misleading. He appears to over-estimate the contrast between the medicine of the pre- and post-revolutionary periods in France. His historical discontinuity is, at least in part, an achievement of his own rhetorical skills. There is no guarantee that Foucault's analysis would in any case be equally applicable to medical thought and practice outside France. Nevertheless, medical sociologists have been willing to take on board his general analytic stance. Surprisingly, perhaps, the enthusiasts have paid rather little attention to Foucault's detailed analysis of medical knowledge, practice and education. Foucault's influence has been such that his ideas have often been adopted and incorporated uncritically. His adoption by sociologists is especially ironic, as Foucault's own treatment of his subject matter is especially un-sociological: it is poorly grounded in the detailed analysis of social organization or everyday practice. His 'discourse' is not normally anchored in an adequate representation of the social, but seems to float free of any specific context.

Nevertheless, several major contributors have attempted to build substantial sociologies or social histories of medical knowledge and practice on Foucauldian foundations. Among the more notable British contributions are those of Armstrong (1983, 1990), Turner (1987), and Nettleton (1992), while an American perspective is offered by Arney and his collaborators (for example, Arney, 1982). Turner's review of power and knowledge in medicine is suffused with the spirit of Foucault. His synthesis contains no original research, but is intended to bring a good deal of sociological work within a framework of general sociological theory, and Foucault is proposed as one route towards that goal. Of course, as Turner indicates, Foucault's general concern with the body means that his ideas form an especially important resource for a sociology of medicine:

Foucault's interest in the relationships between the discourse of scientific knowledge and the exercise of professional power, the development of a political struggle around the body, the history of sexuality in relation to medical institutions, and finally the development of various forms of discipline and surveillance under the general notion of panopticism provide a powerful framework for the development of a rhetorical medical sociology addressed to the central issues of meaning, structure, social order and power. (Turner, 1987: 10)

Unfortunately, Turner does not apply these Foucauldian insights in order to generate any detailed analyses. Indeed, despite the centrality of 'knowledge' and 'discourse' to such a proposed sociological programme, Turner's account deals very poorly with the social or historical contexts of medical knowledge and practice. His account provides neither novel analytic frameworks nor new analyses of specific diseases or treatments.

By contrast, Armstrong (1983) uses the insights he derives from Foucault to produce a recognizably coherent and novel analysis of aspects of the development of medicine in Britain. His is a much more precise treatment than Turner's: like Foucault himself, Armstrong starts from close readings of medical and scientific texts. Armstrong traces key transformations in the character of medical knowledge in twentieth-century Britain. He identifies the emergence of medical discourses focused either on particular techniques of classification, enumeration and surveillance, or on particular categories of patient. His series of historical analyses highlights the technical and discursive diversity of modern medicine. Even the Foucauldian perspective need not commit us to a reductionist perspective whereby a homogeneously modern medicine is postulated.

Armstrong's analysis highlights both the strengths and limitations of the Foucauldian approach. On the one hand, it addresses attention to the generation of particular styles of thought within the profession of medicine. It places knowledge firmly at the centre of a sociology of medicine. On the other hand, it does so in terms that all too often remain lacking in sociological precision. It is not clear from Armstrong's analyses, for instance, how the various transformations in discourse are initiated and sustained. There is little or no grounding in the everyday character of medical *work* or the interpersonal relations of medical institutions. The Foucault-inspired approach is undoubtedly one of the most important of contemporary justifications for a recognition of the social or cultural definition of medical phenomena:

> We can no longer regard 'diseases' as natural events in the world which occur outside the language with which they are described. A disease entity is the product of medical discourses which in turn reflect the dominant mode of thinking (the episteme in Foucault's terminology) within a society. (Turner, 1987: 11)

On the other hand, that perspective actually does rather little to document the key processes whereby those 'disease entities' are actually produced as elements within the everyday social reality of actors in medical settings. Turner's reference to the language of medical description hides the fact that the discourse analysis of Foucault does *not* address in detail the spoken language (discourse) through which such everyday work is accomplished. In other words, Foucault provides one among several epistemological rationales for the 'social construction of medicine' but falls short of a thoroughgoing sociological analysis of that process.

One of the more lively debates over the sociological analysis of medical knowledge in recent years was occasioned by Bury (1986) in a major review and critique of what he categorized as 'constructionist' accounts of medical knowledge (see also Bury, 1987). His targets were a mixed bag of sociologists, some inspired by Foucault and post-structuralism, others by a phenomenological or interactionist perspective on the 'social construction of reality'. Nevertheless, he finds in the various positions a common adherence to a 'constructionist' position, underlying the various contributions. And he finds that underlying position untenable. Bury's views are wide of the mark, for the most part, but they merit attention, because they encapsulate many vulgar misconceptions about the sociology of medical knowledge (or indeed of any knowledge). Bury's intervention has been subject to thorough rebuttal by Nicolson and McLaughlin (1987, 1988). I find their responses convincing, and the entire debate is not recapitulated here. One of Bury's basic worries is the supposed 'incoherence' of the constructivist position. He draws attention to the fact that there are various theoretical perspectives that imply a constructivist account. But the constructivist camp, composed of these diverse tendencies, is a creation of Bury himself. The supposed incoherence is a product of his lumping together authors of very different persuasions, and then accusing them of espousing an incoherent position.

More fundamental – and more commonly shared with other sociologists, one suspects – is Bury's complaint that a social constructivist perspective cannot adequately cope with the constraining role played by material reality. In effect, this implies that social constructivism is a purely idealist posture, that acknowledges no reality independent of its socially organized representations. There is, however, absolutely no need for a constructivism to adopt a naive idealism any more than there is for Bury or other critics to endorse a vulgar materialism. There is, in fact, no major problem, for a constructivist view does not imply that social actors whimsically conjure reality out of thin air. Equally (and this is often overlooked) it certainly does not mean that it is simply and solely a mental product. It is necessary to remind oneself that the 'social construction of reality' does indeed refer to *social* processes; that it refers to collective acts, not to individual, much less private cognition. It is not a solipsistic view of reality construction. It is sometimes less easy, however, to remind oneself, or critics like Bury, that the collective acts of reality construction are themselves material. Socially organized transactions with the physical world are themselves real. The everyday social actor and the expert (such as the natural or medical scientist) engage with a material universe in acts of exploration. There is no implication in the work of phenomenologically inspired sociologists such as Schutz (for example, Schutz, 1967) or Berger and Luckmann (1967) that reality construction takes place in disembodied minds that have no engagement with a 'real world'. 'Reality' is not to be viewed as a construct in the sense that 'there is nothing there' independently of social actors.

When the anatomist or physiologist, say, produces his or her accounts of human structure and function, we do not need to deny the existence of bodies in order to attempt a sociological account of their work. We may certainly need to 'bracket' our, and their, assumptions about how 'bodies' exist, or indeed the very category 'body' itself, but that is quite a different matter. The latter – the equivalent of the phenomenologists' *epoche* – is a necessary methodological procedure, which ought to be practised by all but the most crass empiricists. A methodologically inspired scepticism about what we know and how we claim to know it does not necessarily lead to a nihilistic perspective. It is quite wrong to confuse a methodological precept with an ontological position. Nicolson and McLaughlin make the same point:

> The sociologist of medical knowledge need not discount the actors' intuition that the evidence provided by, say, pathology derives, in some sense, from beyond the social. For example, one need not deny that a photograph of the interior surface of one of the cavities of the brain is a photograph of something which is not wholly an artefact – even if the objects photographed could be named and conceived of differently, even if both the term 'ventricle' and the significance attached to it are social conventions, even if a medical photograph is itself a conventional representation, the making of which requires years of training and specific socialisation. It may be agreed by sociological observer as well as scientific actor that medical knowledge is, generally speaking, about the physical reality of human bodies. (Nicolson and McLaughlin, 1987: 11)

There is, therefore, no major problem in recognizing that socially organized practices of investigation, perception, description and manipulation are transactions with and within a material universe.

Equally, however, there is no need to endorse the view that those transactions are totally governed and constrained by that material domain. One hardly needs to engage in systematic cross-cultural and historical comparison in order to realize that if there is a more or less uniform and stable material world, then our perception of it, to say nothing of our consequent understanding of it, must be underdetermined. The ordering and evaluation of observations of the natural world are inextricably cultural *as well as* natural events. That surely is one of the most important lessons of Foucault's stark exemplar at the beginning of *The Birth of the Clinic*, whatever the shortcomings of that particular work. Foucault reproduces the recorded observations of a pre-modern physician in which is described in great detail a physical structure – a membrane – which is not recognized by modern anatomy or physiology. Clearly the earlier and the contemporary observers are engaged in transactions with the biological realm; each is indeed engaged in real physical work in manipulating material tissues. It may reasonably be assumed that there have not been massive and irrational changes in that material universe. Yet what is observable changes. It does so because each observer operates with a different stock of knowledge – shared with other members of their respective occupational networks – and a different repertoire of descriptive, linguistic resources.

If one adopts a constructivist perspective, therefore, one is not proposing the patently absurd view that biological or medical phenomena are purely mental constructs, any more than one is committed to the view that pathology is somehow a projection of such cognitive acts. Indeed, when Merleau-Ponty used the 'phantom limb' phenomenon to explore the phenomenology of perception, there was no suggestion that the rest of the material body was mysteriously absent, or a figment of the amputee's imagination; nor indeed was there any suggestion that the missing limb had not in fact been amputated (Merleau-Ponty, 1962). A phenomenological perspective on the body in sickness and in health should not be taken to mean that material bodies do not exist in a material world.

There is, perhaps, a problem in terminology. For all its inadequacies Bury's critique captures many misunderstandings (or incomplete understandings) of the broadly constructivist position that are shared among a number of sceptics. In what follows I shall generally avoid the use of 'construction'. That term does undeniably carry connotations of mental and individual activity. It does sometimes fail to convey the sense of material transactions with the world. Equally, the invocation of constructivism (just like the invocation of biomedical culture) can too easily be used as a gloss, rather than being used to open up detailed sociological analysis of *how* those transactions are accomplished. In an attempt to avoid those unwarranted and unnecessary connotations, I prefer to refer to the social *production* of medical knowledge. In doing so, I hope to draw more explicit attention to precisely those socially organized practices and transactions by which facts, findings, representations, opinions, diagnoses – all the elements of practical medical knowledge – are produced and reproduced. Emphasis is thus placed on medical knowledge production as *work*. It acknowledges that it is embedded within a social and technical division of labour. It reminds us that medical knowledge is grounded in material as well as cultural resources.

Stress on the social production of medical knowledge may also – again, by avoiding unhelpful connotations – help to preserve the principle of symmetry in approaching any and every aspect of medical understanding. The principle of symmetry has been advocated by sociologists of scientific knowledge, especially in the context of the so-called *strong programme* (Bartley, 1990; D. Bloor, 1976). The principle of symmetry in this context insists that it is necessary – as a *methodological* imperative – to apply the same sociological analyses to domains of knowledge that are conventionally regarded as 'orthodox' as to the 'rejected', the 'failed' or the heterodox. The task of sociological inquiry is not to explain away error in social terms, while assuming that correct belief is adequately explained by reference to nature itself, and the inexorable progress of scientific research. We must, in other words, apply sociological scholarship to any and every aspect of specialist knowledge, irrespective of its supposed adequacy (as judged by non-sociological criteria). In the field of medical knowledge, therefore, it is the task of the sociologist (or anthropologist) to pay equally serious attention to the practices of orthodox cosmopolitan medicine as to the non-orthodox or non-Western. Against that background of methodological precept, therefore, there is no difficulty in recognizing that *all* knowledge – including scientific and medical – is *socially produced*. In this book I do not achieve a full account of the local production of medical knowledge and opinion. To do that would involve more extensive fieldwork in many sites, including much more sustained attention to medical laboratories (Bartley, 1990).

The principle of symmetry requires that we acknowledge how knowledge is made, legitimated, shared and transmitted within socially organized contexts. Attention to the processes of knowledge production implies no particular commitment *vis-à-vis* the validity of the knowledge in question. As a matter of *sociological* inquiry, therefore, it is proper to confine research precisely to the realm of the interpersonal and the cultural. It is irrelevant to any intrinsic or extrinsic evaluation of medical or scientific knowledge, for instance, to note that it is located and distributed within a social and technical division of labour; that authority and expertise are differentially distributed within that social framework; that aspects of knowledge and skill are contested within and between different segments, specialties and networks. And so on. Insoluble problems arise for the sociologist when he or she mistakes the nature of the disciplines, becoming a second-rate philosopher. My argument, therefore, is not simply that one may, but that one should bracket ontological problems of scientific and medical knowledge in order precisely to concentrate on their distribution, transmission, legitimation, representation and, generally their *production* in everyday settings of work. In this context it is important to stress that sociology should not be invoked in order to explain away particular aspects of medical knowledge. As Berg (1992) points out, medical sociologists have too often separated out the medical and the social in order to treat as sociologically problematic issues of bias and ideology. In such sociological work,

> it is 'simply' biomedical knowledge that directs the physician, through logical steps, from individual findings towards the right diagnostic and therapeutic decisions. The 'cognitive' domain of medical action was thus regarded as self-explanatory, not needing and defying sociological scrutiny. (Berg, 1992: 153)

The view that Berg criticizes here fails to do justice to the social organization of everyday knowledge production and reproduction. We need to pay adequate attention to how routine knowledge is made and shared.

In contrast to the rather jejune nature of epistemological disputation, empirical research gives considerable weight to the view that contemporary biomedical knowledge is socially produced and culturally specific. First, the nosologies and nosographies that are the stock-in-trade of modern Western medicine are not merely characteristic of a scientific capacity to describe and enumerate the natural world. They are dependent on certain fundamental features of medical culture, which is itself produced and reproduced through processes of socialization (Atkinson, 1977, 1981a, 1981b). It is, for instance, revealing that medical students are apparently increasingly predisposed to use the category *disease* as they are progressively socialized into the culture of the clinic (Stefan and McManus, 1989), and the specificity of diseases or syndromes is itself historically and culturally specific.

Moreover, specific disease categories themselves are subject to processes of definition and negotiation that are inescapably rooted in social processes and interests. Amongst many medically identified conditions and problems one may instance the identification and attribution of Alzheimer's disease (Gubrium, 1986), premenstrual syndrome (Rodin, 1992), menopause (Lock, 1985), genetic diseases (Yoxen, 1982), tardive dyskinesia (Brown and Funk, 1986), hirsutism (Ferrante, 1988).

The processes whereby particular disease labels are attributed are far from clear cut, and they are certainly not determined by naturally occurring categories and phenomena. For instance, Hunt (1985) uses the example of hypoglycemia to show a degree of indeterminacy in the attribution of that biomedical term. She argues that contrary to the commonsense view of diagnosis as a description of facts, a term such as hypoglycemia expresses the physician's concepts of 'anomaly' or 'dysfunction'. The attribution of the disease label is highly variable among physicians, and Hunt concludes that one must regard such diagnostic labels as cognitive constructs; as such they are subject to the influence of culture and context (see also Fujimura and Chou, 1994).

The use of culturally prescribed disease categories is itself dependent on the socialized competence of practitioners to recognize and describe the relevant signs of a given disease. As I have tried to show elsewhere (Atkinson, 1988), clinical observation and recognition do not come naturally to neophyte medical students: the students must be socialized into the culturally and locally appropriate ways of looking, and the required vocabularies of description. This is as much a matter of apprenticeship as any other culture-specific way of knowing and telling (cf. Lave, 1988; Lave and Wenger, 1991). The senses and instruments alike must be socialized into the production of reliable (that is, reproducible) clinical descriptions.

Such accomplishments are underpinned by characteristic modes of practical reasoning and work. Although sometimes described in apparently cognitive terms, they are primarily socially shared and organized methods for the accomplishment of the clinic. Freidson's characterization of the *clinical mentality* (Freidson, 1970) is a classic formulation in this vein. The production and reproduction of clinical knowledge or opinion are grounded in characteristic modes of perception and legitimation. Knowledge is justified primarily in terms of the personal knowledge of the physician, and his or her professional experience. In other words, the practitioner claims a particular warrant for his or her actions in which personal knowledge is a paramount reality (Schutz, 1967). As Freidson himself puts it:

> In having to rely so heavily upon his personal, clinical experience with concrete, individual cases . . . the practitioner comes essentially to rely on the authority of his own senses, independently of the general authority of tradition or science. After all, he can only act on the basis of what he himself experiences, and if his own activity seems to get results, or at least no untoward results, he is resistant to

changing it on the basis of statistical or abstract considerations. He is likely to need to see or feel the case himself. (Freidson, 1970: 170)

In later chapters I shall present and discuss data that help elaborate and improve on such a view of clinical practices – in particular by suggesting that personal, traditional and scientific knowledge interpenetrate in clinical discourse in more complex ways than Freidson's brief characterization accommodates. Nevertheless, his formulation is valuable in providing an outline of one of the most important features of modern medical culture. It is a culture which celebrates the individual practitioner's autonomy and the existence of clinical judgement. It is, therefore, resistant to the uniform exercise of knowledge and skills. This goes some way to accounting for the persistence of knowledge which may be – from other perspectives – discredited; and equally, for practitioner resistance to innovation. Lipton and Hershaft (1985), for instance, document the acceptance of flawed clinical research, while Brown and Funk (1986) exemplify the resistance of clinicians to the recognition of a particular condition. Individualized styles and preferences, derived from and warranted by the clinical mentality, may go a long way towards explaining sources of variability in diagnosis and treatment preferences (for example, Denig et al., 1993). It also provides a framework of legitimacy within which treatments may be provided that are not necessarily justified by other criteria (for example, Bates, 1990).

Freidson's account of the clinical mentality is paralleled and exemplified by various sociological accounts of practical reasoning by physicians and others in everyday work settings. In many ways the best of those studies, by virtue of its rigour and theoretical sensitivity, is Bloor's study of ENT specialists and their recourse to adenotonsillectomy (M. Bloor, 1976b). Bloor adduces, from a phenomenological perspective, that the clinicians in question operate with particular stocks of recipe-knowledge and typifications of their patients' problems. His analysis of clinicians' practical reasoning stands in sharp contrast to the decontextualized approach of too many decision-making analyses. So too does Katz's analysis of surgeons' work (Katz, 1985). Both Katz and Bloor show that 'decision-making' rarely occurs as a discrete action. Rather, Bloor's ENT specialists and Katz's surgeons operate with a repertoire of recipes, often used in such a way as to resolve clinical work into one self-evident course of action. Their treatment decisions are not based on considering and weighing all the available information. As Katz shows in particular, outcomes are produced in shared discourse among surgical teams, and she comments on the distribution of expertise and opinion between different specialties. She also comments on how 'non-medical' factors impinge on surgical decisions, even though the discourse of consultations – formal and informal – between colleagues is couched entirely in medical terms.

It must be emphasized in this context, however, that a sociological analysis is not concerned exclusively, or even primarily, with the extra-medical. The organization of medical discourse, and the clinic as an ecology of knowledge, call for sociological commentary in their own right. Such sociological work is contrasted with the tradition of 'decision-making' analysis that has informed a good deal of recent commentary on medical practice.

Deciding and decision-making

In recent years social scientists – in partnership with medical practitioners and others (such as statisticians) – have devoted considerable attention and energy to the study and modelling of *medical decision-making*. There has been a rapidly growing literature in this area, and the implications of this new specialism now have practical consequences for the practice of medicine and the training of practitioners. Major contributing disciplines include psychology and artificial intelligence. To some extent, this literature might appear to remedy some of the absence of studies of disease behaviour to mirror the sociology of illness behaviour. It fails to do so, however, but some of its contributions and – more illuminating – its shortcomings are of general relevance to the micro-sociology of medical knowledge.

It is not possible systematically to review all of the literature here. I shall begin with a consideration of a few major studies from *psychological* perspectives. As a starting-point the work of Elstein, Shulman and Sprafka (1978) will be used as an influential and important exemplar. (A similar study from the United Kingdom is reported by Gale and Marsden, 1983.) Their experimental procedures embody one common approach to the investigation of decision-making by physicians and medical students.

Interestingly, Elstein and his colleagues identify their approach as having an ethnographic flavour, deriving from previous research on problem-solving by chess players. Such an approach, the authors claim, is based on the following characteristics:

1 The systematic description of cognitive phenomena rather than hypothesis-testing.
2 No attempt at machine simulation.
3 Experimental contrivances that approximate to 'real life' situations.
4 Extensive use of 'introspective' techniques, such as subjects' verbal accounts of their own cognitive processes.
5 An emphasis on the interpretation of such accounts.

The experimental methods used by the authors included what they referred to as 'high fidelity simulations'. Such simulations were based on actors' presentations of complaints to a series of physicians, coupled with information provided in response to the physicians' inquiries (such as lab results). The physicians themselves were encouraged to verbalize their thoughts as they progressed through the diagnostic process of history-taking and subsequent investigations. Elstein et al. note that the spoken activity of reflecting on their thought processes did not appear to be troublesome or disruptive for the physicians 'since it was a minor variation of their conduct on ward rounds or when reviewing cases with their students' (1978: 48). This remark gives us a clue as to a broader institutional and analytic framework for these and similar phenomena. (Unfortunately, those verbal protocols were coded and scored, but were not analysed *as talk*, and extracts are not reproduced in the published account; consequently we cannot inspect the discursive arrangement of reflection.)

In general, Elstein, Shulman and Sprafka represent the physician's decision-making process as one guided by hypotheses. They argue that hypothesis-formation occurs early in the process, and the physician's thought process is not characterized as one of inductive reasoning. They characterize the process thus:

> The structure of medical problems is varied and complex. Some are handled by generating specific hypotheses early, others by a more regular progression from general to specific. The consistent finding is that some hypotheses are always generated early and that medical diagnosis does not proceed in a strictly inductive fashion . . . Information processing theories of problem solving may be viewed as hypothesis-testing theories . . . analysis of diagnostic reasoning as a series of intermediate decisions is also consistent with this view . . . Some diagnostic decisions are reached by an orderly progression through stations, while in other cases a diagnostician may move directly to a terminal point. (Elstein et al., 1978: 79–80)

In discussing their own and others' results, Elstein et al. make mention of a number of methods of practical reasoning drawn on by physicians. They include:

1 The use of medical information based on its availability or ease of recall.
2 The perceived similarity between two events ('representativeness') may be used as a method to recall and organize information.
3 Reliance on the 'law of small numbers', or faith in trends that appear early in the collection of data.
4 Elevated estimates of probability of a given condition based on recent exposure to a rare case.

Again, therefore, the authors hint at the practical reasoning likely to be found in naturally occurring settings of medical work, but they are not able to examine directly such aspects of mundane medical reality.

It is characteristic of the approach adopted in this and similar studies that such modes of reasoning are treated primarily in terms of error and bias. Consequently they are not translated into systematic appraisals of clinicians' methods of practical reasoning, rules of thumb, recipes of knowledge, or whatever. Rather, in keeping with a more general normative perspective, Elstein et al. treat these methods as sources of error or interference in the reasoning process.

The same normative approach may be discerned in their approach to variation between physicians. For their main 'high fidelity simulation' the investigators attempted to compare two groups of physicians: those who had been nominated by their peers as outstanding diagnosticians, and others. They were unable to document any major differences that consistently distinguished the two samples' cognitive styles. This failure to demonstrate outstanding diagnostic skill apparently reflects the fact that problems differ more significantly than do problem-solvers. Despite the finding of high variability among physicians and from problem to problem, however, one can detect a tendency among authors of this persuasion to construct general characterizations of decision-making. The emphasis on information-processing and hypothesis formation reflects this tendency.

Even more explicitly and consistently normative in outlook is that body of literature concerned with the computational representation or simulation of clinical decision-making. These may be based on a number of alternative models, including regression and Bayesian methods. Here the desire is not simply to understand the thought processes involved in diagnosis, but to improve upon clinicians' otherwise unaided reasoning. The specialized literature in the field of medical decision-making is now replete with expert systems and the like for the 'solution' of a wide range of diagnostic and management problems in clinical medicine. (See Dowie and Elstein, 1988 for a cross-section of papers in this general area.)

I have mentioned contemporary approaches to medical reasoning for two reasons. First the topic itself is of fundamental importance to the sociological understanding of medical work, and the contributions already alluded to are important in their own right. Secondly, the specific limitations of those approaches help one identify the distinctively sociological concerns that require elaboration. Both the psychological experiment and the statistical model or computer simulation have in common that they are representations of decision-making in the real world. Hence we can gain some purchase on the broader issues by looking at *how* they represent matters, and how they necessarily over-simplify or otherwise distort. To do so is not just to engage in cross-disciplinary polemics. The point here is not to criticize the psychologists for using techniques of experimental social or cognitive psychology, nor to denigrate the intrinsic value of expert systems. Rather, at this stage, the purpose is to use those models and simulations as if they were ideal types, against which one's own observations and reflections can be set for heuristic purposes. (Collins, 1990a, 1990b provides an extensive contrast between expert systems and practical reasoning from a sociological perspective on scientific knowledge.)

The first observation to be made recapitulates one made earlier about most sociological and psychological studies of doctor–patient interaction. That is, virtually all work in this area represents diagnosis or decision-making – like the consultation itself, within which it is often embedded – within a very restricted framework. They observe, that is, a strict set of Aristotelian dramatic unities. Decision-making activity is restricted in terms of its *actors*, its *duration* and its *setting*.

First I draw attention to the treatment of social actors. This in itself is a misnomer, for in much of the literature the medical practitioner is represented as anything but social or an actor in the conventional sense. Indeed, the decision-making process tends to be portrayed as a private and individual affair. As we have seen already in other contexts, the model is that of the initial diagnostic encounter – the consultation – between one patient and one practitioner in the consulting room. This is, of course, the actuality for many encounters; it is also a reasonable simplification for experimental purposes. Viewed sociologically, however, it is a very partial view of medical work. Much medical practice goes on in complex organizational settings. In many organizational settings (not just clinics or hospitals) decision-making itself is a collective, organizational activity. Moreover, as we shall see, 'decisions' may be subject to debate, negotiation and revision, based on talk within and between groups or teams of practitioners. In medical settings, the exercise of diagnostic decision-making may be the focus of interaction between house staff and their superiors, between teachers and their students, between medical and nursing professions, between clinicians and laboratory staff, between primary care teams and consulting specialists. Consequently, medical decision-making may involve not just more than one doctor, it may also bring into play more than one medical specialty, members of which contribute different views of expertise and different organizational interests. The silent inner dialogue of single-handed decision-making, therefore, is by no means the whole story.

Secondly, the representation of *time* is, too often, unduly restricted. For thoroughly comprehensible reasons, the decision-making process tends to be represented as bounded in time. It has the appearance of a more or less unitary act, of short duration, accomplished in a single sequence of cognitive acts. Again, one must acknowledge that many 'decisions' are made in that way. In many contexts, however, the timing of 'decisions' may be much more diffuse, or protracted, or cyclical in character. Just as the decision-making process may be dispersed through a division of labour, so different segments of medical work may bring to bear different tempos, schedules, routines and deadlines. The division of labour itself implies not just the differential distribution of expertise, but also the dispersal of tasks on different time-tracks. The timing and dove-tailing of 'decisions' and actions by the house staff (say) may be grounded in a temporal order quite different from, say, a team of specialists consulted to produce crucial 'information' or advice concerning diagnosis and management. The time of and for 'decisions' and 'deciding', then, is complex and multiple in the modern clinical setting. Models that incorporate only a single practitioner operating in a restricted time-frame do little to capture the complexity and diversity of the modern clinic.

Thirdly there is the issue of the *setting* for decision-making activities. Deciding on diagnoses and courses of treatment is not confined to a single site. Within a complex division of labour, work relevant to diagnosis, and to management is dispersed over many sites. Again, this is a reflection that many types of actor may be involved. But it is much more than that. For each social setting in the organization of the clinic will generate its own information. The disease may be assembled out of a plethora of decisions, that are the outcomes of work in diverse settings: clinical laboratories, radiographic departments, consulting specialties and so on. Each setting may generate its own 'information', embodied in various forms of representation: print-outs, films, frozen sections, written notes, spoken consultations. Each of these texts and inscriptions is itself the *outcome* of processes of 'decision-making'. In turn it calls for further interpretation, which may involve its *translation* – physically, from one setting to another, and discursively from one linguistic or representational register to another. This latter point throws into relief one of the most obvious conceptual limitations of much of the decision-making literature. That is, a distinction between 'information' and 'decisions'. All too often information (such as laboratory results) is treated as *given*, while the exercise of judgement or decision-making is applied to that information. The elements of information may be accorded different weight (for instance, in probability-based representations) but each is still seen as an antecedent input. In organizational terms, however, medical work may be somewhat different. First, as indicated above, the information is itself an interpretation, a reading of the representations generated in the relevant site. It is itself a judgement, albeit often furnished by an expert. There is, therefore, a range of organizational features which come into play. Of course, the advocate of a strict information-processing model might well argue that this is readily accounted for: any piece of information is simply treated as the outcome of a prior stage of decision-making. The problem with this is that the outcome is no better than an infinite regress of decision-making. In reality, distinctions between information and decisions are untenable.

The sequential ordering of the decision-making model becomes especially troublesome when it is realized that the credibility of the information may rest upon the credibility of the diagnosis, rather than vice versa. Or, to be more precise, in the practical reasoning and organized work of the physician, diagnosis and information are mutually constitutive. Both are judgemental issues.

Some of these general considerations can be illustrated, though not demonstrated, with reference to my fieldwork with the haematologists. In the first place, as I have indicated already, processes of medical work and decision-making are dispersed across different personnel, different hospital or clinic sites, and may be temporally distributed. With the complex organization that is the modern hospital and its divisions of labour, patients and their cases are discussed and worked up by many doctors and others. The very fact that – especially in the US setting – haematology is a consulting discipline underlines the collective and dispersed character of clinical work. Information and opinion are likewise dispersed, and often must be collected (or fragments of it collected) under the auspices of particular occasions of talk.

In contrast to the essentially de-contextualized versions of clinical decision-making, sociologists have repeatedly drawn attention to ways in which social characteristics and cultural context impinge on clinical decisions. It has been shown, for instance, that patient characteristics such as

gender, ethnicity or perceived social worth can affect processes of evaluation and outcome. Clinical decision-making is not the outcome of
individual minds, operating in a social vacuum. It is not disinterested,
therefore, and is as susceptible to shaping by social influences as any other
knowledge.

Further, as Anspach (1987) notes, it is shaped not just by general norms
and typifications, but by the very organization of medical work itself.
Anspach's analysis of life-and-death decisions in neonatal intensive care
treats the clinic as an *ecology of knowledge*. She stresses how the
organization of work in the clinic differentially distributes knowledge and
interests among health professionals. The division of labour distributes
expertise. Processes of decision-making are not individual acts. Anspach's
argument is summarized thus:

> the newborn intensive care unit *qua* organization allocates different types of
> information to those who work within it, and, in so doing, defines the character of
> the 'data' that each group brings to the life-and-death decision. Each occupational
> group has a different set of daily experiences which define the contours of the
> information used in making prognostic judgements and in reaching life-and-death
> decisions. (Anspach, 1987: 217)

Anspach addresses the differences between three such occupational groups
– attending physicians; residents and fellows; nurses. The same argument
may readily be extended to encompass other lines of professional segmentation, such as differences between clinical specialties, or the distribution of
knowledge between clinicians and non-clinical specialists. For a similar
analysis of life-and-death decisions, see Slomka (1992), who again emphasizes the social distribution of knowledge and experience among
different parties to the process.

The general argument here is directly analogous to the analysis of
awareness contexts in the social management of death and dying (Glaser and
Strauss, 1964). Glaser and Strauss identify their awareness contexts in terms
of the distribution of information among the parties. A context is defined in
terms of the information-state of a small social network: it is not reducible to
the state of awareness or understanding of the individual participants.
Contexts are created, sustained or transformed by virtue of social interaction and changes in the information state. The shift from one awareness
context to another is equivalent to a Gestalt-switch or a catastrophe-like
change in that local social system. Likewise, in the analyses that follow, the
emphasis on the exchange of talk in face-to-face encounters should not be
misunderstood: this is not a micro-sociology of individualized actors. We are
always dealing with local manifestations and accomplishments of *social
organization*. Equally, we are witnessing the use of *socially shared discursive
resources*.

Some of these issues are glimpsed in the following accounts of everyday
work at Beacon Hospital. They reflect the peripatetic and discursive
accumulation of facts and opinions about the patients who were the subjects
of consultation. To underline these general considerations it must also be

kept in mind that while the haematology team were engaged in their work together, others – usually the team of residents on the ward – were doing their work on the same patient elsewhere (probably at other times).

The following short passage from an early morning is by no means atypical of how a fellow's working day might start. The fellow, Heather Wendell, the students, Lillian Drill and Jean-Paul Dumont and I were due to check on the progress of a number of patients (consults) before the weekly review meeting. The students had not arrived by 8.10 am, and Heather left to begin visiting patients, leaving a note for the students to page her and follow on. I waited for the students. Lillian arrived a little later, but Jean-Paul did not appear. Lillian paged Heather, found out where she had got to, and discovered she was up on Floor 8. She and I headed off in pursuit. The following extracts from the fieldnotes continue the account.

As normal, we had to wait for an elevator, and then travelled in it squashed against the wall – the bulk of the space being occupied by a bed. We arrived on Floor 8 at about 8.43, and found Heather seated with the patient's case notes. She finished writing her own note in it and we set off immediately for Floor 7. There we immediately looked at Mr Helmer's case notes. Lillian mentioned something about parasitic organisms that were referred to in the notes. Heather said she's mentioned them to another of the doctors. Between them Heather and Lillian had some difficulty in remembering the names of both parasites. And when they found the relevant note, Heather giggled that she'd told the other doctor the name of the wrong thing. Never mind, she consoled herself and us, he would look at the notes.

We then went to Mr Helmer's room [Mr Helmer was a young man with AIDS]. Heather stuck her head in the door; the room was dingy as he hadn't got the light on. 'What are we on here?', she asked, 'Masks, gloves, gowns?' 'Nothing', the patient replied. 'Oh, nothing. Well I'm just gonna wash my hands.' As she did so she muttered to me 'We have so many patients here on different systems . . .'. Heather and Lillian both washed their hands, took off their white coats and went in. They were in there for only a couple of minutes. Heather asked Mr Helmer how he was feeling today, and he said he felt a lot better than yesterday.

Heather and Lillian both came back out, looking solemn. As we were about to leave, Heather went back to check the temperature chart, in order to make sure that Mr Helmer wasn't febrile. Back at the nurses' station, where we stopped, Heather explained to Lillian that before the Tuesday conference they have to go round and check the details of their patients.

We set off again, arriving at the next floor by 9.00 am. Heather found the patient's notes and looked at them, then passed them on to Lillian, and went to check something with one of the surgeons. Lillian said she didn't know who the patient was. I said I thought it was Mr Fiores, 'the below-the-knee amputation from the heparin-induced problem'. I appeared to have got it right, judging from her reaction. Lillian commented that there is really nowhere to stand or sit to look at the notes. We were certainly in the way, as doctors and nurses pushed past us. Lillian balanced the notes somewhat precariously on the corner of a desk, nearly dropping them in the process. Meanwhile Heather had been paged and was on the phone. It was obviously Jean-Paul [the other medical student] and she was telling him to wait by the Haematology office for us.

Lillian seemed to be having some difficulty making sense of the chart. When Heather came over and joined us she commented 'The lab sheets here are terrible', as she helped Lillian to decipher the notes. She pointed to a value on one of the haematology lab printouts. 'They don't do it every day as they're supposed to'.

And so our little round continued as we checked up on the progress of all the consults. Later that morning the patients were presented at the review conference, as well as at subsequent morning rounds with the attending physician, Dr de Kalb. We shall encounter one of these more formal presentations in a later chapter. When a patient (in this case Mr Fiores) is presented his case is, as it were, gathered up into one more or less coherent narrative, and a plausible series of investigations and interventions. As we have already glimpsed, however, the clinical fellow with responsibility for the consultation must deal with fragmentary and unsatisfactory information, often gleaned from cursory inspections of the notes and equally brief encounters with the patient and other physicians. Not infrequently others' sins of omission or commission mean that the necessary information is unavailable or has been recorded inappropriately. Numerous hands contribute to the patient's chart, including the haematologists themselves. They do not always record the same facts and interpretations. Sometimes they can mislead one another (as Heather had inadvertently done over the possible parasites).

It was by no means uncommon for the haematologists to request something in the patient's chart, only for the request to be ignored or imperfectly complied with. In the example given above, tests that should have been repeated daily were not being done by the ward staff. Indeed, the social and technical division of labour in the hospital often results in teams or individuals working at cross purposes. Action and knowledge do not dovetail smoothly together to produce a seamless web of decision-making and action. Different specialists define their work and their interests in quite contrasting ways, and hence may define the clinical problem or problems they are addressing quite differently. Further, the exigencies of everyday work may be responded to differently by, say, the physicians or surgeons exercising primary responsibility for the patient and by consulting specialists such as the haematologists. In particular, it is noticeable that they may operate not just with competing definitions of the problem, but with different and competing timetables as well.

From the point of view of the haematologists with whom I worked, the surgeons were most frequently seen as operating at odds with them. In particular, their temporal frameworks seemed to be different in many cases, and their clinical priorities seemed to differ. It was quite common for the haematologists to be consulted by surgeons. Before surgery a patient would be evaluated, and – amongst other things – their haematological status assessed. For instance, bleeding time would be calculated: obviously one cannot proceed with surgery if there is a major problem with blood clotting, indicated by a prolonged bleeding time. But as a consequence of a consultation from a surgical service, the haematologists could find themselves embarking on a prolonged search for the root causes of haematological problems and their possible solutions. As they did so they would grumble that the surgeons were pressing them for a speedy response, and an un-equivocal indication of whether surgery was precluded, or could go ahead.

As a consequence of such differences in style and interests, clinical 'information' would not necessarily be taken at face value. The degree of trust put on a given piece of data in the patient's chart, or piece of advice, or differential diagnosis, would depend very much on *whose* observation or opinion it was. If the author were known to the haematologist, then such personal evaluations could even extend to which laboratory technician had been responsible for making a particular measurement: for some purposes special counts of blood cells need to be taken, and some laboratory technicians are known to be over- or under-estimators. Such local knowledge may provide grounds for discounting an apparently anomalous value, for instance.

By contrast, the technical division of labour and the differential distribution of expertise among specialists and subspecialists means that particular kinds of worker – and hence of the information they provide – is granted particular privilege. The clinical pathologist is a case in point. As a *type* the pathologist is entitled to adjudicate about a specimen, a lesion and so on. As individuals, they may be granted more or less expertise. As we shall see later, at Beacon Hospital, one pathologist in particular was additionally endowed by her colleagues in haematology with all but infalliable competence. If she made a pronouncement one way or the other then her opinion would be treated as definitive; equally, if she said that it was impossible to make a definitive identification, then that opinion too would outweigh any other (pending further investigations, better specimens, clinical developments and so on).

The consulting team would find themselves moving physically and discursively through the clinic as an organization. They were highly peripatetic, and I have already tried to convey a sense of their movements. Consults could come from any service in the hospital. The daily work of responding to new consults and following old ones could thus precipitate the clinical fellow and the student(s) on circuits of the hospital: from an Intensive Care Unit, to Burns, to General Surgery, to Internal Medicine. They also saw patients in the Haematology–Oncology clinic for follow-up consultations, or for chemotherapy. The fellows and students would also need to seek out information elsewhere – from radiographers and other producers of images to pathologists, from the haematology laboratory to the library. Networks of information-gathering reached to other hospitals in University City, especially for research findings and developments in treatment. The latter sources should not be overlooked. Medicine in such a setting is a literate and research-oriented activity. Recourse to relevant medical journals in the library was a recurrent feature of work. Medical students were often sent to the library not just for their own benefit, but also to 'devil' on behalf of the haematology team. Offprints of relevant articles were often circulated, and occasionally left in patients' charts for the benefit of the resident staff.

There is, then, a rich array of sources and types of 'information' that may be fed into the 'decision-making' processes. Some of that information is in the form of 'facts and figures', such as laboratory values. Others are in the form of professional opinions, research reports and personal anecdotes. As we shall see, they are intertwined in the collegial discourse of clinicians in complex ways. The sharing of such knowledge is always mediated by the interpretations and values attached to it by the clinicians themselves at any given time. It is also formulated into accounts and discussions about cases through the narrative and rhetorical acts that are shared among physicians and others.

Throughout the case accounts and presentations I participated in and recorded – some of which are excerpted throughout this book – decision-making could not be captured as a unitary act. Like the 'information' that is dispersed in time and space, and distributed across several teams or individuals, so the processes of discussion, argumentation, review and deciding are similarly dispersed. There are numerous and repeated occasions on which patients are discussed, with greater or lesser formality, at greater or lesser length.

While these discussions and presentations are certainly germane to the treatment of patients during their hospital admission, they cannot be captured under the simple rubric of decision-making. At least, the conventional, often implicit, models of the processes involved are too restricted to do justice to the events recorded and observed. As I have suggested already, the actual events fracture the spatial and temporal frames implied by most decision-making models. What we see, indeed, are multiple occasions of spoken interaction, often in multi-party settings. It would often be hard to put one's finger on specific points at which 'decisions' had been arrived at. I suggest this – though it is hard even to illustrate, let alone demonstrate – not because I believe that the physicians and their colleagues were indecisive or because their work was unproductive. On the contrary, a good deal of work got done in the course of their collegial talk, and through other means – including the collection and inspection of physical traces such as bone marrow aspirates, biopsies and blood samples. On the other hand, the speech acts that were accomplished in the course of their work were multiple, often weaving together into dense and complex skeins of talk. As will be seen in the chapters that follow, the presentation and discussion of cases, working them up, and reporting on them, rested on narrative, description, persuasion and disputation. Colleagues could debate about evidence and interpretation. They would exchange and elaborate on precedents, often couched in terms of anecdotes and maxims. They might implicitly query courses of action already embarked upon, and criticize their fellow practitioners. They would trade personal preferences and exchange information about the latest research findings. Some courses of action, past or future, might be endorsed, but others might never reach clear resolution. Throughout the talk that informs this book, therefore, there is a good deal of socially organized activity that relates to diagnosis and patient management. There is, in other words, a good deal of deciding and the projection of action that is being enacted. But it is far from clear that it can be equated with decision-making, if that is conceptualized in terms of individualized information-processing. On the contrary, I shall be concerned with socially organized medical work. This has little to do with essentially psychological processes. It has everything to do with the social exchange of talk, the social distribution of knowledge, and the everyday ceremonies of medical work.

The circuits of discourse

The social, discursive organization of the modern hospital may be described in terms of an elaborate round of formal and informal spoken performances. They constitute a liturgical order in which are accomplished medical work and the reproduction of medical knowledge. Clinicians themselves circulate within the clinic, coming together from time to time to rehearse and to reconstruct their cases. N.J. Fox (1992) has written of the 'circuits of hygiene' in the clinic. One might extend the trope and write of 'the circuits of discourse'. The ancient ceremonies of the round already capture the intimate connections between medical work and medical talk. The complex arrangements of modern medicine implicate its personnel in a repetitive round of rounds. The formal orders of time in the hospital (Zerubavel, 1979) are partly mapped out by the periodic enactments of these secular rituals. Rather than the closed-ended model of decision-making, the liturgy of the clinic is more aptly captured by the figure of repetition. Patients and their cases are repeatedly, though not endlessly, visited. Patients are visited physically in the bedside examination and history-taking. They are visited figuratively in the socially shared talk among professionals. In the course of the more detailed discussions that appear in the following chapters, therefore, it will be necessary to trace some of these complexities. We shall not be looking at them with a view to evaluating the adequacy of diagnostic and therapeutic work in this particular setting. The intention, rather, is to examine some features of this liturgy of the clinic. In order to do so it will be necessary to pay rather close attention to the organization of talk. As will become apparent, I hope, this is not directed at a purely formal description of discourse structures. It is meant to demonstrate some of the locally accomplished, socially organized ways in which medical knowledge is produced and reproduced. In the chapters that follow I shall consider in more detail some of the ways in which everyday medical work is accomplished through the spoken performances of medical practitioners and others. I shall explore how language is used in the clinic to represent and narrate the facts of disease and illness, and to persuade fellow practitioners as to those facts or opinions.

4

Reading the Body

The body and the clinic

The cultural history of modern medicine clearly identifies an orientation to the body as a key feature in its emergence (Lupton, 1994). This view is articulated in Foucault's treatment of the birth of the clinic (Foucault, 1973). The epistemological break that marks the foundation of modern medicine is to be identified in the inspection of the patient's body, and the privileged revelation claimed for the *clinical gaze*. This mode of seeing was part and parcel of a technology of surveillance and monitoring. In this political anatomy, the patient's body became legible. Moreover, the observable signs and the patient's symptoms were increasingly matched to the findings of pathological science. A new discipline of pathological anatomy enabled the physician to treat disease in terms of localized lesions and processes. The body in modern medicine is thus constituted as a site for *inspection*. The techniques that helped to establish this modern medicine included palpation, auscultation and percussion. The body is thus read as the localized setting for disease processes that are themselves traced to specific organs and systems. As Armstrong summarizes this view of modern political anatomy:

> The modern body of the patient, which has become the unquestioned object of clinical practice, has no social existence prior to those same clinical techniques being exercised upon it. It is as if the medical gaze, in which is encompassed all the techniques, languages and assumptions of modern medicine, establishes by its authority and penetration an observable and analysable space in which is crystalised that apparently solid figure – which has now become as familiar – the discrete human body. (Armstrong, 1983: 2)

Armstrong himself documents further ways in which modern medicine has developed new modes of organizing patients' bodies within a social and conceptual space of medical inspection. He suggests that various medical specialisms in the twentieth century have 'invented' different versions of the human body, and of relations between those bodies. Through a close analysis of specialisms such as paediatrics, geriatrics and general practice, Armstrong argues that the twentieth century has invented a new 'body', which is treated in social and biographical contexts. As he puts it in introducing his argument: 'these various medical events have served to fabricate, not, as in the nineteenth century, a discrete passive physical body, but an essentially relative and subjective one' (1983: xiii). On the other hand, the techniques of inspection of the physical body continue to generate, legitimate and inform the 'clinical gaze'. Armstrong himself acknowledges the co-existence of the 'passive body' with the 'social':

> indeed, with the growth in medical technology and super-specialities, the panoptic gaze has focused on an even more detailed analysis of the body. Thus at the same time as the community gaze constructs identities and relationships, the Panopticon produces ever more discrete and individualized bodies. (Armstrong, 1983: 111)

In other words, the modern hospital still reproduces a clinical gaze in which the body of the patient is rendered legible via a detailed scrutiny of its constituent parts.

Indeed, the modern clinic continues the dissection of the body for pathological anatomy by means of multiple technologies of inspection and enumeration. The techniques that saw the birth of the clinic began to outline the patient's body as a space to be inspected and probed. The contemporary clinic extends those technologies to such an extent that, in principle, every organ and every system may be inspected and sampled. These diverse technologies mean that the body of the patient is no longer localized in the discrete, integral body of the actual patient. The discursive space of the body is no longer coterminous with the bedside – that physical and interpersonal locale in which the clinic finds its birth and its rationale.

The bedside and the patient's corporeal presence remain important, of course. In my own work on bedside interaction and instruction for medical education, I made that point most strongly (Atkinson, 1977, 1981a, 1981b, 1988). I showed just how dramatically the ceremonial progress of the teaching round is deployed to recreate the consecrated space of the clinical encounter. The clinical gaze is focused on the patient, whose presence is the literal embodiment of medical rationality. The dramaturgical enactment of the teaching round is a daily reconstruction of modern medicine. Through it, the clinical gaze is reproduced and warranted.

Yet the clinical gaze is no longer anchored to the bedside itself. The clinic's gaze is now dispersed. The gaze is not confined to the local inspection conducted by the individual physician or his/her entourage of assistants and students. The bedside remains as the original site of clinical understanding. It is to the bedside that the clinical investigation returns: it is visited repeatedly by clinicians. But the space of the bedside does not bound the clinical gaze. The bedside itself becomes a site of data-collection. The body is sampled, invaded, measured and inspected, in order to yield images and information. Those data can then be scrutinized and interrogated elsewhere – in the specialist departments and laboratories of the modern hospital. It is a commonplace to note that the hospital is an organization of extreme complexity. It is marked by a high degree of social and technical division of labour. The body is dispersed through multiple sites of investigation throughout this organizational complexity.

It is in this way that the body is rendered legible. It is made to render up its signs by means of a variety of technologies that produce traces, images and enumerations that can be interpreted by physicians and others. The special senses of sight, touch, sound and smell are supplemented by intermediary technologies.

In other words, the body yields its clues by means of a wide range of clinical methods. The modern history of medical technology has furnished the clinic with a powerful armamentarium of investigative machinery. Through that machinery of investigation and description, the body is disaggregated into numerous traces and fragments. Each of them may then be read by competent observers. Each specialist offers his or her special gaze, which in turn may inform the generalized gaze of the primary care physician or team. In other words, the body of modern medicine has entirely ceased to be coterminous with the physical presence of the individual patient. The body may be read and interpreted *in absentia*. The traces and signs of the body's structures and functions may be taken and read elsewhere.

Indeed it is pertinent to be reminded that the attending physicians' rounds that I participated in and recorded among the haematologists were not necessarily physical tours of the patients. They were frequently conducted at a table, and consisted of the presentation and discussion of findings, results, measurements and other accounts. The latter were assembled from a diverse range of sources and technologies. The history and bedside examination of the patient were supplemented by many other elements of the clinical gaze – including 'lab' reports of various sorts.

The body is thus transformed into a series of signs and representations, by means of a complex array of technologies of inspection. The technical division of labour within the modern clinic is, in part, a diversity of specialized means for visualizing and enumerating the fragmented body. In this way 'information' about the patient and his/her condition is dispersed in time and space. The physical complexity of the modern hospital, and its equally complex temporal order, provide a matrix in which clinical knowledge is constructed and lodged.

The body is represented in various departments, divisions and laboratories. Each specialty claims expertise in a representational technique and its own organs or systems. The modern body has been appropriated and reconstituted by a diversity of experts. In this system of medical inspection and surveillance, the integrity of the body is dissolved into a series of more or less discrete domains of knowledge and technique. Moreover, as new technologies have developed, as their availability and use has spread, so the body itself may be ever more fully probed, more delicately visualized, and more finely enumerated.

The modern clinic has multifarious means and devices whereby the body's constituents and configurations are rendered visible and legible. Among the most dramatically obvious to the contemporary observer are the various mechanisms for the production of *images*: X-rays; ultrasound; computed tomography; magnetic resonance imaging; nuclear tracing. Each of those imaging techniques reveals differing aspects of space, tissue and motion.

The different imaging modalities . . . clearly provide some overlapping services in terms of the information they convey, and to that extent they are substitutes for each other in diagnostic procedures. CT scanners, diagnostic ultrasound, and nuclear imaging devices, for example, are all capable of providing images of specific organs of the body. Because many imaging modalities also provide different services, to that extent those different modalities are also complementary to one another. For example, the CT scanner provides data on brain tissue, nuclear medicine can be used to examine microcirculation, and an important application of ultrasound is the measurement of the velocity of blood flow. (Bronzino et al., 1990: 455)

Each technique generates a different image; each constructs a different version of anatomy and physiology.

Each means of imaging just referred to constitutes what Lynch (1990) calls 'the externalized retina'. (My borrowing of his phrase changes the usage somewhat.) Each of medicine's non-invasive techniques for rendering the body 'legible' constructs a *representation* of the body. Each representation selects and transforms particular features of the body. The general principles involved have been identified in the context of scientific 'representations' (cf. Lynch and Woolgar, 1990), or 'inscriptions' (Latour and Woolgar, 1986). In scientific laboratories, the work of 'research' is largely conducted through the production and interpretation of such representations – which may, in turn, lead to further representations. The working scientist does not manipulate 'things in themselves'. He or she uses techniques and equipment to make representations; the representations (DNA radiographs; X-ray crystallographs) constitute the data available for inspection and explanation (Amann and Knorr-Cetina, 1990).

What is true of laboratory science is also true of the medical laboratory and the work of medical specialists. The inscriptions of medical imaging become the object of 'the clinical gaze'. These representations are, of course, *conventional*.

Nature is *rendered* in ways that accentuate certain features of interest. It is imaged, in a transitive sense, by operations on it. For such images to be relied on as evidence, there must be general agreement as to their value and reliability, and there must exist a set of procedures for generating them. (Yoxen, 1990: 282)

Yoxen's own treatment of the development of ultrasound technology illustrates his point. He clearly demonstrates the complex interrelationships between the interests of clinicians, the representational strategies that were tried and the manufacture of the equipment itself.

there was a diversity of approaches to the technical and representational problems in using sound to visualize internal organs. Different groups pursued different strategies and explored the utility of different graphic conventions, even though a common aim was improved diagnosis. What seemed an acceptable engineering solution was somewhat variable, although in each case the basic challenge to be faced was the validation of the resulting image through some sort of visual comparison. (Yoxen, 1990: 26)

In other words, there is a process of consensus-formation as to what will 'count' as an adequate representation (whether for research or for practical purposes). By the same token, the recognition and interpretation of a competent representation depends on a knowledge of its very conventionality. The conventional nature of the inscriptions, taken with the sheer technical complexity of realizing the techniques, means that they are not at all 'transparent'. They are, in many instances, difficult to interpret: sometimes, indeed, it may be hard to relate the inscription to the known 'facts' of human anatomy and physiology. The images produced by, say, ultrasound do not automatically translate into medical practitioners' taken-for-granted assumptions and interpretative frameworks.

We know, for example, that the interpretation of X-rays is by no means straightforward. The technique is not novel. The X-ray effect was demonstrated by Röntgen in 1895 and has been used extensively in clinical medicine for many decades. Nevertheless, the X-ray film does not reveal its information unproblematically. Pasveer (1989) has addressed problems of X-ray photography in medicine. There she examines what explicit and tacit rules go into the rendering of the various images, and what transformations they imply. Pasveer also argues that such images themselves embody tacit knowledge, in that the knowledge is *used* and shared without necessarily being linguistically articulated in a propositional form. Pasveer also emphasizes the extent to which the production of images and representations does not merely mirror the reality of the body, but constructs the body itself. Writing of the historical introduction of X-ray techniques into the practice of medicine, Pasveer says:

> The X-ray images were trusted for their ability to represent reality, but in the pre-Röntgen era reality looked enormously different from the shadows that were now said to be mirroring the inner parts of patients. (Pasveer, 1989: 361)

In a similar vein is Daly's treatment of echocardiography. She tends to emphasize the *ideological* character of imaging techniques:

> The enormous capacity of imaging devices to probe the living body and diagnose asymptomatic disease makes them powerful technologies of surveillance, important for generating that medical knowledge of normality which creates docile bodies and sustains medical power. (Daly, 1989: 101)

She also goes on to note that the resultant images always require interpretation. They do not provide self-evident information.

> In practice . . . echocardiography has not resolved uncertainty. It requires interpretation of a complex moving image according to sometimes uncertain professional criteria. The image is recognized as being operator-dependent, rapid advance in the technology means constant changes in techniques and there is seldom evidence from autopsy or operation to substantiate the diagnosis of disease in the well patient. (Daly, 1989: 104)

These various imaging techniques by no means exhaust the means available to render the body visible and legible. There are many other ways to remove and render traces of the body. Many – unlike imaging – depend on the removal of sample tissue and its further preparation and treatment.

Many of the techniques employed by clinical pathologists and haematologists depend on the close inspection of small samples of body fluids and tissues.

The haematologist will typically use a number of routine procedures for the examination of blood and other systems or organs. The most obvious is the examination of a smear of peripheral blood under the microscope – which is used to gather a great deal of information about the composition and morphology of the blood and its constituent parts. Equally basic to the haematological investigation is the inspection of a small sample of bone marrow. The latter is important for the reason that bone marrow is the site of manufacture for red blood cells (erythropoesis). Hence the presence or absence of young cells can be detected in the marrow as can abnormality in their maturation.

The haematologist who works with related cancers (such as the lymphomas) will have occasion to work with biopsies taken from tissues suspected or believed to be malignant. The products of a biopsy will be subject to visual inspection, possibly in collaboration or serially with a clinical pathologist. Larger tissues may also be sampled for frozen-section preparation and pathological inspection.

With each of these techniques – and others like them – the haematologist helps to disaggregate the body into finer and finer discriminations. Each is removed from the patient in time and space, and each sample becomes a kind of 'text' which can then be read by competent investigators. Blood, bone marrow, lymph nodes and the like are thus sampled and dispersed. Their information is therefore de-contextualized from the patient, and reconstituted as the object of knowledge in the complex organization of the clinic.

The visible body

In many instances the tissues of the body require preparation before the sample can be read and interpreted. It needs to be fixed and enhanced as a legible text. In some cases, therefore, it needs to be prepared by *staining*. The staining of blood samples is one way in which body tissue is rendered visible to the clinical gaze. Each stain fixes and makes apparent particular haematological features. Each therefore corresponds in a general sense to the sort of image enhancement that has interested sociologists of scientific knowledge. In one sense, microscopy appears to be technology for the direct and detailed inspection of human tissues. And, to a limited extent, that is true. The microscope has, historically, furnished a potent extension of the clinical gaze. It allows the clinician or the pathologist to peer beyond the gross features of structure and function. It permits a close-up view of pathology and an examination of structures not available to the naked eye.

On the other hand, the microscopic gaze is not unmediated. The tissues need to be rendered visible to the microscope's lenses; and the images so yielded need to be interpreted, in the light of the means used to render them legible in the first place. The competent microscope user must, for instance, know about the properties of reflected and refracted light; about the relative thickness of specimens and preparations; about appropriate levels of magnification. Equally, the microscopic gaze is mediated by the conventional methods used to make certain structures or contents visible. The practice of staining microscope slides is an old one. Sometimes the stain's value is primarily in just rendering visible otherwise translucent tissues. Where there is a virtual absence of 'natural' colour, then the addition of artificial colours enhances the visibility of the tissue. Such staining introduces one element of *contrast* – between 'light' and 'dark', or 'opaque' versus 'translucent'. Other modes of staining may introduce further elements of contrast by revealing structures or substances that would not otherwise be visible. In some cases, for instance, the haematologist will need to use a special stain to reveal the presence of iron. The choice of stain, of course, will depend upon what visual information is being sought.

The staining of a slide is, therefore akin to some of the processes described by Lynch in various contributions on the production and interpretation of scientific images (Lynch 1985a, 1985b, 1990). Lynch points out that natural scientists deploy varieties of 'rendering practices' through which scientific images are produced. Amongst other things, he draws attention to practices of image-construction (such as the use of computer enhancement) that employ arbitrary false colours in order to mark particular domains, and in order to enhance contrast. An excellent example of this latter rendering practice is the visual representation of differential heat in organs such as joints. Inflammatory processes (arthritis) are represented by computer-enhanced images in which contrasting arbitrary colours are attached to areas of different temperature. In much the same way, the specialized stains that are applied to a peripheral blood smear introduce conventional, arbitrary colours and contrasts in order to reveal otherwise invisible traces.

The practised haematologist or pathologist is, therefore, adept at seeing the evidence revealed to microscopic inspection. He or she is familiar with the conventional reading practices used to produce legible traces. The laboratory has available a variety of general and special stains that enhance the visibility of particular features. The laboratory staff use various recipes to produce stains, or use commercially prepared standard preparations. The modern use of microscopy is thoroughly dependent on stains, and it would be virtually impossible without the visual enhancement they allow.

The use of natural dyes to stain microscopic specimens did not become widespread until about 1850.

> It is safe to say . . . that the use of stains revolutionized microscopic technic. The early microscopists were able to make much progress without stains because of their painstaking diligence. The work without stains must have been extremely difficult, and it is hard on reading some of the old publications to believe that some of the minute structures described were actually seen. Few users of the

microscope today would be likely to have either the patience or the eyesight to do the work described in those early days. The fact that the microscope is now being used successfully in the hands of so many students who would not think of comparing themselves with the pioneers in microscopy is due to the use of stains more than to any other factor – although, of course, no one can deny that modern improvements in the microscope have also played a part of great importance. (Conn, 1961: 2)

As Conn indicates the modern habits of scientific vision are virtually 'unthinkable' without the enhancements of histological staining.

This is not the place for a full history of stains and visibility, although the relationship between technology and descriptions in disciplines like haematology and clinical pathology is clearly an important area for exploration in the social history of medical knowledge (see Bracegirdle, 1978). Their contemporary use in clinical and scientific laboratories, together with other techniques of fixing and rendering undoubtedly deserves more extensive treatment, and would be a crucial aspect of any strong programme in the sociology of medical knowledge production. Many of the stains used in haematological work have early origins in histological staining techniques. Romanovsky, for instance, combined eosin and methylene blue, and modern blood stains 'are often spoken of as modified Romanovsky stains' (Conn, 1961: 253). Later developments include Wright's stain (1902), widely used in its contemporary commercial preparations. Giemsa's modification (also 1902) is also widely used still.

The processes and products of histological staining all have in common the same function. They render visible what otherwise would not be so. They enhance or create colours whereby particular features of cells and tissues (for example, a cell nucleus) become manifest. They are therefore but one element in the processes whereby 'biomedical reality' is produced. Such enhancement does not mysteriously create the objects in an ontological sense. It does, however, render them knowable. In that sense, therefore, they constitute or construct the phenomena as objects that can be seen, discriminated, understood and described. They are thus rendered up as objects in the specialized register of medical talk, and amenable to the specialized clinical gaze. They are produced and reproduced as stable phenomena through conventional means. The 'artificial' colours of biological staining themselves constitute an arbitrary but socially shared set of conventions for biological representation. They render their objects in more or less standardized dyes of blue, red, purple and so on. The stains themselves (such as Wright or Giemsa) are themselves standardized. There are industry standard recipes for their preparation. The various colours and shades (of azure, for instance) are parts of a *system* of colours and contrasts. They thus form a system of signifying practices whereby a legible body is reproduced. Even the 'direct' observation of histological phenomena via the optical microscope depends on various techniques without which inspection would be vitiated.

The topic takes us beyond the scope of the present work and into another project altogether, but one must note that the laboratory practices that render the body visible are themselves 'craft' work, often dependent on tacit, embodied knowledge. The laboratory scientist or technician is routinely engaged in the day-to-day preparation, administration and checking of things like special stains, or the routine inspection of body tissues and samples. The everyday work of the clinical laboratory scientist has been almost totally neglected in sociological investigations of the modern hospital or medical school. Yet their backroom work – for all that it takes place in the backstage regions of the clinic – is of fundamental importance to the social organization of modern medicine. The visibility of the disaggregated body depends on a technical division of labour, whereby the practices of 'revealing' and 'seeing', 'counting' and 'classifying' are socially and spatially distributed.

Seeing is not straightforward. Whether or not the smears and traces have been prepared in special ways, the specimen does not automatically and self-evidently yield its clues to the scientist or clinician. Competent observation is predicated on tacit, embodied knowledge of how to 'see' and 'what to look for'. These implicit competences are also supplemented by external sources of reference. In particular, the haematologist (or laboratory scientist) can refer to the illustrations in textbooks or 'atlases' of haematology. This includes various kinds of printed representation against which observed instances can be compared. These atlas representations provide especially important reference-points for students and less experienced practitioners.

There is nothing novel, even 'modern', about the use of the 'atlas' as a medical *aide-mémoire*. The representations of human gross anatomy, for instance, have been incorporated in major printed works of scientific and aesthetic significance for centuries. Barnes takes an anatomical illustration (the musculature of the human arm) as one of the type cases of scientific representational devices (together with diagrams, a city map, and contours on an elevation map). Of those representational devices in general, Barnes comments:

> Representations are actively manufactured renderings of their referents, produced from available cultural resources. The particular forms of construction adopted reflect the predictive or other technical cognitive functions the representation is required to perform when procedures are carried out, competencies executed, or techniques applied. Why such functions are initially required of the representation is generally intelligible, directly or indirectly, in terms of the objectives of some social group. (Barnes, 1977: 6)

The medical illustrations included in many textbooks and other guides are no exception to this general characterization. They are a pervasive feature of the reproduction of medical knowledge. Textbooks and lectures are replete with photographic and diagrammatic representations of anatomical features. The atlas of gross anatomy has been supplemented, of course, by diagrams and photographic plates at a histological level. Computerized images have in turn been used to an increasing extent for instructional and diagnostic purposes.

These representations are useful for the practitioner who needs to recognize and classify features of a given specimen. The exemplars in printed representations may be used as a point of reference, or as a set of templates, against which 'reality' is contrasted and composed. The representations of the textbook or atlas are actual types (such as photographs of particularly clear examples) or ideal types (such as diagrams constructed to illustrate 'classic' forms). Whether or not they are constructed or reproduced, such illustrations 'simplify' in various ways. Since even photographic illustrations are carefully made and carefully selected, they normally contrast with the complexities and ambiguities of what is 'actually' seen under the microscope.

The function of the anatomical or histological atlas is, therefore, analogous to that of the 'field guide', as described by Law and Lynch (1990). They discuss the use of 'manuals' among bird-watchers, and suggest that they provide 'a descriptive organization to the craft of *seeing* species in the field' (p. 293). The field guides – which use either drawings, paintings or photographs – simplify in different ways: 'Each guide thus employs a tacit "picture theory" of representation: an idealization of the potential correspondence that can be achieved between a representation in the text and the "bird in the field"' (pp. 273–4). In other words, the field guide or manual is not just passive or inert in the act of seeing. The manual's representations inscribe implicit instructions for how to look and what to look out for. The recognition and discrimination of the right sort of features will only be achieved by looking for what one hopes to see. The guide thus draws attention to the kinds of distinctive features that should be attended to (relative sizes, shapes or colours).

In just the same way, the anatomical or histological atlas can direct the gaze towards the most appropriate kinds of distinctive features. It encodes and reproduces its implicit theory of knowledge. The bird-watchers' manual inscribes the theory of *species*: mechanisms for the differentiation and enumeration of types. The haematologist's manual likewise inscribes a theory of types of phenomena such as blood cells. In a manner just like that of the naturalist, the haematologist must act as a 'spotter' of cells, and be able to relate what is noticed to significant types. The presence and distribution of key types of blood cells in turn helps to allocate the blood itself to a type, which may imply a diagnosis (in turn dependent on another theory of disease types).

The haematologist therefore uses the atlas (from time to time) to produce descriptions and categorizations of phenomena such as blood-cell types. His or her concerns include the capacity to perform the following perceptual and cognitive tasks: identify the shape, colour and relative size of blood cells; use appropriate linguistic categories to generate descriptions of those phenomena: categorize and classify those cells into types (developmental lines); estimate relative frequencies of cell types; produce accurate counts of cell types.

In these ways – as in many other areas of clinical medicine and pathology –

the expert (primary physician, specialist, laboratory scientist) acts as a practical phenomenologist. He or she is concerned, as a matter of everyday work, with the nature of *appearances* and the production of *descriptions*. Those descriptions need to be adequate for the practical purposes of sharing and recording biomedical observations. They need to be sufficiently delicate to capture sometimes subtle variations in the appearance of tissues and traces. Equally, they draw on a register of occupationally given vocabularies that are a socially shared medium of description.

These matters are by no means confined to the work of haematologists. All medical work is dependent on the use of the senses, and the observation of the patient's body is grounded in the construction of medically relevant descriptions. I have, for instance, documented elsewhere some of the problems encountered by junior medical students in their attempts to produce descriptions of patients and their bodies that are regarded as adequate and accurate by their clinical teachers. The novice does not immediately see a pertinent description of, say, a patient's complexion. It was apparent during my earlier fieldwork with Scottish medical students that confronted by an instruction to 'observe' a patient they could easily flounder (Atkinson, 1988). They could not always produce satisfactory descriptions of the clinical signs – even the most apparently obvious kind. (Obvious, that is, to the teaching clinicians.) Observations are not self-evident to the 'uninitiated'. In the absence of a conceptual framework and a descriptive vocabulary there is no socially shared 'observation': there is no agreement as to a stable world of phenomena. Hence, even agreement to describe a patient as 'pale' or 'jaundiced', or 'tanned' or the like is dependent on the situated vocabularies of clinical medicine.

In precisely the same way, the haematologist or clinical pathologist assembles descriptions of potentially significant phenomena out of a common stock of descriptive categories. At first sight, the shared vocabulary of the clinical laboratory may seem unremarkable – no more nor less than a technical, neutral language of scientific description. In practice, however, there is nothing natural about the haematologists' or pathologists' descriptions, and nothing given about the descriptive categories or their use. On the contrary the language of the pathological gaze is, like any other such specialized register, a socially shared collection of conventions. The linguistically defined categories of medical description provide the cultural resources for the production of facts. The trained clinician or pathologist draws on a vast repertory of descriptors in order to generate accounts of what has been seen, what has been noticed or observed. Many of those terms are in common usage – not restricted to clinical or laboratory settings. Others are far more domain-specific, and characteristic of pathology discourse.

The choice of an appropriate description has implications for how phenomena are categorized, and hence for possible differential diagnoses. The following exchange between clinicians (in this case a fellow and an attending) and a pathologist (P) is illustrative:

F: Yeah, there weren't that much then when we went back and looked we were more impressed with it, so it would be good if you could review it and see if it is atypical

At: Because the thing that we were noticing, you know, when you see the Wright stain of the lymphocytes, quite often the cleft is right down straight and deep, right through the middle.

P: Yeah

At: Well a lot of these cleftings looked more like circumferential cleftings.

P.:   Mm

Pathologist and clinicians go on discussing the tests they want to carry out on the tissue. Later in the interaction, looking now under the microscope, they return to the issue of 'cleft' cells:

At: Those are clefts. There's a cleft

P: A *notch!*

F: Hahehh

St: Hehnhnhum huhuhm

P: Well, I'd hate to have to make it on this. I think the *bone* marrow's very suspicious

At: There *were* some there

What is at stake here is whether the cells that have been seen, and are not being scrutinized by the pathologist, can properly be described as 'clefts'. The clinicians are in some difficulty in establishing a diagnosis concerning this patient, on the basis of a wide range of information, and the evidence of the microscope and of the laboratory remains equivocal in their eyes. It is puzzling enough a picture. Here, as we can see, it remains obscure. The clinicians want to describe the presence of 'clefts' in the lymphocytes, even though they do not seem to claim them as straightforwardly present. On the other hand, the pathologist – to whom appeal has been made for a more definitive opinion – remains equivocal as to the general characterization of the specimen. Moreover, the pathologist challenges the clinicians description of what they all 'see' under magnification. The description 'notch' is preferred to 'cleft', with unstated but implied consequences of undermining further the clinicians' attempts to characterize the case.

The identification of distinctive features, such as clefts or notches, in the samples of bone marrow or blood cells, is one major task for the clinical pathologist or clinical haematologist. The observer needs to be able to characterize sizes, shapes, colours, degree of symmetry, texture and internal morphology of cells. These characteristics, of course, constitute the 'normal' types and lines of cell maturation. Equally, they are used to construct 'abnormal', sometimes pathognomonic, cell types. (It must be borne in mind that while deviations from the normal may be described as 'atypical' cells, their descriptions are – from one point of view – equally typified, and often associated with ideal-typical disease entities.) Likewise, other tissue samples (lymph nodes, for example) require the same sort of histological description. The following exchange illustrates the point. It also demonstrates a further issue in the clinical division of labour – the privileged gaze of the clinical pathologist:

At: We will find you another node
P: Only if you can find yourself another pathologist!
       [*Laughter*]
F: If you don't like it we'll change it.
P: But I don't think anybody could get around this node. It's full of germinal
       centres.
At: The nodules of nodular lymphoma would be bigger than that?
P: Well, no they would be this size, but they don't have this very nice mix of cell
       types with a lot of mitosis.
At: Mitosis suggests reactivity, do you reckon on that?
P: Yeah, I mean, that's *soft*, but the very high mitotic rate tends to suggest
       reactivity. . . .
F: [*to the pathologist*] You know, Carol, it was a very *large* node, so you know
       the node *clin*ically was pathological you know, so I don't think we just missed
       and got a bad node or something 'cos it was a pa*thologic*ally large node.
P: It's *strik*ingly granulomous, isn't it?
F: There's granulomas with *giant* cells, lots and lots of giant cells.
P: Well there're more *giant* cells and fewer regular peculiar cells than you
       normally see . . .

In this and similar sequences, then, the clinicians and the pathologist
together seek to negotiate an acceptable description of the specimen itself
(the product of a biopsy). The vocabulary of pathological description (for
example, granuloma, giant cells, mitosis) provides a framework for the
shared perception of the tissue, and out of that vocabulary emerges
descriptions that will fit other, relevant descriptive frameworks. In this way,
the description of the node can be used by the clinicians and the pathologist
to enter it into possible disease categories. For instance, the sequence
quoted above continues:

P: . . . Um and there *is* no ne*crosis* and you usually see necrosis in well-
       established Fletcher granulomas.
F: So it doesn't look like TB
P: It wouldn't be your first choice. . .

In the course of the fieldwork with the haematologists it became apparent
that the clinical pathologist quoted above held an especially privileged
position in the technical and moral division of labour locally. Pathologists in
general have special rights in adjudicating on the presence and character of
disease processes or entities in the body's organs and cells. They have a
special place in the discourse of the clinico-pathological conference at which
different specialists contribute their distinctive perspective on a given case.
Not all are granted equal powers of observation and adjudication by their
clinical colleagues, however. The pathologist just referred to, Carol Greene,
however, was strikingly revered by her colleagues. She was granted special
powers of vision, and was appealed to to render pathological judgements
when clinicians or other pathologists were in a quandary and unable to arrive
at a mutually acceptable description. By the same token, if Carol Greene
decided that a given specimen of tissues such as a bone marrow aspirate or
biopsy, could *not* be adjudicated on unequivocally, then the degree of
uncertainty was treated as the definitive state of understanding concerning

that particular case, pending further investigation or further clinical developments. The privilege granted to that one individual pathologist suggested that over and above the shared competence of practitioners, there was a personal element whereby particular individuals had a 'gift' or an 'eye' for recognition and description.

The development of a vocabulary of haematology or of clinical pathology is reminiscent of the shared vocabulary of, say, wine buffs and experts. As Lehrer (1983) has documented, the taste and the bouquet of wine are recognized and marshalled in accordance with a vocabulary of sensory categories and analogies. The wine taster, whether professional or lay, selects from an enormous repertoire of everyday descriptors in order to convey to others the elusive character of taste. Many such terms, though used in a particular way in the domain of wine tasting, consist of everyday descriptive and evaluative terms that are extended into wine usage. They are thus transformed into more esoteric terms within the register of wine. In just the same way, the haematologist needs to be able to describe blood, its constituents and traces. These registers of practical recognition are learned and reinforced through the shared talk of instruction and rounds. They are organized socially through the vocabularies and imagery that are shared among physicians and scientists. Medical work and medical science, indeed, are striking for their rich array of descriptive terms. The production of images is accompanied by descriptive languages for their interpretations. Since images and specimens cannot speak for themselves, physicians must draw on shared descriptive resources.

Take the following brief episode, for example. An attending physician is looking down a microscope together with one of the medical students. The attending, Dr de Kalb, says to the student, 'That's a helmet cell, a German helmet.' The student does not cotton on immediately, and the physician repeats, 'That's called a helmet cell. It's shaped like a military helmet, and I said it looks like a German helmet . . .'. They go on looking at the peripheral blood smear. Dr de Kalb says, 'One of the things you're told to look for in megaloblastic anaemia is hypersegmented neutrophils. I think that's one there.' The other student on the round, who is looking at the same smear through another eye-piece says, 'There's an eosinophil . . . Is that a little drumstick there?' Dr de Kalb replies, 'I think it may be', and explains to the first student that it is so named after the leg of a turkey ('like at Thanksgiving') rather than a real drumstick. In concluding their examination of the smear, Dr de Kalb says, 'I bet if you did a marrow you'd see a lot of megaloblastic activity'. Here we can gain some preliminary sense of how technical language and everyday terms are linked in the shared discourse of inspection and description. Like Lehrer's tasters of wine, the physicians and students use a great many descriptive terms to cover shape, size, colour and texture. The vocabulary itself is important in organizing the shared perceptions.

In the second half of this chapter, therefore, I look more closely at the linguistic organization of visual perception and the production of clinical descriptions. I concentrate in particular on the work of the haematologists in inspecting samples of blood and bone marrow under the microscope.

Seeing and talking

The observation of bodily traces and images is crucial to the organization of contemporary medical work. The clinical gaze at the bedside is supplemented by the laboratory gaze. The clinician or clinical pathologist inspects a host of images and specimens. That is not a straightforward activity. The competent practitioner must learn to see. The 'raw data' of clinical observation and inference are shaped by implicit assumptions and explicit instructions that furnish frameworks of what to see and how to see it. They help to define not only what is seen, but also indicate how to *look*. Looking is an active process. It is discriminating: figure and ground are separated, the essential and the accidental are distinguished, and the characteristic differentiated from the idiosyncratic. Looking, seeing and describing are linguistically organized activities.

There is ample evidence in the haematology data of how the student or junior doctor is guided in seeing. There were, for instance, several occasions when I was able to locate the tape-recorder immediately below the microscope that was used during morning rounds. The microscope had four sets of eye-pieces: consequently, if there were three or two participants it was also possible for me to look at the slide too. If there were four that was not possible, though a helpful student might give me the chance to take a peek through his or her lens. The detailed talk about the specimen is often preceded or accompanied by talk and instruction about the skills and mechanics associated with the manipulation of the microscope itself.

The following example also begins with comment about the press of bodies around the microscope. One must imagine four heads bent close together, arms and elbows touching. The discussion takes place while the participants are looking down the microscope, and they are examining a blood smear. The ethnographer on this occasion was able to have his own eyepiece.

At:	Do you want me to drive?
F:	Go right ahead
At:	Okay, I'll just try and get my elbows clear here.
St:	Huhm
At:	Okay, I'll get my right elbow farther over. [*to the student*] I'm sure Hale [*the fellow*] has told you that whenever you look at a smear the first thing you do is you look under low power
St:	Yuh
At:	You do that for several reasons. Can you give me a few?
St:	Well, first of all just to get a general you know an overall look at it. Then you also um
At:	Yeah whaddaya get from the overall look *for*?
St:	Oh the ratio cells you know the red blood cells to you know white cells to um just get the per*centages* of each you know just a general look at it mm?
At:	Well let's take each in turn

St:	Okay
At:	What am I looking for in the red cells?
St:	Red cells, you're looking for uniformity of size and whether they're hypochromic or hyperchromic and
At:	= Right you can make some *guess*timates at low power
St:	Right
At:	On those issues but you're not gonna be . . .
St:	You'd really get a better look under high power
At:	Anything else?
St:	As far as the red blood cells?
At:	Yeah
St:	Umm
At:	Something very simple and obvious
St:	How many of them there are?
At:	*No*. That hehehm
St:	Alright, simple and obvious
At:	Well what can we achi*eve* at this power? What if we free associate once, how's that?
St:	Okay
At:	I'm cruising along here and several things are registering in my head consciously and unconsciously. The most important thing I'm looking for at this stage is the staining quality of the smear and where I can go down under under oil.
St:	Yuh okay
At:	You know I've had arguments with Henry Kretschmer who never uses oil immersion and I've proved him wrong on several occasions. See oil immersion, I never use high dry as a power, a pathologist uses high dry but I go for low to oil.
St:	Mhm
At:	And as haematologists we need this. So I'm basically looking, I'm making some overall judgement of the quality of the smear.
St:	Mhm
At:	And my judgement on this on a scale of *ten* is and I'm gonna give this smear at least an eight. It looks like a beautifully spread and beautifully stained smear.
St:	Mhm
At:	With automation this is this is great praise from me. You can get garbage you know slipping through ah not uncommonly.
PAA:	D'you get a lot of problems with the stains?
At:	Well these are automated now
PAA:	Mm
At:	And a lotta times the screening process fails. Technicians will accept it rather than band smearing or make another one. Okay, so I'm looking, number one on that. Number two, I'm looking to see whether the red cells in addition to being nicely stained and nicely spread are there any abnormalities are there– is there any malformation?
St:	Mhm
At:	The answer is no
St:	Mhm
At:	You know, there's no clumping at all and from this long distance away there does not appear to be any significant degree of microcytosis that I can see, it may be a little anisocytosis *and* from this distance these cells may be a tad hypochromic. I can't be sure. But that's a *call* we make under a higher power from immersion, and then while I'm cruising al*ong* obviously I'm seeing all the *white* cells.

St: Mhm
At: And I'm looking to see for heterogeneity or monotony. All these decisions on all these cells that I'll be making at a higher power. And what I see is heterogeneity and I see the yeah segmented neutrophils being the most prominent cells, which is what we want it to be.
St: Mhm
At: And at this power you can see plaques that see platelets but again that's something that we'll get down to later on. Okay this is pretty much what *I'm* looking for at this power we *can* recognize nucleated reds we *can* recognize homogeneity in a white cell population suggesting you know a leukaemia.
St: Mhm
At: Ah and also we can see if there's a fair amount of anisocytosis evident, we can see sickle cells uh oh why not play the ball game on our own home field and let's get down to *thou*sand power rather than hundred power.
St: = Mhm
At: Hale, do you wanna add anything at least at this power?
F: No, I–
At: Pretty much you're looking for an area on which you wanna go down on
St: Mhm
At: And this is such a nice smear we can go down anywhere
St: Mhm
At: Some areas you get a lot of *artifact* and some will look hypochromic, others will look normochromic
St: Hhm
At: This smear we have to say is *superb* . . .
. . .
At: Is this in focus for everybody?
St: Mhm
At: And now we get down to the red cells at this time now we see platelets and we see them. You don't have to look hard to see them, they're in every field. And my guesstimate at the moment I'll hold back on, because I want to see how things are here . . . but I do know right now there's no thrombocytopenia with certainty because you wouldn't be seeing platelets of this number you known on survey.
St: Mhm
At: Now that cell in the middle is what?
St: Erm a lymphocyte? Hm?
At: Ex*actly*
St: Okay hhe hh
At: Would you say that's a typical lymphocyte or an *a*typical lymphocyte? Is that the way it looks seen on the drawing board or is it
St: = It's a little atypical isn't it. Or is it totally atypical?
At: Now wait, what's atypical about it?
St: Well does it have a little more cytoplasm that might make it
At: = Well I would think the cytoplasm and nucleus
St: = Is right
          [   ]
At: is quite right
St: = Good okay
At: = for a lymphocyte. That's all right, but there are at least two atypical features
St: Okay
At: that I can see
St: But the nu
At: = Maybe *three*

St:	[ ] cleus
At:	And they're all, I'm gonna make this distinction. If you look at a *normal* smear and you apply rigorous criteria you will find a small percentage of atypical lymphocytes
St:	Hhm
At:	That's good, and baggage, that's the *substrate*. That's, whenever you look at a smear expanding your range of normality so that you don't go hopping and say this has to be that because you see one cell
St:	Mhm
At:	This is atypical for a few reasons. One is it has vacuoles in its cytoplasm. Secondly it has some serration, you know it's like the corona radiata round the sun
St:	Hhm
At:	Of the cytoplasm. And third is the little indentation in that nucleus
St:	= Right
At:	And the nuclear chromatic may not be *quite* as closely packed as you'd expect
St:	Okay
At:	So there are three criteria for atypicality
St:	Mhm
At:	That doesn't mean this should automatically trigger in our differential diagnosis all the things that cause atypical *lymphs*
St:	Mhm
At:	Um what I'm looking for really is a *typical* lymph because Oh look at this, that comes down the pike. Now my head's beginning to trigger. What do you think, now what's *that*?
St:	That's also a lymphocyte
At:	Well it–er
St:	Uh?
At:	Yeah, I admire your frank–, your zeroing in on it. Exactly
St:	Well that– that also has that kind of a corona radiata thing the other one does. And um doesn't really have any indentations but it's not, it's like the other one it's not condensed, as condensed as you'd expect it to be
At:	Right, and *also* there's a nucleolus in that
St:	= That looks like right there in the
At:	= Right, lower left
St:	= lower left corner that there is
At:	It's lower left for me, is it lower left for everybody?
St:	= Yeah lower left for me
At:	= about seven o'clock
St:	Uh I have a nucleolus
At:	Okay, so NOW I'm saying what the hell's going *on* here
St:	Mhm
At:	What I'm really looking for is a typical lymphocyte that all of us will agree on which will be one marker because *that* nucleus would give us the diameter, baseline for to assess whether these cells are microcytic or not. Certainly on the basis of those two cells we have to say all the red in these microcytic but here's, now they're getting a little better
St:	Mhm
At:	Okay? So there's a typically typical lymphocyte and not being too *picky* both of those would be you know
St:	Mhm
At:	= with our X-ray vision we could see maybe vacularization of the cytoplasm

St: Mhm
At: and now with *that* there as a *marker* we can say that the *red* cells . . . we can
         make a better judgement that the reds approximate a mild degree of
         anisocytosis while over *here* is a small cell right in the centre
St: Mhm mhm
At: And there's a little cytosis, this cell *here*. Can hedge on that very nicely by
         saying Dr Lollard [*the attending*] got it smudged so I really can't commit
         myself.
St: Mhhm
At: And I'll have to *accept* that, but you could also could try to *guess*timate
                . . .
St: I'm not sure if it er I'm not sure
At: Well we know it's not a lymphocyte
St: Right
At: We know it's not a neutrophil. We know it's not an eo*sino*phil. We know
         it's
St: = Like a mast?
At: = not a basophil
St: hehehm
F: Can't be a mast
At: It can't be a circulating mast. You don't get circulating *mast* cells
St: = Yeah huhm Ahm
At: = And that leaves us with one other denizen of the peripheral *blood*
St: Peripheral blood Umm
At: Like a monocyte, right?
St: = Monocyte
At: Okay?
St: Okay
At: It has the size, it has the tinctorial qualities it has the nucleus and the
         cytoplasm of a typical monocyte
St: = Okay
At: A monocyte that's been squashed
                . . .
At: Is that typical lymphocyte?
St: Well, it looks like there might be a little bit of nucleolus left in the
At: = That's hard to tell, yeah
St: That's hard to tell 'cos of the stain
At: Right
St: Um I think it looks *pretty* typical
At: It's not *bad*, but there are so many vacularizations in the cytoplasm

This extended extract displays the oral transmission of the craft skill of
recognition. As I have explained earlier in the book, I make little or no
apology for imposing such a lengthy extract from the data on the reader. It is
rare to encounter such a sustained sequence preserved in which instructions
in 'how to see' are explicated. It is a microcosmic interaction, in that it
represents a myriad of similar occasions when experienced practitioners
coach their juniors in ways of seeing and describing. This particular extract
from the field data is especially useful in one sense: the student involved is
not very confident in her responses to the attending physician, and the latter
engages in a good deal of prompting, correcting and repair. While one may
enter no claim as to the typicality of such an exchange, therefore, it is a
particularly useful one. The student's reticence and lack of skill prompts the

senior physician himself to articulate his own activities at some length. He seeks to explicate some of his normally tacit knowledge in talking through the smear with the novice student.

What is noticeable is how the act of visual recognition is achieved through speech acts. As the participants share a single microscope with multiple eye-pieces, they can operate with the practical assumption that they see the same field. As practical phenomenologists, they operate with the sort of assumptions identified by Schutz (1967). That is, they may assume, for all practical purposes, that they inhabit a world of shared objects. They simultaneously scan the same sectors of the blood smear, and the same cells are visible to each of them simultaneously. In other words, this particular technology provides a method that strengthens what Schutz described as the prerequisite for intersubjective understanding:

> It is . . . essential to the face-to-face situation that you and I have the same environment. First of all I ascribe to you an environment corresponding to my own. Here, in the face-to-face situation, but only here, does this presupposition prove correct, to the extent that I can assume with more or less certainty within the directly experienced social realm that the table I see is identical (and identical in all its perspective variations) with the table you see. . . . Therefore, when I am in a face-to-face situation with you, I can *point to* something in our common environment, uttering the words 'this table here' and by means of the identification of lived experiences in the environmental object. I can assume the adequacy of my interpretive scheme to your expressive scheme. For practical social life it is of the greatest significance that I consider myself justified in equalling my own interpretation of my lived experiences with your interpretation of yours on those occasions when we are experiencing one and the same object. (Schutz, 1967: 170–1)

If this basic assumption is a prerequisite to the natural attitude of everyday interpersonal life, it is especially important – and problematic – in the social exchanges of experts. The experience of the 'man-or-woman-in-the-street' of pointing to a table and expecting his or her companion to experience the same object is very different from that of the expert who works with esoteric knowledge and judgements. The aesthete or professional art critic or historian cannot point to an art work and assume that even another expert – let alone a lay person – can in any practical sense be said to see the same object(s). The purely physical visual field may be assumed to be a shared one, and the arrangement of objects to be recognizably the same. Yet they cannot be held to constitute identical objects in any meaningful fashion. In the absence of a shared frame of reference, and a shared language of special descriptions, then even physical objects themselves may not be discerned in the same way.

In this sense, therefore, the shared visual field of the microscope may ensure that in a purely physical sense the same phenomena are under inspection. On the other hand, as we have seen in this data extract, that does *not* mean that the same things will be seen. Expert vision depends on the capacity to recognize and to describe. These capacities are socially – that is, culturally and linguistically – organized. The competent practitioner will be able to discriminate and to describe phenomena using complex series of categories and descriptors that are not available to the lay person or to the novice. There is no need to subscribe to a strong version of the Sapir–Whorf hypothesis in order to recognize the importance of descriptive labels or categories in the acquisition and use of expert discrimination.

The physician or medical student – in common with practitioners in other fields of expertise – faces repeated problems of practical phenomenology. The objects of the clinical gaze repeatedly present problems and puzzles of description and recognition. The haematologist, as we have seen, has his or her special set of signs and fields that must be scanned, read and decoded. As I discussed in the previous chapter, the haematologist reads the patient's body – its gross features and its local manifestations of deviations from normality – in order to render professionally adequate descriptions. On the basis of my earlier work in the Edinburgh medical school, I have documented some of the everyday problems encountered by medical students and the pedagogical devices that may be used to inculcate appropriate descriptions (see, for example, Atkinson, 1988). Here I focus on more of the data from the haematological settings in order to explore some of the issues involved.

It is readily apparent that the novice and the practitioner alike must deploy a wide variety of terms in order to describe key features of blood. Blood cells are described and classified; their relative frequencies are estimated. Likewise, bone marrow aspirates must be decoded. In capturing and sharing their descriptions of blood, haematologists learn and use a varied vocabulary in order to characterize distinctive features, such as blood cells. They are described in terms of shape, size and colour. On that basis they can be stored into different cell types, and developmental sequences (*lines*). Rather than recapitulate features observable in the data presented already, these general remarks can be illustrated by further extracts from the case conferences. For instance:

F: Do you wanna go under oil?
At: Mm were you um are you adjusted there?
F: Er no
At: Why don't you just
F: I can just adjust this
At: Okay
F: That's good for me
At: Ri–ight
St: (Focus)
At: Well you have to focus up and down
F: Yeah
At: That's a Mott cell, and that one also
F: Yeah and we saw just tons of 'em. Some had nucleoli, some were more immature than others.
At: Mm
F: Some looked like plasma *blasts* with very open nucleus and we saw some mitoses
At: Mhm, nice
F: Yeah. There's clusters. You know, in areas like *here* if you don't count the erythroid cells there's like fifty per cent
At: Yeah

F: Oh there's a couple of nucleoli over the other way, the other way

At: There's one there

St: Hhum

F: Yeah there's clusters. *I* you know in areas like *here* if don't count the erythroid cells there's like fifty per cent

At: Yeah, and if you turn to the other side, yeah this one has also

F: Right

At: Yeah, that really is a good one

F: Yeah, there, there's one with a huge nucleolus

At: Oh yeah, wow, phew, and the one next to it has too

F: Yeah

At: More pink

At: [*to the student*] Lloyd, supposing you saw plasma cells like this but they had sort of irregular cytoplasm sort of *flaring* out and had a sort of reddish line, otherwise known as flame cells, what would that tell you?

St: They're still plasma cells, I mean they look exactly like that?

At: Well no, they don't look exactly like this. Instead of sort of round neat cytoplasm they more go out in a sort of jaggy pattern and a sort of reddish coloured cytoplasm rather than bluish does that tell you anything?

St: Erm, I'm not, I don't know

At: [*to the fellow*] Charles, you don't know?

F: I don't know either

At: = called flame cells?

F: Uh?

At: They're characteristic of IgFA myeloma

F: Oh

St: Ah

At: A rare entity

F: There's a nice nucleolus in that one

At: Better look it up

F: That's probably a plasma cell too, huh?

At: Mhm

F: Even though it's less coloured

At: Yeah

At: Oh look at that one. Some of them are really nasty looking. Now, is the peripheral smear available here?

F: I haven't actually had in and seen the peripheral smear, we should get that

At: Would be interesting and because . . .

F: = Make sure she doesn't have any

At: = Make sure she's a plasma cell leukaemia

F: Yeah, I'll get that today

. . .

F: Er we don't see any dividing ones right here but they certainly were around

At: Yeah

F: So what do you estimate, around thirty per cent?

At: Yeah I woulda said greater than thirty per cent, you see I mean it always varies depending

F: Yeah

At: = ON

F: We were, we saw

At: Would be nice to see the bone marrow biopsy, it ought to be quite impressive

F: Yeah, I hope that that'll be ready now

At: Um there are quite a lot of megakaryocytes

F: = Yeah

At: = She obviously has adequate of those, and
F: And she's not
At: Still, hard to estimate the ratio, because there are so many
F: Would you call this sheets, though? I guess you
At: No
At: = They're pretty close they're not really sheets
F: Well
At: No, sheets you normally talk about like (   ) arrangement
F: Right
At: The way it looks like the cytoplasm are merging into each other
F: Right
At: Um and that is truly pathological but no, this isn't pathological (but)
F: Yeah
At: No, I wouldn't call it sheets. Very nice, very nice indeed.

In this extract we can see repeated examples of the negotiated, even disputed, character of clinical descriptions. Those descriptions are not simply matters of personal perception, and their significance goes well beyond what is just seen on the microscope slide. The selection and attribution of the appropriate descriptive terms has direct implications for the diagnosis. Many such signs are treated as *pathognomic*. That is, the presence of such signs is a virtually certain indication of a particular disease entity. The consensual identification and use of appropriate descriptive terms is therefore highly consequential for the haematologists (and indeed any medical practitioners).

In establishing and sharing their histological descriptions, then, the haematologists must try to establish agreed benchmarks and reference points. These include verbal labels and pictures or diagrams that can be pointed to in order to provide ostensive definitions of the relevant phenomena. The following extract shows an interplay between a reported description, a reported photographic representation, a blackboard sketch recapitulating that photograph, and inspection of a patient's smear. These various sources and layers of signification all relate to the appropriate identification of cells or cell fragments, and hence their potential diagnostic implications.

F: Yeah. I'd like to look at the smear because the one thing that disturbed me is I saw a few more *tears* than I would like to see and so I thought that once we get this solved and once the crit comes back to normal and all this chaos calms down if there's still a lot of tears it might not be unreasonable to do
At: Teardrop red cells you mean?
F: Yeah. It's not over*whelm*ing but I couldn't really, I don't know, can I explain that on the basis of a delayed transfusion reaction?
At: Well what are you thinking of? Myelometaplasia or something like that?
F: Something like that

This sequence is followed by several more seconds of discussion about the patient and her condition in the preceding days. The clinical fellow again prompts the attending physician to look at the slide for himself. He does so while the fellow responds to a 'bleep' that has interrupted the case conference.

At: Are these so-called tear drops *new*? I mean were they there before?
F: I never saw them red before

At: Well, I mean, There are a few of them there and I sure don't know what to make of them

F: Mm

At: Now which stage was this?

F: This was the day before I saw her

At: Well let's see now. Now I'll try to figure out when that was

F: >Okay it was< you know way after the surgery

At: Yeah

F: <And then her>

At: Had she already had the transfusions?

F: Had had

At: Two of them

. . .

At: Yeah, Right half. There's a hypersegmented poly

F: Yeah that was (   )

At: Well that fits in with the the haemalyt– = well if it's probably *folate* or she's using up her folate very rapidly. That's usually a very early finding in severe haemolysis

F: So. In other words you should– you might that maybe before you'd see that they can't retic?

At: Yeah

F: Okay

At: = I mean she's using up her folate and I dare say she's gonna have a megalobastic *marrow* now. Well I'm not too impressed by this . . . It may be that you know, have you ever seen that famous *photograph* of a red cell wiggling through the =

F: = (   ) screen?

At: No no not that, that's another one, the the fenestrations of the *spleen*. No I mean, you know it pushes through a small *hole*

F: Yeah

At: And I suspect when the spleen is working *over*time that a person with many antibody coated red cells, that some of those are gonna get *pinched* off

F: Mhm

At: And I think that would reshape the red cells to some extent. It may be that those are antib– and if the *next* time that goes through its gonna get *another changes* and it eventually will be a spherocyte

F: Mm, yeah

At: And it may be that we're just seeing this grow here. You don't often get a chance to see a Coombs positive haemolytic anaemia in its *early* evolution. By the time we see them they're usually well established and a lotta spherocytes which are due to *nips* of red cell and cells that *escape* the spleen but aren't gonna escape it the next time they go through. So I suspect that that's going on here you know

. . .

At: Let's get a piece of paper here. Here you are on the blackboard.
[*He draws with chalk on blackboard*]

At: The picture looks something like this. These are spleen cells, here's a red cell which is on its way through this *way*

F: Mm. Right

At: And for example there are Heinz bodies there and that would be pinched *off* and the cell would come out with, and look like *that*

St: Mhm

At: But I think that when the spleen really gets *going* and er some of the cells don't quite *make* it, you may end up with a piece taken off something like so. A piece like *that*, eventually it will be a spherocyte.

In this sequence, then, the observable phenomenon itself – the presence of tear-shaped cells – is contested by the attending physician. He draws (from memory) on a classic textbook photograph of the spleen, and constructs an alternative description of what may have been seen. What he claims is seen under the microscope is related to other images, such as his report of the photograph and his drawing on the blackboard. In other words, what is visible is recognized only in the context of other representations – seen or imagined. In the course of this discussion, therefore, the visible characteristics of blood cells are explored in relation to classic types, and to possible physiological processes. Shape is seen and interpreted simultaneously. The meaning of cell morphology is explored in relation to possible frameworks of significance. It is also noticeable here that the senior physician, Dr de Kalb, engages in personal speculation on possible causes and processes. As we shall see in a later chapter, it is characteristic of rounds that the senior participants (attending physicians) often express themselves in this personalizing way.

The work of seeing is, at least in part, the work of naming and describing, as we have seen. The facts of the body and its appearances are produced via richly descriptive vocabularies. Likewise, the significant appearances of the body are shaped and conveyed through these shared linguistic repertoires. It is self-evident that clinical medicine and the clinical laboratory sciences have their own linguistic registers and situated vocabularies. Like all socially organized specialisms they have distinct vocabularies, which encapsulate the distinctive concerns and procedures of the trade in question. For cognitively skilled occupations, the registers of craft knowledge are fundamental elements of their stock-in-trade. The clinical gaze and the laboratory gaze are mediated by such linguistic registers.

On the one hand, the haematologist, or equivalent specialist, has mastery over an enormous range of technical terms. These cover the basic and the medical sciences – such as biochemistry, histology, pharmacology. The average textbook in a field like haematology will be full of specialized terms, covering structures and processes, pathologies and preparations, organic compounds and their constituents. In addition to this huge vocabulary of technical terms, however, there is a further range of descriptive terms that the competent practitioner must learn to *use* in order to deploy his or her competence. In other words, there may be a contrast between knowing *that* a particular cell-type is characteristic of a specific disorder, and knowing *how* to recognize and describe such cells. It is one thing to know the relevant criteria (size, shape, colour) and quite another to be able to apply those criteria in common with other practitioners in the production of appropriate categories and attributions.

The following extracts provide examples of students or clinicians reporting their observations in the course of case presentations and discussions:

St: Okay we did the bone marrow biopsy, well tolerated
At: Yes yes yes!
St: The aspirate revealed twenty to thirty per cent of atypical plasma cells

At: How atypical?
F: Er very
St: = Very not well at all
At: Sheets
St: Not sheets
F: Um not *sheets* but er
St: = Mostly their appearance is atypical. They had large nucleoli
At: Mhm
St: And multiple nucleoli
At: So, young looking
St: = They're mitotic
F: = Numerous mitoses. Many many mitotics
At: Okay
F: Many separating
St: Large cytoplasm
At: Mhm
St: Yeah
F: Prominent nucleoli and in certain areas marked (   ). Up to sixty, seventy
        per cent of the cells seen were plasma
At: Mhm okay
F: But it wasn't subtle
At: Impressive

In the following extract, the same group are actually inspecting a bone
marrow aspirate, identifying similar phenomena. Here Teresa, the attending physician, draws the sociologist into the process of observing and
describing

At: [*to PAA*] Know what you're looking at? Hehh
St: Pretty
At: This this is an aspirate out of the bone marrow cavity
PAA: That's right, I know that much
At: Yeah and um normally what you *see* is the myeloid and erythroid cell lines
          in a ratio of about three white to one of red
PAA: Mhm
At: Precursors, they're called precursors
F: Here's a nice one, Teresa
At: In this patient um oh yeah, yeah, in this patient who has plasma cell, who's
          myeloma about thirty per cent of the cells are plasma cells
PAA: Mm
At: And they're replacing the normal elements [*Telephone rings*]
F: And right in the centre here
At: They know you're here too! [*Attending goes to answer phone*]
F: Yeah Right in the centre there, that binucleated cell is a dividing plasma
          cell, which is very atypical. You really shouldn't see that
PAA: Aha
F: And in all those big large cells would be blue cytoplasm, like there's
          another atypical one with two nucleoli
PAA: Right
F: = Two nucleoli, are *all* abnormal plasma cells
PAA: Mhm
F: And normally you should, plasma cells should be one per cent or less of
          the number of cells in the marrow, whereas here it's probably up to in
          certain areas above thirty per cent.
PAA: Mm

F:	This is clotted so its not that good. There's probably an atypical one too, if it's a plasma cell. There's another binucleated plasma cell, so this is diagnostic of multiple myeloma
At:	Okay
F:	Alright

Here, then, we get further exemplifications of the *recognition* tasks involved in the seeing and reporting of clinically relevant phenomena. The practitioner must take into consideration such distinctive features as size, shape and colour of cells. The relative size and shape of the cell's nucleus is attended to, as is the appearance of the surrounding cytoplasm. The problems of recognition – especially in the presence of an inexperienced student or an even less expert ethnographer – may often lead the clinician to search for and welcome the presence of clear examples, that may be used as reference points for pedagogic purposes. When they are available, they fulfil the same function as the ideal-typical cases to be found in the textbooks and atlases. The need for clear exemplars contributes to the clinician's frequent use of apparently aesthetic, or similarly evaluative criteria. The identification of a particular cell or of a given field of peripheral blood or marrow aspirate as, say, 'nice' reflects the practitioner's need for concrete examples that are demonstrably and desirably clear. Of course, that very clarity itself is an appearance that is *achieved* by means of the organized work of showing, telling, comparing and asserting. Even the self-evidence of a stark contrast or a striking appearance must be read *as* self-evident, and that status pointed out to novices and neophytes by the senior and more authoritative mentor. Such exemplars will often be greeted with an appreciative comment, such as 'impressive', or 'here's a nice one'. They provide benchmarks against which implicit systems of comparison and contrast can be assembled and invoked.

I have drawn attention to this aspect of the reproduction of medical knowledge, drawing on my research on medical students (Atkinson, 1988). The pedagogical devices I described there rest on systematic contrasts between distinctive features, so that the 'signs' of disease entities are distributed in semantic spaces. Similar processes can be detected in these haematological rounds, although they are less consistently and explicitly articulated, since the recorded episodes are not exclusively aimed at the instruction of medical students. Nevertheless, it is easy to detect the elements of practical reasoning that are invoked in the course of such recognition exercises.

The novice is encouraged to base his or her judgements on basic criteria or dimensions of contrast. The cells in question may be larger or smaller, more or less pigmented, with nucleus present or absent, with regular or irregular margin, symmetrical or asymmetrical, and so on. From such elementary, practical features the novice and the more experienced practitioner together can establish the frameworks for competent descriptions and the identification of clinically relevant deviations from the normal.

The theme of this and the preceding chapter takes us beyond the narrow confines of haematology. It reflects the contemporary interest in the body as a topic of sociological discourse. I have suggested already that authors such as Foucault and his followers, such as Turner (1984, 1987, 1992), have sought to place the body at the centre of a sociological discourse that deals not solely with health, illness and medicine, but with a broader consideration of the rationalization and disciplines of modern society. To a considerable extent their influence has been a beneficial one. They have successfully drawn attention to the disembodied character of so much classic sociological writing. Indeed, Turner has pointed out the extent to which even the sociology of medicine has managed to overlook the body in much of its literature. It is also arguable that the recurrent preoccupation with the consultation has in some quarters led to an unduly cognitive orientation, with insufficient attention to the physical manifestations of health and illness.

Turner himself advocates a recognition of the centrality of the body to a sociology of action in general, and to the sociology of medicine in particular. Turner suggests, for instance, that

> the sociology of the body not only provides an important focus within sociology as a whole in contemporary work, but offers medical sociology, or more specifically the sociology of health and illness, an opportunity to become the leading edge of contemporary sociological theory. (1992: 162–3)

On the other hand, Turner does very little to document the treatment of the body in contemporary medicine. The overall theme of his sociology is clearly pertinent to the current discussion. Turner argues, in parallel to Foucault and others, that the regulation of the body is an important aspect of the 'rationalization' process of modern society. Historically, the regulation of the body can be traced through the institutional arrangements of religion, law and medicine. Unfortunately, Turner's own analysis does not touch on the empirical investigation of contemporary and medical practice. It remains the case that detailed examination of the investigation and management of the body is lacking from a great deal of medical sociology.

In the terminology of Strauss and his collaborators (for example, Strauss et al., 1985), there is a recurrent need to address the 'body work' that is the most characteristic set of tasks in the modern clinic. We have sociological analyses of the historical significance of the emergence of laboratory science in the division of medical labour (Jamous and Peloille, 1970), and some very limited analyses of the modern relations between clinicians and pathologists. We now have an emergent literature on the medical and life sciences as *work* (Clarke and Fujimura, 1992). Yet we know far more about anatomy in its historical context (Turner, 1992) than we do about contemporary practices of understanding the body. We know more about 'the lesson of the hospitals' (Foucault, 1973) in eighteenth- and nineteenth-century medicine than in the organization of medical education in the late twentieth century.

Body work

This and the previous chapters have attempted to provide a preliminary account of how members of one medical specialty set about the assessment of the body. This descriptive account of haematological work illustrates a number of fundamental issues. First, it highlights the importance of the principle of 'symmetry' in the sociological treatment of the body in medical knowledge. We have now become accustomed to historical accounts that demonstrate the understanding and representation of the body in past periods. It is a commonplace to note that 'the body' has not been a stable, fixed entity. Historical distance undoubtedly helps us to appreciate the social and culture specificity of bodies and their representation (Gilman, 1988; Lupton, 1994; Stafford, 1991). One must not, however, pay attention primarily to the 'other' bodies of history, while neglecting the socially constructed bodies of our own specialized knowledge. The body (or, more properly, the bodies) of contemporary biomedicine are just as much social products as those of, say, Tudor obstetrics, seventeenth-century anatomy, eighteenth-century surgery or nineteenth-century pathology.

Secondly, it draws attention to some of the processes and procedures whereby the body is surveyed within the framework of a rationalized technical division of labour. The glimpses of haematology and clinical pathology afforded by the fieldwork and recordings illuminate some of the socially organized practices whereby the body is dispersed within that division of labour. Bucher and Strauss (1961) outlined the distinctive Chicago-school view of the professions by stressing the extent of *segmentation* within elite occupations like medicine. They emphasized – in contrast to sociological perspectives that stressed a homogeneous professional 'community' – that occupations like medicine could be thought of as coalitions of interest-groups and specialisms. Each segment identified itself, in contradistinction to other segments, in terms of its distinctive mission, its knowledge-base and its characteristic approach to work. In just the same way, one can think of the body as being segmented into shards and fragments, tissues and traces. The fragmentation of the body directly mirrors the segmentation of the modern medical setting. Each professional group, each segment, lays claim to its distinctive knowledge; each lays claim to particular bits of the body. The haematologist, of course, claims the blood, the bone marrow and the lymph nodes. Elsewhere, the other specialists ply their trade with their own body framework. Furthermore, this division of labour rests upon a further collection of specialist workers – the laboratory scientists and technicians who transform the body's tissues and products into values and readings.

Thirdly, therefore, we must recognize that this work goes into rendering the body legible and visible in various ways. The body of the modern clinic is not merely fragmented and dispersed: it is manipulated, transformed and fixed into a series of representations and enumerations. The surveillance of the body is thus intimately connected to the existence, location and use of medical and scientific laboratory technologies. As yet we lack a thorough-going sociology of medical technology and instrumentation. It is, however, abundantly clear that the possibilities and limitations of a medical understanding of the body are coterminous with the limits and possibilities of the technologies and techniques that render the body's traces readable, visible, recordable and countable.

As I have indicated above, we have a few excellent studies of the means whereby the body is rendered into images. The history of X-ray imaging and the recent history of the other imaging techniques have been explored, and they are among the most striking examples of how the body is rendered as an object of expert knowledge and scrutiny. They are indicative of how the modern body is transfigured into shadows, shapes, spaces and traces. There are, however, many other techniques and methods whereby the body may be inspected, its manifestations indexed and permanently recorded. We have already encountered methods of inspecting and counting features of the blood, and the methods used to make the blood or bone marrow visible. The body of the modern clinic, therefore, is to be thought of – at least in part – as a series of representations. Those representations are themselves dispersed in time and space within the complex organization of the clinic. They are inspected, interpreted and reported by different cadres of specialized personnel. In a paradoxical manner, therefore, one should think of the modern clinic as producing a disembodied body. That is, a body – as an object of medical scrutiny – that is divorced from the body of the patient. The body may therefore be read at different sites. The bedside itself is one such locale, of course, and the patient's own body is always available for surveillance. It is, however, one among many possible versions of the body that may be assembled in the modern clinic. The patient thus may have a multiple existence within the clinic. As we shall see, the various fragmentary aspects of the patient and his or her body are brought together under the auspices of *the case*. This is achieved through the work of the medical practitioner or practitioners in the construction of the case, by means of narrative reconstruction. It is to the narrative reconstruction of clinical cases that I turn in the next chapter.

5

Constructing Cases

The everyday accomplishment of medical work – the production, reproduction and use of medical knowledge – is dependent on the competent use
of a wide range of skills. They include the physical manipulation of
diagnostic and scientific instruments, the skilful use of medical technology,
the techniques of inspection and investigation of the patient's body. Many of
these competences are embodied skills that are part of the craft knowledge
of the practitioner. In large measure they are tacitly acquired through the
apprenticeship of the student and the junior practitioner.

Medical work is further dependent on other skills and competences. They
are equally tacit – equally indeterminate – in that they are rarely, if ever,
subject to codification, prescription or explicit instruction. Those skills are
largely rhetorical. The competent medical practitioner translates the skilful
work of clinical investigation, laboratory tests, radiographic imaging or
whatever into plausible and persuasive accounts that justify past actions,
current understandings and future plans.

Medical work and medical knowledge are enacted within an oral culture.
It is, of course, a literate culture too: journals and textbooks are important
resources, while, case notes and other documents are constantly produced in
relation to each patient and each consultation. Nevertheless, medical
knowledge is grounded in a great deal of talk between colleagues, or
between teachers and their students. There are, indeed, many occasions
within a busy teaching hospital when talk and debate about cases, opinions
and received wisdom are culturally required. The occasions for such
collegial talk include: clinical lectures and demonstrations; ward rounds,
teaching rounds and grand rounds; mortality and morbidity reviews; regular
seminars and conferences; the surgeon's commentary to juniors and
students. Occasions such as rounds are complex occasions wherein instruction, social control and social status are enacted (cf. Arluke, 1980; Weiss,
1993). In addition to those more or less formal scheduled occasions for talk,
there are numerous other working encounters during which collegial talk is
exchanged.

The cynical observer might well speculate that the patients and their
complaints are primarily the pretext for medical talk. Indeed, it is certainly
arguable that a 'case' is constituted by the written and spoken accounts that
surround the patient's body and its physical traces. Clinicians – especially in
North America – talk of 'working up' a case. By that they normally refer to
the performance of a range of available clinical investigations, tests,
procedures and the like. From one's observations of routine hospital work,

however, one might equally infer that a case is worked up through repeated tellings. To be more precise, there is a complex set of relationships between actions and accounts in the accomplishment of a case.

'Telling the case' is an elementary type of work in many professional, people-processing contexts. There are many occupational groups who routinely produce spoken and written accounts of 'the facts of the case', who reconstruct their client's biography and moral character, and who persuade others as to the credibility of those facts and the appropriateness of preferred courses of action. The production of case-talk is, for instance, the stock-in-trade of lawyers and social workers. As Pithouse and I have argued, social workers characteristically account for their clients and their own interventions by recourse to narratives. Through stories about clients' families and professional encounters, the social worker gives a good account of him- or herself, the adequacy of the work performed, and the client or family in question. Causes and consequences are couched in terms of narrative. The social worker's narratives render otherwise invisible work accountable to colleagues and superiors (Pithouse and Atkinson, 1988).

In much the same way, it may be argued that medical work is constantly produced and reproduced through narrative and other language skills. The work resides in written and spoken rhetorical formats. The competent practitioner is adept at describing his or her work and persuading others to share opinions on the cases in question. There is in the everyday organization of medical work a close relationship between written and oral accounts constructed by medical practitioners for their colleagues. Physicians refer to written materials in the production of their spoken performances; the latter may provide the basis for subsequent written texts. As Tannen (1985) has pointed out, a sharp distinction between 'literate' and 'oral' aspects of culture is misplaced in many instances: it is undeniably true of the culture of medicine.

There has, indeed, been a certain amount of sociological attention to the production and reception of written documents and records, some of it classic. Garfinkel's original contributions of ethnomethodology contain his account of clinic records (Garfinkel, 1967); Raffel's work on medical records and documentary facts offers a parallel perspective (Raffel, 1979). Macintyre (1978) and Rees (1981) among others also develop our understanding of the organizational contexts and consequences of record-keeping in clinical settings. They all show how the organization of medical work is partly achieved through the construction of written records, such as the folder of case notes. Likewise, those documentary sources are read by members of the organization against a background of tacit knowledge about everyday work in the local setting.

Most recently, Pettinari (1988) has made an important contribution to the investigation of written clinical discourse. Pettinari devotes her attention to surgeons' written reports of their operations. She shows how the work of the surgeon is translated into the textual format of the operation report. She also demonstrates how surgeons in training learn to produce written accounts that conform to organizationally required types. The production of an adequate report is thus part of the competence acquired by young surgeons. It is one of the many demands of situational learning required of trainee practitioners. In addition to 'learning the ropes' in the course of their occupational socialization, Pettinari's young surgeons need to 'learn the texts'. The surgeons' operational reports – which are written or dictated after the completion of operations and procedures – transform what was done and what was seen into a restricted frame and a restricted occupational register. Those reports are, in turn, available for other surgeons to read and interpret in the light of their shared knowledge of those self-same conventional constraints. Barrett (1993) also focuses on writing in the production of schizophrenia as a diagnosis; he examines how the processes of reading, writing and interviewing are interwoven in clinical work. He emphasizes the 'movement back and forth between oral and written discourse' (p. 266). He traces the transformation of the patient's lay constructions to the clinician's professional constructions in terms of the translation from an oral to a written mode of discourse. What is interesting from my point of view is the reverse movement – from professional records to professional narratives, as cases are reconstructed as oral performance in rounds and conferences.

The sociological analysis of medical records is not extensive. It is, however, much more substantial than the sociological literature on spoken interaction between medical colleagues. This point about the bias in social-scientific research on medical discourse has been made by Anspach. She notes the extensive research on the medical interview or consultation, and continues:

> This very extensive literature on medical discourse contains a significant omission. Although much has been written concerning how doctors talk *to* patients, very little has been written about how doctors talk *about* patients. . . . This analytic focus on the medical interview occurs even though the way in which physicians talk about patients is a potentially valuable source of information about medical culture. Rarely do doctors directly reveal their assumptions about patients when talking to them; it is in talking and writing to other doctors about patients that cultural assumptions, beliefs and values are displayed more directly. A consequence of this omission is that with few exceptions, much information about medical culture is inferred indirectly or introduced ad hoc into discussions of medical discourse. (1988: 358)

Anspach goes on to note, quite rightly, that virtually the only area of research in which there has been consistent interest in the language of medical knowledge has been the sociology of professional socialization. But she also notes one generic limitation in this area:

> While addressing the cultural meaning of medical language, studies of professional socialization are limited by their exclusive reliance upon ethnographic methods. Medical slang is often presented out of context and is divorced from the actual occasions in which it is used. Moreover, these studies have been confined to slang words and humour, often glaring violations of the service ethic which are readily apparent to the field worker. Rarely do ethnographers address the more subtle

assumptions embedded in physicians' routine talk. For these reasons, the ethnography of professional socialization would be enhanced by the more detailed approach of discourse analysis. (1988: 359)

Anspach here draws attention to studies that have documented some of the more exotic features of medical school culture – often with connotations that contrast sharply with the public face of professional work and values. Situated vocabularies of patient typing, for instance, have been recorded, which encode pejorative views of patients and their problems (for example, George and Dundes, 1978; Jeffery, 1979; Mizrahi, 1984; Scully, 1980). (Anspach is, perhaps, a little too dismissive of this whole area of research. While some of the published work is unduly biased towards a simplistic folk-lore approach, several major studies do embed their discussions of folk-terms within the broader conceptualization of medical knowledge and medical culture.)

In general, however, Anspach's observations are entirely pertinent. There is every need for the ethnographic study of medical work to incorporate detailed analyses of everyday talk by clinicians and other parties to medical work. Equally, however, there is need to retain a broadly ethnographic treatment of medical settings and social action within them. There is a danger that the extraordinary possibilities of permanent recordings, audio or video, may lead analysts to rely on nothing else (Atkinson, 1992b). The temptation is to define 'the field' as consisting solely in whatever may be *recorded and transcribed*, so that the products of such recording techniques themselves become decontextualized, and broader social processes lost to view. A broader ethnographic treatment also helps to guard against a sterile formalism in the analysis of spoken discourse.

Descriptions, narratives and conversations about 'cases' are, as I have suggested, aspects of everyday medical work. Such talk is not simply *about* the work of the hospital. It *is* medical work. Likewise, we are not dealing with descriptions of medical conditions and interventions that exist independently of these discussions. The cases are produced by the case-talk itself. That does not mean, of course, that diseases and treatments are magically conjured up out of thin air by physicians' incantations. Rather, the case-like quality of all that is reported, seen and done is shaped by linguistic exchange between physicians. The descriptions and other accounts are given their shape and consequence by the many and various spoken actions that are taken for granted in modern medical settings.

The modern teaching hospital provides numerous more-or-less formal settings in which cases are presented and discussed. They form part of the everyday ritual of medical work and instruction. The metaphors present themselves repeatedly – dramaturgical and liturgical. There is always an element of the theatrical about modern medicine, and cases always present something of the spectacular. Physicians and their students repeatedly provide one another with knowledgeable audiences, before whom the practitioner may demonstrate, describe, justify and persuade. Equally, one may think of this repeated round of cases (and indeed of rounds) as furnishing the equivalent of a ritual or liturgy. There is a highly formalized set of occasions and procedures through which the practitioners and their students reveal to one another the mysteries of their craft. Through the daily and weekly enactment of their ritualized recitations, physicians repeatedly produce the cases they discuss, and they discuss the cases they produce.

The liturgical or sacred quality of case-talk varies from context to context. Some are of relative informality; others are extremely formal. As Anspach notes: 'Case presentations vary on a continuum of formality, ranging from relatively informal presentations on daily rounds to formal presentations in large conferences, attended by the senior staff of a department' (1988: 360). In all relatively formal case presentations, however, there is a liturgical element. The presentational rhetoric is prescribed by medical and organizational culture. Anspach's work provides a general characterization:

> Although the specific features of the history vary according to the purpose of the occasion, the case history – whether presented in written or in verbal form – tends to follow an almost ritualized format, characterized by the frequent use of certain words, phrases, and syntactic forms and by a characteristic organization. Histories presented in rounds generally begin with a sentence introducing the patient and the presenting problem. This is followed by a history of the patient's problem and its management and then by a list and summary of the present problems in each organ system, presented in order of importance. Because social aspects of the case are always presented (if at all) only after medical problems have been discussed, the semantic structure of the base presentation attests to the relatively low priority accorded to social issues in the reward structure of residency programs . . . (1988: 360–1)

Anspach herself goes on to document several distinctive features of such presentations. She notes four major ones. First, she draws attention to 'the separation of biological processes from the person' – what she herself refers to as 'de-personalization'. Secondly, she notes 'the omission of the agent': the use of the passive voice, that is. Thirdly, she describes 'treating medical technology as the agent'. Fourthly, she notes that they contain numerous 'account markers', 'which emphasize the subjectivity of the patient's accounts'. Anspach performs an invaluable service in her substantial analysis of such case presentations. Hers is a more substantial data-base than mine on haematologists, and she is able to provide quantitative content-analyses of the case presentations (written and oral). Unfortunately, although she lists and exemplifies several important features of the case presentation as a genre, she fails to capture just how these features are deployed by medical practitioners to produce 'a case'. Several presentations are reproduced by Anspach, and one must read those in order to grasp just how a case is put together. In other words, she makes references to a generalized format and some specific rhetorical features. But she misses the poetics of the case presentation itself. She does not describe how the various features are combined to produce a particular kind of narrative and descriptive performance. What is needed here goes beyond the enumeration of a few distinctive features of case-talk (important though they undoubtedly are). We need to see just how case narratives and descriptions are produced, as *narratives* for instance. We need to understand just how the presenting physician draws together the various elements – from the patient's account, from laboratory findings, from clinical bedside observation and examination – into a plausible and persuasive account. The physician who presents a case produces a narrative, through which the patient's career is not merely recapitulated, but produced *as a career*. The story of the case, therefore, encodes the variety of events and observations into a single, more-or-less coherent account, through which events themselves unfold. The story itself may or may not be resolved, in that the case may be on-going. There may be unfinished business and unresolved problems. The story may, indeed, prove to be one of the insoluble puzzles. Nevertheless, it is a narrative mode in which the career is assembled and rehearsed before the medical audience.

It is, moreover, a narrative that does not merely draw together information and opinion. It sets them into an organizational context that is itself inscribed in the narrative structure. It establishes the credibility and plausibility of that knowledge and opinion. It distributes credibility between the narrator and other *dramatis personae*. Several of these issues will be explored in some detail in later chapters. Here attention will be paid primarily to the poetics of case narratives. Rather than enumerating features in terms of a content analysis (however illuminating), I shall try to show, with reference to extended examples, how patients and their conditions are constructed through physicians' collegial discourse.

The identification of narrative modes in medical contexts is not novel. Indeed, in recent years, there has been a burgeoning interest in narrative. Accounts of narrative forms and contents include several sustained analyses of narrative in the expression of health and illness. Kleinman (1988) is an important case in point. Kleinman's lengthy treatment is predicated on his perspective on 'suffering', and the 'meaningful' nature of the illness experience. Concentrating on the personal and interpersonal consequences of chronic illness, Kleinman stresses the sense-making work of narrative reconstruction. For instance, he gives a summary account of such an interpretation in the following passage:

> The chronically ill become interpreters of good and bad omens. They are archivists researching a disorganized file of past experiences. They are diarists recording the minute ingredients of current difficulties and triumphs. They are cartographers mapping old and new territories. (Kleinman, 1988: 48)

And Kleinman goes on shortly after that passage to argue:

> Thus, patients order their experience of illness – what it means to them and to significant others – as personal narratives. The illness narrative is a story the patient tells, and significant others retell, to give coherence to the distinctive events and long-term course of suffering. The plot lines, core metaphors, and rhetorical devices that structure the illness narrative are drawn from cultural and personal models for arranging experiences in meaningful ways and for effectively communicating those meanings. Over the long course of chronic disorder, these model texts shape and even create experience. The personal narrative does not merely reflect illness experience, but rather it contributes to the experience of symptoms and sufferings. (Kleinman, 1988: 49)

In pursuit of a humane and interpretative approach to illness, therefore, Kleinman pursues a biographical and narrative approach. He reports life-history accounts from a series of patients. He emphasizes the work of meaning-production that they accomplish through their personal narratives. Unfortunately, despite the rich sources of data he draws on, Kleinman does not capitalize on his original inspiration. He does little or nothing to delineate the formal features of the narratives themselves. The 'plot lines', 'core metaphors' and 'rhetorical devices' are never subject to systematic analysis in their own right. Kleinman always seems more content to let the narratives 'speak for themselves'. His emphasis on meaning-creation through narrative follows his more general anthropological commitment to the analysis of illness experience. There is a danger of assuming that the patient's illness experiences are shaped by narrative, while by implication 'disease' is not regarded from the equivalent analytic viewpoint. Such a view rests on the medical anthropologists' particular emphases on illness as meaningful experience. A number of commentators have paid more attention to the formal qualities of illness narratives than did Kleinman (Riessman, 1990). They include Williams (1984), and Garro (1994), on the narrative reconstruction of chronic illness, and Robinson (1990) on multiple sclerosis. As Bury puts it, illness is a form of 'biographical disruption' and is itself a biographical phenomenon. Illness is retrospectively accounted for in the course of everyday autobiographical work on the part of lay persons (Bury, 1982).

By and large, we encounter the familiar asymmetry in the social scientific literature: disease production is much less likely to be regarded from a narrative perspective. Hunter (1991), by contrast, provides one of the few treatments of doctors' narratives. She comments generally on the narrative accomplishment of medical understanding. For instance, in a passage typical of the approach in general, Hunter proposes that:

> In medicine the case is the basic unit of thought and discourse, for clinical knowledge, however scientific it may be, is narratively organized and communicated. As the medical account of a malady constructed from the patient's words and body, the case is a doubled narrative: the patient's story is encapsulated and retold in the physician's account of the process of disease in this one individual. The act of telling the medical story is likewise a redaction of the patient's own earlier presentation . . . As a fundamental ritual of academic medicine, the narrative act of case presentation is at the center of medical education and, indeed, at the center of all medical communication about patients. (Hunter, 1991: 51)

Hunter provides an extended account of the function of such narratives and performances in the accomplishment of medical work. She emphasizes, among other things, the interweaving of spoken and written accounts, such as the patient's chart or case notes. She also stresses the ritualized or formulaic aspects of such narrative productions. In Hunter's treatment, everyday medical knowledge is inextricably grounded in 'narrative knowlege' (p. 65). Medical practice – especially in the context of academic medicine in the teaching hospital – is predicated on the regular round of story-telling about patients. It is, Hunter suggests, fundamental to the production and reproduction of medical thought and culture:

> The case presentation is the fundamental medium of clinical thought and discourse. Guiding the methodical acquisition of information about the patient's malady and the consideration of its hypothetical interpretation, the narrative representation of the patient's plight is the opening summary in the process of medical care. It constitutes the foundation of medical attention, the goal of which is the recognition and treatment of the disease that is the source of its narratability. (Hunter, 1991: 68)

In contrast, however, to anthropological treatments of illness narratives, Hunter's discussion of physicians' narratives contains no analysis of actual case presentations or similar medical discourse. There remains, therefore, considerable need and scope for the empirical investigation of doctors' narrative practices (Mattingly, 1991).

In the course of making a 'presentation' of a case, the student or junior physician needs to give a good account of him or herself by giving a good account of the case. He or she needs to deploy narrative and descriptive skills in order to recount the case appropriately. A 'good' account will normally need to satisfy the following criteria: it should provide sufficient detail to allow the audience to follow the chronological development of the illness in question; it should be sufficiently *eventful* to permit the hearer(s) to identify and reconstruct the most salient findings and to follow the course of management; the course of the case's telling should display the clinical reasoning and action that have shaped the career of the case. An adequate grasp of detail simultaneously provides visible – or at least audible – testimony that the responsible clinician or clinical team has a sufficiently close and sure acquaintance with the case. On the other hand, the skilful account will not be unduly loaded with detail. The adroit account-giver will judge and select those results and findings likely to be deemed relevant and informative by peers and superiors. By that I do not mean that information is inherently 'relevant'. The relevance of the narrated information is judged in the context of the account in which it is embedded. The cogency of the case presentation and the value of the information imparted are mutually implicative in the hearers' evaluations of an account. Within the spoken case narrative, therefore, are inscribed socially and locally interpreted assumptions concerning the relevance of its contents. As Schutz repeatedly reminded us, the everyday world and our practical knowledge of it are structured in terms of domains or 'zones' of relevance. The detail with which one needs to know about some actor, object or event is a function of its relevance within our world of experience. There is, in other words, a mundane principle of 'need to know' with which we normally operate (Schutz, 1970; Schutz and Luckmann, 1974). Hence a narrator should construct his or her account in accordance with the schemes of relevance that relate to the audience. A successful story, in other words, will convey enough information as to satisfy a requirement for 'newsworthiness', but not so much as to overload the hearer with information that will become treated as 'irrelevant'. The narrative should not, therefore, explore in detail things which the hearer may take as read, or recapitulate background features that are entirely familiar to the hearer, and hence devoid of interest or relevance (see Sacks, 1992). In receiving a case account, therefore, the professional colleague or superior may reasonably expect due attention to relevance structures. A superior may sharply instruct a junior colleague to prune a long-winded account and to report 'just the positives', rather than reporting, say, the 'unremarkable' features of a physical examination.

Moreover, the presentation and discussion of a case are not simply the recitation of a series of facts and findings. The cogency and persuasive power of a case account also rest on the appropriately judicious weighting of the evidence to be rehearsed. Evidence must be evaluated, and discussed accordingly. (I explore this aspect of things in more detail in the next chapter.) Equally, the competent account should weave together information from different sources and of different types. These elements should be brought together under the aegis of a narrative that imposes a cogent, clear unfolding of the chronology of the reported events. Indeed, it is one of the most important aspects of the narrative quality of case presentations that they provide chronological and evaluative frames of reference, and bring the two together in one single spoken performance. In a sense, of course, these are not 'personal' narratives in the sense applied to illness narratives by authors such as Kleinman. They draw on a restricted range of formats and types. The physician is tightly constrained as to how narratives may be assembled. On the other hand, there can be no doubt that through the often ritualized forms of the round and the conference, medical cases are constructed and shared.

The following is a fairly characteristic case presentation that comes towards the formal end of the stylistic continuum. It is one of several delivered to the weekly Haematology–Oncology lunch-time conference. There the week's most notable cases were presented by the fellows and the medical students. Senior members of the service, as well as more junior colleagues attended regularly, listening to the case presentations while eating sandwiches made up from bread and cold meats provided. After each case was formally presented there would routinely follow a question-and-answer sequence.

The following case is being presented by one of the students:

> *St*: Er Mrs Thayer is a fifty-eight-years-old white female who's got a history of rheumatic valvular disease including mitral regurgi- mitral stenosis, aortic insufficiency and chronic afib. Her disease has been progressive over the last two years with two recent admissions for biventricular failure. She had a planned admission for sometime later this fall and early winter for mitral replacement, and routine er electrolytes over the past few months showed an increase in creatinine. In August . . . her creatinine was one point six, which was elevated from zero point eight a year ago. That was *then* increased to three point five on on the ninth of September accompanied by three plus protein with white blood cells and *red* blood cells in the urine. She was ad*mitted* on the fifth of October for a workup of acute renal failure . . . The

patient denied that she'd had any fever, night sweats, or recent fracture before the admission. She did have a ten to fifteen pound weight loss over the past year. On physical *exam* she was very sallow, thin, and she's very anxious. The only *positive* findings were her cardiovascular exam. She had an irregularly regular rhythm and she had an opening snap with a . . . *systolic* murmur heard at the left sternal border at the apex, and a diastolic murmur at the apex. She *did* have distension eight to ten centimetres and she has an HJR. She also had two plus sacral oedema. Her admission chest X-ray showed that she has bilateral pleural effusions and an increased heart shadow. She did have a kidney biopsy soon after admission, but they failed to obtain any usable tissue, they only had any that showed a tubular atrophy which has been sent for special scanning. She had an ultrasound on the kidneys which was normal, she's had retrograde scan which was also normal. Her most *recent* laboratory values – she's got an ESR of thirty-seven, calcium of eight point four, her BUN is eighty-three, creatinine five point six, her protein was five point five and her globulin was two point four. She did have an IEP, a serum IEP, sent which was read initially as normal but then they found a small kappa chain in both the serum and they also found it in the urine. So we were called to do a bone marrow biopsy. I should also mention that her white blood count is fourteen point two, the latest one, the haematocrit is thirty-two point two and her platelet was forty-four . . . Protein was two grams. The bone marrow aspirate showed a thirty per cent atypical plasma cells. Given her deteriorating renal status she began her chemotherapy on Saturday, the *bone* marrow was done on Friday and she's had Lincristene, Prednisone and Malfolan.

This is a fairly unremarkable case presentation in which the patient's career and the trajectory of one or more disease processes are constructed. It helps us to identify several of the important features of routine clinical narratives.

It is entirely characteristic of this style of presentation that it establishes the chronological narrative as one frame of reference. The physician's tale is an unfolding chronicle. It constructs a relative chronology of events, that is tied in to the absolute chronology of days and dates. The time-frames vary. The account is set within a broad temporal framework, with somewhat vague and general categories: 'over the last two years', 'with two recent admissions', 'sometime later this fall and early winter', 'past few months'. Against this broad, fairly impressionistic, background the current episode is established with greater clarity and precision: 'in August'. 'That was *then* increased to three point five on the ninth of September', 'She was adm*itted* on the fifth of October'. The narrative production of the current episode is notable not just for its more precise timing, but also for the two marked emphases. They respectively announce the critical change in the patient's electrolytes, and the point of admission. The turning-points in the narrative of the career are thus discursively marked, both in the prosodic features of the case presentation and in the temporal categories employed by the physician.

Set within this chronological career is an evolving narrative which is a story of mystery and revelation. The import of the story becomes apparent to the audience of haematologists/oncologists, and it is not fully explicated in so many words by the presenting medical student. It calls for further elaboration here. The career that is constructed in the presentation of the case is not straightforward. The patient has a history of heart problems, for which treatment – in the form of surgery – had been planned. Prior to her current admission, however, quite different medical problems were indicated and she was admitted for a 'workup' for renal failure. The physical examination confirms cardiovascular problems, but adds little. The investigations of the kidneys themselves reveal no pathology – either by biopsy or ultrasound. At this point in the narrative, therefore, the career is problematic. The known cardiovascular problem is confirmed; the new problem remains puzzling, however. Finally, however, further investigation yields a clue: the identification of a light chain. This is suggestive of a lymph problem, and for that reason the primary case team called in the haematologist for consultation, requesting the conduct of a bone marrow aspiration. The narrative presents the results of the bone marrow biopsy and the immediate consequences. Immediately, chemotherapy has been initiated, using a standard combination of powerful agents. It is notable that the narrative has reached a denouement of sorts: the puzzle has been partially resolved. It is equally notable, of course, that in this context, and on this particular occasion, the narrator does not find it necessary to state precisely what the diagnosis is. The narrative itself builds towards the unstated diagnosis, which is confirmed in the recitation of the combination chemotherapy. The latter is not justified or marked in any special way. The signs that have been recounted by the medical student in rehearsing the case are sufficiently pathognomic for the actual disease label to go unspoken. Discursively, it is treated here as unremarkable and straightforward. It is, however, remarkable from another point of view that the most salient issue – what is wrong with this particular patient – is precisely what remains unsaid.

This narrative follows a standard format, drawing on the formulae that generate such oral compositions. It follows the pattern common to many such cases: an introductory statement that introduces the patient; the recent history prior to the current admission; the physical examination of the patient; laboratory findings and other investigations; the initiation of · treatment. It is obvious, of course, that the presenting physician or student does not report to peers or superiors everything that has been reported, said, seen and done. On the contrary, these accounts are highly selective and compressed. The many details that could be recounted are, for the most part, omitted. The presenter gives the physical findings that are 'remarkable' or 'positive'; others may be passed over as 'unremarkable' or omitted altogether.

It is not surprising that this case presentation reflects the stylistic features identified by Anspach (1988). It will be recalled that she writes of four: depersonalization; omission of the agent; treating technology as the agent; the use of account markers. The 'de-personalizing' aspect is readily apparent. The patient appears as a named person, with personal attributes only in the opening phrase (in accordance with normal rhetorical requirements). From then on, the patient's identity makes but a fleeting appearance, as part of the physical examination: her 'anxiety' is noted, in addition to her physical appearance. Otherwise, the case is narrated almost exclusively in terms of the impersonal categories of findings such as laboratory values. These accounts are far from being personal narratives of illness; they are impersonal narratives of disease.

Equally, the case presentation displays Anspach's second feature – the 'omission of the agent':

> Case presentations not only fail to mention the patient's personal identity; they also omit the physician, nurses, or other medical *agents* who perform procedures or make observations . . . (Anspach, 1988: 366)

As Anspach notes, this usage may include use of the passive voice. In this example, for instance: 'She was ad*mitt*ed on the fifth of October'; 'the bone marrow was done on Friday'.

Here it is also expressed in terms of the patient as recipient or object of the actions of unnamed and unspecified others. For instance 'She did have a kidney biopsy'; 'She had an ultrasound on the kidneys'; 'She began her chemotherapy'. These examples show a slightly different discourse strategy from that identified by Anspach. It is what we might call the displaced subject of medical action. The real agency (for example, the physician) is presented as if it were the patient. Here, of course, the patient did not 'begin' her chemotherapy as the active subject or initiator of the action. One may also instance the following aspects of the account. Here the patient appears as the 'owner' of a set of physical, medical attributes. These contribute, however, to the overall effect of 'impersonal' and 'passive' modes, in line with Anspach's characterization: 'She *did* have distension'; 'She did have a ten to fifteen pound weight loss'; 'she had an irregularly regular rhythm and she had an opening snap with a murmur'.

These latter examples are closely linked to Anspach's third category – the treatment of 'technology as agent'. Here, the account makes no reference to the agency of medical personnel: findings are attributed solely to techniques or procedures. The data are not so much discovered as revealed by the technology. Here for instance: 'routine electrolytes showed'; 'On physical exam'; 'Her admission X-ray showed'; 'The bone marrow aspirate showed'.

In some cases, indeed, it is not necessary to account in terms of any agency, personal or technological. Information – especially laboratory values – is simply presented with no reference to its source: 'Her most *recent* laboratory values she's got'; 'her white blood count is fourteen point two the latest one the haematocrit is thirty-two point two and her platelet was forty-four'.

Finally, one can note the fourth and last of Anspach's main characteristics – the marking of accounts. Here the physician marks the patient's reports in ways that cast doubt on their validity, in contrast to the factual data of physical examination or laboratory results. There is a very clear example in this case presentation: 'She was ad*mitt*ed on the fifth of October for a workup of acute renal failure and the patient denied that she'd had any fever, night sweats'. This usage is identified specifically by Anspach, who notes a 'frequently used account marker "denies", actually calls the patient's account into question or casts doubt on the validity of the history' (Anspach, 1988: 368).

'Denial', Anspach notes, is used typically in three ways. First when the patient reports abstention from behaviour that might compromise health, such as alcohol or tobacco. Secondly, it is apparently used when patients say they have no allergies. Thirdly, '"denies" is used when a patient reports a symptom which usually belongs to a larger constellation of symptoms, but does not report the others that he or she would be likely to have' (Anspach, 1988: 368).

In the example considered here, from the Haematology–Oncology conference, the term seems to have the third function. Given the emerging story, symptoms such as night sweats or fever might have been entertained as likely components of the story by the audience. Consequently, the absence of predicted – or at least, likely – symptoms is marked. One may note in addition a possible function of 'denies' in such contexts, not suggested by Anspach. The use of 'denies' may be held to imply that the negative information has been sought. The implication is that the physician – or the physician whose report is included in the narrative – has been thorough enough and perspicacious enough to ask the patient about these things in the course of taking the history. It establishes more than the unvarnished fact that the patient has not reported such information. Denial implies an active response from the patient to elicitation on the part of the medical personnel. The use of 'denial' thus establishes an appropriate distribution of responsibility and credibility within the account. (As I shall explore in the next chapter, this is an extremely important function of such medical accounts.)

Finally, it is testimony to the typicality – or at least the ordinariness – of this case presentation and to the generality of Anspach's findings that this Haematology–Oncology presentation was not originally chosen with the intention of illustrating any of her observations. It is therefore noteworthy that a case presentation originally selected with other criteria in mind so well captures the main features identified in Anspach's more extensive survey of equivalent speech events.

The present example does, however, display some important character-istics that are not specifically addressed by Anspach. First, it is evident that medical agency is not eliminated altogether. Some reference is made to the actions of physicians. In this first example, indeed, the narrator uses a self-repair to introduce an anonymous 'they':

> She did have a kidney biopsy soon after admission but er failed to, they failed to obtain any usable tissue . . .

That 'they' contrasts a little later with 'we':

> but then they found a small kappa chain in both the serum and they also found it in the urine. So we were called to do a bone marrow biopsy . . .

As will be seen in subsequent discussions, the contrast, and the introduction of the first person plural is not accidental. It is a feature found in other narratives. Sometimes the contrast is drawn in order to juxtapose the shortcomings of others compared with the expertise of the consulting team of haematologists. Otherwise, as here, it provides a more neutral point of reference to indicate precisely how and when 'we' were consulted. Although the close proximity of 'their' failure to obtain a usable biopsy introduces an evaluative flavour to this local contrast, the audience of haematologists will probably hear such a contrast lying behind the invitation to the haematology team to intervene as consultants. In general terms, such a contrast may mark an important transition in the career narrative, separating the pre-consultation from the post-consultation phases. For a discipline like haematology – in this as in many other hospitals, largely a consulting specialty – this is an important element in the narrative of care specializ-ation. The introduction of medical agents, and the splitting between 'they/them' and 'we/us' is also an important feature of this collegial discourse. The homogeneous impersonality of specialized medical discourse here is overlaid by a more personalized (albeit anonymous) attribution of action and responsibility. There is, therefore, embedded in this narrative a concatenation of two frames of reference – the temporal order and the division of labour. It will be seen in later discussions that these aspects of the case presentation may be especially important in the discursive encoding of 'certainty' and 'uncertainty', and the establishment of credibility. (It will be seen that it is not only the patient's account that becomes marked and treated as evidentially problematic.)

Case presentations, especially those of the more formal types, normally follow some of the basic narrative elements identified by Labov (1972; Labov and Waletsky, 1967). Labov outlines an *evaluation* model of narrative events (Cortazzi, 1993). Labov suggests that narratives consist of ordered utterances that reflect the temporal order of a sequence of events, and he derives an elementary structure for narratives. The basic structural units are: Abstract (optional – a prefatory summary); Orientation (locates the story in terms of persons, places and times); Complication (what happened, expressed as a sequence of events); Evaluation (conveys the point of the narrative, and the point of view of the narrator); Result (or the resolution of the story); Coda (optional – a closing summary, or recapitu-lation signalling a closure of the story sequence). These basic building-blocks of narrative structure can be repeated and nested to generate complex structures, and they do not always have to be present. They do, however, characterize a wide variety of spoken narratives (see Cortazzi, 1993: 47–8).

Clinical presentations frequently follow such a pattern or structure. An orientation gives a brief introduction to the patient and his or her presenting problem. The complication is often the most extended part of the case narrative, recounting the past history of the current admission. It may indeed, in common sense terms, recount 'complications' if the case is not straightforward and has necessitated multiple investigations, complex differential diagnoses and prolonged treatment. Complication will be

developed through concatenations of outcomes such as laboratory test
values and the findings of physical examinations. The Evaluation may well
be implicit, or may be incorporated into the Result, where the outcomes of
clinical diagnosis and management are reported. The evaluative aspect of
such narratives is used to convey the moral of such a case story to peers,
superiors or students (Atkinson, 1992a).

Case presentations normally follow such narrative patterns. The clinical
picture is allowed to unfold through this discursive strategy. It is noticeable,
for instance, that the crucial clinical information and its interpretation are
held back and appear as the outcome of the narrative. In some ways,
therefore, the case presentation can be made to come out as a mystery story
or cliff-hanger (Atkinson, 1992a). Brown (1993) has made a parallel point
about *patients'* stories in psychiatric intake interviews. He suggests that
whereas patients may just be recounting their story, therapists may need to
interpret it as a *mystery story*, searching for clues in the attempt to determine
its significance. Here I am suggesting that the reverse is also true: clinicians
may retrospectively reconstruct their cases as puzzles or mysteries to be
unravelled, and so tell their stories accordingly. Such narrative formats
recapitulate one of the characteristic thought-styles of modern clinical
medicine: that diagnosis is a kind of puzzle-solving activity.

I have suggested that in the course of its telling the case presentation is
noteworthy for the concatenation of values and estimates. The facts of the
case are largely conveyed through *enumerations*. As Anspach's analysis
would suggest, these are certainly devoid of human agency for the most part.
Unmarked, they constitute the hard data of most medical cases. It is,
however, noticeable that even in the domain of such findings, there is some
room for variation in their presentation. The objective reality of such values
is not totally homogeneous. The case presentation suggests some changes in
nuance. For instance, the following values and findings are presented as
entirely factual in that they are unmarked or unqualified:

> she's got an ESR of thirty-seven, calcium of eight point four, her BUN is
> eighty-three, creatinine five point six, her protein was five point five and her
> globulin was two point four . . .
> . . . a thirty per cent atypical plasma cells . . .

On the other hand, a number of such 'findings' are marked. For instance:

> She did have an IEP a serum IEP sent which was read initially as normal, but then
> they found . . .

Further, some values are given in terms that are less 'precise' than those
above:

> She did have a ten to fifteen pound weight loss . . .
> She did have distension eight to ten centimetres . . .

In other words, the impersonal facts of biomedical knowledge themselves
may be subject to variation or imprecision. In context, these less precise
numerical expressions contrast with the extreme precision usually reserved

for laboratory values and counts. Here they are used to refer to clinical observations rather than laboratory-based findings. The contrast between precise and imprecise numerical expressions may thus be used to mark the division between the clinical and the laboratory. The usage recalls the analysis by Dubois of imprecise expressions in scientific presentations (Dubois, 1987). Working with presentations at scientific meetings and conferences, Dubois identifies a rich vocabulary for estimates, approximations and the like. In those presentations, she suggests that imprecise expressions function to foreground the more precisely expressed values. Rhetorically, therefore, approximations, ranges and estimates can be used to contrast what is significant from what is not, to mark findings as preliminary, or to discredit the work of others while celebrating that of the presenter.

Values, findings and narrative detail

Of course, the rhetorical construction of the case is not achieved through narrative alone. Or, to be more precise, there are many rhetorical features that may be said to contribute to the construction of a plausible case. As has already been suggested, the case presentations and discussions dealt with here include frequent and detailed presentations of figures and *values*. As a discipline, whether as a consulting service or as primary care physicians, haematology is heavily dependent on the clinical laboratory. It is one of those clinical areas *par excellence*, in which there is a clear articulation between the laboratory and the clinic.

The case presentations observed and recorded therefore contain frequent reports of values from laboratory investigations. Those may be 'routine' tests performed on virtually all patients on whom the clinicians are consulted or whom they are treating. They may also be special tests requested and performed for more specific diagnostic purposes, relating to one given patient, and a particular differential diagnosis. There are fundamental aspects of the chemical composition of the blood – the 'labs' of various important constituents and indicators – that are routinely measured and monitored on the haematology service. There is, therefore, a complex process of assembling, reporting and interpreting of 'the labs' for any given patient. The nature and significance of the laboratory findings may vary over the course of a patient's career; indeed, they may be used as major landmarks in the rhetorical construction of an illness career or trajectory. Nevertheless, throughout the assembly and report of a patient 'case' or 'career', there is repeated reference to lab *values*.

A number of examples will illustrate further how those quantitative data are entered into the accounts:

> *St:* On admission she was just noted to have some upper extremity ecchymoses which she says she's always had due to her chronic coumarin therapy. She was noted to be in right and left sided congestive heart failure, with a question of liver congestion . . . She was also noted to have occasional

asterixus. Now what's very interesting about this woman is that she's also had an elevated BUN and creatinine when she first came in now her BUN was a hundred and three and her creatinine was four. These elevated values go back to at least prior to her surgery.

At: In 1977?

St: In June of this year. No, in June of this year

At: Uh in June of this year

St: When her BUN was twenty-four and her creatinine was one point two in May this year.

At: Is this the first time it's been checked since?

St: No it had been checked before but it actually had been found to be within normal limits

At: What is the BUN now?

St: Now? Now it's in the sixties I believe it six-

At: = Twenty-four?

St: Yeah, on admission. Now it's down to the two point seven range. She also told me that she always bruised easily even prior to her coumarin therapy and that she bled from the gums at dental procedures, had never been worked up had never had a family history of the same as far as she knows and at 1977 she underwent catheterization prior to surgery and developed a massive right groin haematoma, into which she bled requiring something along the lines of three or four units of red blood cells and multiple transfusions of fresh frozen plasma and albumin. At that point she was also noted to have developed afterwards an increase SGOT and was thought to have a transfusion related hepatitis although her surface antigen was negative.

At: Well

St: And it might have been a non-B erm er

At: Has that quieted down? I mean it's not been a problem since then?

St: Well she currently has an elevated SGOT although her other liver parameters are within normal limits

At: = Slightly elevated or?

St: Yes slightly elevated, sixty-one, probably consistent with the congestive condition. Anyways in this hospital er during this hospitalization she's noted she's been noted to be in right and left sided heart failure er she has had some fluid overload. Renal ultrasound was done, which was found to be normal, and the rest of her workup is consistent with some tricuspid regurgitation and apparently some dysfunction of the valves.

At: Well, I'm a little bit disorientated here. What are they working her up for?

St: She's being worked up for her left renal failure and right sided failure.

At: Oh

F: And her renal failure

At: And not the original complaint, the diarrhoea

F: Right

St: No that actually stopped when she came in

F: No I think I that that was dig[italis] because she also came in with a dig level

St: That's right

F: = of over three

St: three point four

F: and I think that's what a lot of the diarrhoea was from

At: So that's cleared up and the problem is failure

St: The problem now is failure and a question of whether her renal function deterioration is due to the massive diuresis that she's on, and she's not putting out much urine, or whether it's due to intrinsic renal problem

At: Which it probably is. Massive diuresis, I don't follow that.

St: She's on a diuretic
At: Oh diuretic
St: Er so
At: You're suggesting that that's damaging the kidney?
St: Well she's on three different diuretics and she's not putting out much
F: Mm well
St: The question is whether she was pre-renal
At: Yeah
St: Or whether this is a natural renal failure. Her laboratory results are remarkable for a haematocrit of about thirty – of thirty point eight, white count of six point seven, a differential that includes seventy-seven polys, fourteen lymphs, nine monos, a PT of sixteen, between sixteen and twenty-one of this admission a PTT
At: She's on coumarin
St: She's on coumarin, of fifty-four point one, and a sed rate on admission that was seventy-six. Let's find the notes of her labs. Her most recent BUN and creatinine were sixty-three and two point three respectively, and her platelet count runs chronically greater than a hundred thousand. She's had anywhere from a hundred and sixteen thousand to a hundred and seventy thousand. On this admission she's never gone below a hundred thousand except when she was on bypass for her surgery and she always came back immediately afterwards. So much for her platelet counts. Her admission is remarkable for a nose bleed noted on the first, also stopped spontaneously, chest X-ray remarkable for pleural effusion which was tapped and thirteen hundred ccs of bloody fluid were withdrawn.

In accounts such as this, the key features of laboratory findings are expressed as numerical values, embedded in the reconstruction of the patient's medical history and his or her current hospital admission. They form part of the formulaic element of case construction. While not invariably present, and while not always present in the same form, the lab values are a 'standard' part of the account. They constitute a regular 'litany' of medical facts or findings. More than any other types of information, perhaps, the lab values constitute evidence of the investigations or 'workups'. Since a patient (a case) is typically worked up through a battery of investigations, the reported evidence – in the form of numerical data – guarantees the extent of the investigation of the patient's condition. Moreover, the patient appears as the 'owner' of a set of physical, medical attributes. These contribute to the overall effect of 'impersonal' and 'passive' modes, in line with Anspach's characterization.

In many ways the 'facts' and 'values' that are reported as the 'labs' are directly analogous to the products and discoveries of research laboratories (cf. for example, Latour and Woolgar, 1986). There is a complex division of labour within and between the clinical laboratories, and as we have seen, there is a homology between the technical division of labour in the clinic and the biomedical disaggregation or distribution of 'the body'. Like the experimental laboratory, the clinical laboratory processes large numbers of investigative procedures. A high number of 'runs' or 'experiments' take place in both contexts. The personnel and the physical plant are deployed together in time and space, in order to produce a daily round of 'findings'.

In the clinical service laboratory, however, those 'findings' themselves constitute the *products* of that socially organized work. The service laboratory is not oriented to the generation of scientific discoveries. The routine processing of tissues and samples is not intended to produce new scientific insights and theories. There are, of course, often research laboratories closely associated with clinical service work, with overlapping personnel: clinicians, researchers and laboratory technicians may all be involved in research and service work. Moreover, research developments often translate into service applications, and there are often periods in the trajectory of any given innovation when research and service have blurred boundaries. Nevertheless, there is a vast amount of everyday laboratory work, much of it repetitive skilled 'craft' work, that is by any criterion routine.

Laboratories that produce findings for clinical haematologists process large numbers of tests for various medical services within the hospital. They receive specimens such as blood or bone marrow and report key values in standard formats – normally on pre-printed forms that are computer-printed with the lab values. They measure the levels of key indicators in blood, bone marrow and other tissues. Their findings, which are themselves socially produced via craft work, furnish important materials for the clinicians. Those laboratory values are often significant for the work of diagnosis and treatment. But they are also important elements in the narrative reconstruction of ill health. As may be surmised from some of the data extracts that have been reproduced here, the reported lab values help to anchor the case in narrative detail. The competent case narrator should be able to recount the significant findings, just as he or she should be able to report on what, if anything, was remarkable about the patient on physical examination. The case narrator should also be able to marshall further quantitative evidence about the patient's values when asked about them by a colleague or superior (as often happens during the cross-questioning that accompanies case presentations at weekly conferences). Furthermore, the fact that such values are available to be reported is itself testimony that appropriate workups have been undertaken. The request from a senior physician for a specific value is also an implicit investigation of whether the right investigations have been ordered on the patient and carried out successfully. This in itself is evidence of good and diligent work on the part of the fellow or student: tests must be made to happen, and sometimes the haematologist must press the ward personnel to ensure that they do. Also, the results may sometimes have to be chased up. (Many tests and values are pretty routine, of course.) A satisfactory narrative, which in itself represents satisfactory clinical work, therefore, is often replete with numerical data. It is not necessary for the clinician to remember all the values for all the patients who are being consulted on at any given time: 3×5 cards tucked into a shirt or jacket breast pocket routinely provide *aide-mémoires*.

My contention is that narrative is not confined to the interpretative methods of lay people in their construction of illness experiences. The production of biomedical knowledge and understanding also includes the use of narrative formats. The rhetoric of case presentations is one mechanism whereby biomedical understanding is achieved and communicated among medical practitioners. Of course, the language of everyday narratives is different from that of case presentations. They are produced in different social contexts and reflect very different orientations or frames of reference on the part of the narrator. Those differences should not blind us to the fact that narrative productions are not the sole prerogative of lay sufferers.

In other words, to use the orthodox dichotomy, narrative is not confined to illness. Disease is accomplished through narrative as well. Most importantly, it is precisely the narrative that establishes the story *as a case*. For a story to count as a case, it is not merely a listing of signs, symptoms and test results. The narrative provides a framework within which that story takes shape; it furnishes sequence and consequence for the recounted phenomena, it constricts the case as a topic of medical discourse, and establishes the parameters of what is noteworthy. It is commonplace to note that the idea of the medical history already implies a narrative construction. It is worth adding that the notion of an *episode* of ill health is equally achieved via the narrative inscription of an appropriate temporal and cognitive framework. The designation of a case *presentation* also conveys some sense of the rhetorical, even theatrical, performance of that case. The achievement of a biomedical case therefore rests on the distinctive rhetoric of medical talk. The case presentation reconstructs events and inferences into a career for the patient, and the course of a disease.

6
Voicing Opinion

This chapter deals with one of the most pervasive themes in the sociology of medical knowledge, and recapitulates part of my own earlier treatment of it (Atkinson, 1984). That argument – outlined only programmatically in that earlier paper – is developed here with relevant data. The theme is that of so-called 'uncertainty' and its management in medical settings. Over the years, it has become something of a commonplace in medical sociology that medical knowledge is suffused with uncertainty, that medical practitioners and students have to confront the 'problem' of uncertainty, and that clinical uncertainty impinges directly on clinical encounters between practitioners and their patients. My argument is that far too much of the sociological commentary has used uncertainty as a catch-all term. It has been used to characterize diverse phenomena, and has not always been subjected to sufficient conceptual scrutiny or empirical inquiry. My argument is, therefore, that the very success of the notion of uncertainty in the sociology of medicine has ultimately proved to be a stumbling-block. With repeated use the idea became stale, its use uncritical. I pursue this argument not just for the sake of pedantry. I am not trying to fight old theoretical battles. My concern, is, rather, to promote serious, detailed attention to the social organization of medical knowledge and its discursive production. A serious appraisal of the theme of uncertainty (and, indeed, of certainty) is a necessary step in the micro-sociology of medical knowledge. The problems arise – as I have indicated – from the success of the very idea of uncertainty in medical instruction and practice.

Much of the inspiration and direction of writing in this area is attributable to the early work of Fox (R. Fox, 1957). There Fox contributed to the more general study of medical education under the general direction and inspiration of Merton. In her particular discussion of medical school experience, Fox stressed the theme of 'uncertainty' in the medical students' acquisition of scientific and professional knowledge. In the course of their studies the students encounter a vast field of knowledge, and soon discover that there are limitations in currently available medical knowledge. They cannot master all the knowledge currently available, and irrespective of their individual mastery it is incomplete anyway. In combination, Fox argued, these two problems give rise to a third – 'difficulty in distinguishing between personal ignorance or ineptitude and the limitations of present medical knowledge' (1957: 214).

It was apparent in Fox's treatment of the theme that it was not just a matter of student problems or perspectives, but also reflects the approach to knowledge enacted by the medical staff themselves. This was marked, Fox claimed, by the 'experimental point of view', which 'promotes the idea that an irreducible minimum of uncertainty is inherent in medicine, in spite of the promise of further scientific advance' (p. 213). In Fox's treatment, the theme of uncertainty is an especially important one in the context of clinical instruction. Not least are the students' problems in perception:

> students were often expected to see before they know how to look or what to look for. For, the ability to 'see what you ought to see', 'feel what you ought to feel', and 'hear what you ought to hear', students assure us, is premised upon a 'knowledge of what you're supposed to observe', an ordered method for making these observations, and a great deal of practice in medical ways of perceiving. (p. 214)

Some aspects of uncertainty give way as students acquire greater technical competence and knowledge, Fox argues. They become less insecure in their own mastery. As the residue of personal incompetence diminishes, therefore, students can attribute failure to the limitations in medical knowledge. As Fox summarizes the position:

> In some respects confident and knowing, in others uneasy and not sure, a student feels variously certain and uncertain, as he makes the transition from the preclinical to the clinical years of medical school. (p. 221)

Throughout that early work Fox stresses the centrality of uncertainty to medical work and culture. The theme was followed through in much of her later, equally influential, work. Indeed, Fox identifies her own research and publications as a series of variations on the theme of uncertainty. It is a major part of the research on experimental treatment (R. Fox, 1959) and on organ transplants (Fox and Swazey, 1974). In one essay Fox herself comments on the success of the idea:

> One of the interesting consequences of the publication of my 'Training for Uncertainty' essay . . . was the unexpected amount of appreciative response which it evoked from faculty and students in nursing, social work, law, divinity, and business schools, as well as from medical faculty and students. (R. Fox, 1980: 8)

The idea of uncertainty was taken up by other sociologists of medicine. It resonated with other concepts that related to practitioners' reliance on 'personal experience', 'clinical judgement' and so on, such as are to be found in Freidson's classic formulation of 'the clinical mentality' (Freidson, 1970: 169). As will be indicated later, however, Friedson's interpretation of 'indeterminacy' or 'uncertainty' is diametrically opposed to that of Fox.

It remains the case, however, that the idea of uncertainty in medicine has become part of the conventional wisdom of medical sociology (cf. Calnan, 1984). It is taken for granted by many commentators that medical knowledge and medical practice are shot through with uncertainty; that medical students and practitioners need to cope with a great deal of uncertainty; that medical socialization and occupational culture are predicated on the management of uncertainty.

The theme has, for instance, been built on and developed by Light (1979), who elaborates on Fox's analysis. Light suggests that there are even more sources of uncertainty for the medical trainee or practitioner. He identifies uncertainties arising from: instructors and superiors and their idiosyncrasies; limitations of professional knowledge; problems of diagnosis; ambiguities of treatment and outcome; the unpredictability of client response. Light underlines the extent to which the trainee comes to appreciate that 'what appears to be a masterly profession is full of uncertainties'. This identification of 'uncertainty' has been incorporated into several major studies and commentaries on medical practice and professional socialization (for example, Broadhead, 1983; Light, 1980; Shuval, 1980).

The theme of uncertainty has appeared most importantly in recent literature on medical decision-making, on the part of lay and professional actors. Bursztajn, Feinbloom, Hamm and Brodsky (1990) provide a major survey of the topic. They argue for a new science of medicine, a paradigm shift, that recognizes and catches up with the perspectives of contemporary natural science, in which principles of uncertainty are well recognized. In contrast to what they recognize as an outmoded mental approach Bursztajn et al. summarize the main criteria for a probabilistic paradigm in contemporary medical thought. A probabilistic approach replaces a mechanistic search for certainty with a recognition that 'certainty is unattainable not only in fact but in principle' (Bursztajn et al., 1990: 64).

As in much of the literature on medical thinking and decision-making, Bursztajn et al. adopt an essentially normative stance. They wish to advocate probabilistic modes of thinking, and action informed by such a cognitive stance. From the vantage point of the probabilistic paradigm, uncertainty is not a residual problem, nor a symptom of failure. It is to be recognized as a pervasive feature of all decisions and actions. Three criteria for probabilistic thought are proposed: probabilistic causation; experimentation as principled gambling; the continuity of the subjective and the objective (pp. 59–62). These criteria are based on (i) the recognition that a patient's condition may have more than one cause, and they thus avoid monocausal reductionism; (ii) that investigation and diagnosis are part of an exploratory process; and (iii) that the doctor's *and* patient's knowledge, feelings and values are of crucial importance. The authors summarize the matter thus:

> Taken together, the criteria of the Probabilistic Paradigm give us a new way to think about and practice medicine. If in some ways they seem to confound common sense, in other ways they reaffirm it, for they restore a respect for the many-sidedness of reality that was lost in the oversimplifications of nineteenth-century science. It was a wonder that medical practitioners ever could have thought that the causes of complicated conditions *could* be known with certainty; that the doctor–patient interaction would *not* influence the course of an illness; that knowledge about microbes and bacilli *could* be separated neatly from knowledge about attributes, feelings, and values . . . (Bursztajn et al., 1990: 63)

These authors document the destructive and self-defeating nature of reductionist, or mechanistic, medical thinking that is founded on the hopeless search for certainty. They advocate a medicine in which inappropriate models of science are replaced: 'Medicine, instead of trying to live up to an outmoded model of laboratory science, can then become a science of action, a science of practice' (p. 61).

At a descriptive level, Bursztajn et al. provide numerous case studies and vignettes of medical practice, many of which are designed to demonstrate the virtues of probabilistic thinking, and the limitations of more mechanistic approaches. They collectively display the complexity of practical reasoning and practical action in many medical settings. Indeed, their naturalistic accounts partly work against the authors' particular advocacy. They demonstrate more than adequately that mechanistic, reductionist thought is inadequate, incomplete and misleading. They show that the search for certainty is misplaced. They are equally persuasive of the need to accept more flexible, more practical habits of thought. Equally, however, they provide a vivid illustration of the equal danger of a kind of reductionism in social-scientific thought about medicine itself. While one may well disapprove of reductionist thought in medical science and medical practice, there is a tendency for social scientists to employ 'nothing but' arguments that are reductionist in effect. We do no justice to the complexity of the phenomena if we resort to blanket categorizations and catch-all explanations. The sociology of medicine, health and illness has been no less prone to this limitation than other sociological specialisms. Appeals to uncertainty as an analytic concept have all too often proved reductionist in their consequences.

This is apparent in Fox's own original and influential contributions. A number of different issues are collected together and glossed under this single heading. While there is an obvious virtue – indeed, to some extent, an analytic necessity – in using such sensitizing categories to produce formal, comparative sociological analyses, there is always a danger that such 'lumping together' may obscure as much as it illuminates. On the one hand, Fox uses the notion of uncertainty to capture a sense of tragic irony at the heart of modern medicine:

> The paradox and poignancy – for both physician and patient – is the fact that our great twentieth-century progress in medical science and technology has helped to reveal how ignorant, bewildered, and mistaken we still are in many ways about health and illness, life and death. (R. Fox, 1980: 1)

In this vein Fox writes of 'the tragicomic hospital world . . . where uncertainty and death were to be only the certainties' (p. 1). This tragic irony is also extended beyond the institutional limits of medicine. Uncertainty is represented as a manifestation or consequence of a more general cultural crisis:

> Health, illness and medicine appear to be epicentres of the increased malaise about uncertainty, and the anxiety about danger and risk that have surfaced in our society. (p. 3)

On the other hand, it is proffered as a feature of medical decision-making, and of the failings of medical understanding. For instance, Fox argues that:

> Awareness of the 'long list of formidable human diseases whose underlying mechanisms are not at all clear and [that] are presently unapproachable by such

precisely targeted techniques as the use of penicillin against streptococci' . . . has grown. Cancer extends this list. Consciousness of 'the frail basis' . . . on which many medical decisions still have to be made appears to have increased both inside and outside the medical profession. The fact that problems that are not only unprecedented but also 'entirely unprecedented' continue to arise in medicine is frequently discussed with a mixture of amazement and alarm . . . (p. 16)

In Fox's analysis, such uncertainty is reflected in 'emotional, moral and existential implications' for physicians and their patients:

> To be puzzled, ignorant, unable to understand: to lack needed knowledge or relevant skill: to err, falter or fail, without always being sure whether it is 'your fault' or 'the fault of the field' . . . is especially painful and serious when the work that you do is medical. (p. 5)

In other words, there are at least four different versions of uncertainty that Fox collects under the one rubric: a manifestation of the Zeitgeist and a focus of social disquiet; a characteristic of medical professional culture; an inherent feature of the present state of biological and medical sciences; a cognitive trait or emotional problem of individual medical students and practitioners.

The net effect of this 'lumping' is to suggest that uncertainty is therefore a pervasive feature of contemporary medicine and medical education. This represents an unwarranted form of sociological reductionism. It is, too, ironic to contrast the accounts of uncertainty offered by Fox and Bursztajn et al. Fox implies that the generality of medical thought and practice is characterized by uncertainty. She suggests that an awareness of uncertainty is part of the general experience of modern physicians; that uncertainty of these various sorts creates problems that must be coped with and accommodated by students and experienced practitioners alike. By contrast, Bursztajn et al. imply that the normal practice of contemporary medicine is characterized by a culture that denies uncertainty as an epistemological or experiential feature. In their eyes, the pervasive mode of thought is that of the mechanistic paradigm. In this context, the reductionist approach of mechanistic thought *reduces* the opportunity for states of uncertainty to exist for the majority of practitioners (cf. Baumann et al., 1991).

Indeed, elsewhere, I have elaborated on the notion that training for *certainty*, rather than training for uncertainty, would be an equally (if not more) apt rubric for the sociological analysis of medical education and practice (Atkinson, 1984). There are many contexts in which uncertainty is not an issue for the actors, because they employ practical reasoning and action in such a way as to produce relatively unproblematic diagnoses and disposals. I have argued that the dominant mode of everyday medical work is closer to what Bursztajn and his colleagues call the 'mechanistic paradigm'.

It is undoubtedly the case that medical students and practitioners make frequent appeals to matters of opinion, or judgement that cannot be validated unambiguously by scientific knowledge. But personal knowledge and experience are not normally treated by practitioners as reflections of uncertainty, but as warrants for certainty. The primacy of direct experience, for instance, is taken to guarantee knowledge which the student or practitioner can *rely* on. Distinctions between theory and practice, or between science and experience are not drawn in order to contrast feelings of certainty and uncertainty, or to justify alternative ways of problem-solving. *Both* are ways of warranting knowledge for practitioners' practical purposes.

Bosk provides a particularly telling account of how the themes of uncertainty and dogmatism may be linked:

> There are many decisions which surgeons are forced to make in the absence of scientifically established criteria. Great uncertainty surrounds much medical behaviour. From their own clinical experience and from medical journals, attendings marshal evidence to support one approach to a particular problem as opposed to another. However, the evidence is far from conclusive, debate continues, and a consensus fails to emerge. Some attendings approach a problem in one fashion with very good results; others have equally good results with a competing approach. Despite the open-ended nature of the question 'which approach is better?', attendings in their everyday behaviour can be quite dogmatic. (1979: 61–2)

A very similar insight is provided by Knafl and Burkett (1975; Burkett and Knafl, 1976), who also emphasize the reliance on personal knowledge and treatment philosophies in orthopaedic surgery.

These views of medical practice and medical reasoning are related to what Freidson (1970) has to say about the 'clinical mentality'. Freidson emphasizes the practitioners' reliance on personal knowledge: 'the practitioner is likely to have to believe in what he is doing in order to practice' and 'Insofar as work characteristically revolves around a series of concrete and individual problems, both success and its causes are rarely ambiguous.' Freidson emphasizes the image of the medical practitioner as a pragmatist. Practical reasoning and action are emphasized. Practical or moral certainty are more prominent aspects of this culture than the management of uncertainty as an intellectual or existential problem.

In other words, there is a potentially complex set of attitudes and relations towards knowledge and practical activity. It is unwise to try to capture them all under the rubric of uncertainty. As I pointed out in my previous discussion of this theme, however, it is equally dangerous simply to reverse the emphasis, and use certainty or dogmatism as a generic category to capture the pervasive ethos of medical thinking. Rather, one needs a more sophisticated and sensitive phenomenology of medical thought than the majority of commentators have achieved. The phenomenology of expert knowledge suggests that there are complex, shifting local definitions of knowledge, thought and action. They imply quite delicate distinctions and definitions, relating to judgement, opinion, certainty, uncertainty, personal knowledge, experience, complexity and the like.

Schutz provides a starting point. He contrasts the attitude of the 'expert' and 'the man (sic) on the street':

> The expert's knowledge is restricted to a limited field but therein it is clear and
> distinct. His opinions are based upon warranted assertions: his judgements are not
> mere guesswork or loose suppositions.
>
> The man on the street has a working knowledge of many fields which are not
> necessarily coherent with one another. His knowledge of recipes indicating how to
> bring forth in typical situations typical results by typical means. The recipes
> indicate procedures which can be trusted even though they are not clearly
> understood. By following the prescription as if it were a ritual, the desired result
> can be attained without questioning why the simple procedural steps have to be
> taken and taken in exactly the sequence prescribed. This knowledge in all
> vagueness is still *sufficiently* precise for the practical purpose at hand. (1964: 122)

Between these two polar ideal types Schutz constructs a third – the
'well-informed citizen', who does not possess or aim at the expert's
knowledge, but equally does not rely on recipe-knowledge alone:

> To be well-informed means . . . to arrive at reasonably founded opinions in fields
> which as he knows are at least mediately of concern to him although not bearing
> upon his purpose at hand. (1964: 122)

My contention is that the expert can act in the way described in Schutz's ideal
type, but he or she certainly does not do so on every conceivable occasion.
For everyday practical purposes, the expert has his or her 'natural attitude'
or 'thinking as usual'. Its content will not be that of the lay person. It may,
however, be equivalent *formally*: a stock of typifications, recipes for action
that are drawn on in an essentially practical fashion. For most practitioners,
for most of the time, the characteristic attitude is one of trust in 'cookbook'
knowledge and action.

The net effect of such reliance is that for most purposes, the professional
or the expert has faith and relative certainty in tried-and-trusted routines.
For instance, in his discussion of assessments in ENT clinics, Bloor remarks:

> ENT specialists' assessments are comprehensible in terms of specialist-specific sets
> of routines which . . . serve to efficiently process cases to that point where a
> particular disposal becomes *obviously indicated*. (1978: 42)

Bloor's work is particularly apt in the context of this discussion of certainty
and uncertainty. The empirical theme of his specialists' work was performing adenotonsillectomies. Although the procedure is normally straightforward and (in everyday terms) routine, there are grounds for regarding it
from the point of view of medical uncertainty. There are no universally
agreed and consistently applied clinical criteria that unambiguously indicate
surgical removal of the tonsils. Rates vary from time to time, and from
specialist to specialist. From that point of view, therefore, one might well
describe the field as pervaded with ambiguity or uncertainty. But it would
clearly be unwarranted to extrapolate from that so as to impute a sense of
uncertainty, or an uncertain attitude towards knowledge on the part of the
practitioners.

The moral certainty of practical reasoning, experience or routine, and the
uncertainty of theoretical discourse reflect two different orientations
towards knowledge and practice. The orientations or attitudes are adopted

in different contexts and for different purposes. Different orientations may be situationally appropriate in different work settings. The expression of uncertainty or the offer of personal opinion will not be equally appropriate, say, in: teaching rounds for junior students; postgraduate specialist training; the conduct and publication of research; peer review; clinical conferences; routine practice, consultations between senior colleagues; the exchange of views between members of different specialties; the presentation of expert testimony. In such contexts – and others – there may be different emphases on the practical and the theoretical. In other words, it is vital that we be sensitive to contexts and local variations in examining the expression of uncertainty or its variants.

Furthermore, it is necessary to pay rather close attention to *how* uncertainty or certainty are actually conveyed in the course of everyday medical work. It is not enough to account for these things in terms of generic and pervasive features of medical culture. There is need for detailed examination of how medical practitioners, students, scientists and others express and discuss their information, how they voice their opinion, and how they claim particular warrants for the knowledge and interpretations they endorse.

In what follows I shall examine evidence, drawn from the fieldwork and transcripts from haematology, concerning the expression of opinion, and the rhetorics of relative certainty. It will be seen that there are complex and delicate expressions and codings of knowledge and opinion. These are context-sensitive, and in various ways locate the speaker in relation to different domains of knowledge and zones of relevance.

The medical practitioner must speak about and act on knowledge which has various kinds of warrant, and of which the speaker has differing degrees of firsthand experience. The knowledge is derived from varied sources. It may derive from the personal experience of the practitioner; it may be gleaned from research publications, or from textbooks; it may have been reported by other practitioners, or from laboratory technicians. In formulating an account of the case, therefore, the physician does not merely collate knowledge and information, facts and opinions. He or she constructs narratives and opinions which reflect different attitudes towards that knowledge: degrees of trust are expressed; credibility and plausibility of others' accounts are made available to an audience of peers; one's personal interpretations and recommendations are couched in situationally appropriate terms. As Fenn suggests, in a rather different substantive context, when experts and witnesses testify, to their peers or to courts of inquiry, they have to establish their credentials and the credence to be attached to their words (Fenn, 1982).

There is, then, a rich situated vocabulary within the rhetoric of medical discourse. The narratives of clinical cases are characterized by complex usages of language to express to colleagues degrees of certainty. These are certainly not just the statistical expression of probabilities, or even more mundane expressions of chance – though they may both be included. They also include a repertoire of devices to express trust, likelihood and evidence, as well as values or numerical data.

This is not solely related to problems of 'uncertainty' *per se*. It also bears on the even more general issue of personal knowledge and indeterminacy in professional practice. In his account of the clinical mentality, Freidson (1970) stressed the central role of reliance on experience and personal opinion. As Freidson expresses it the clinical mentality commits the medical practitioner to a particular stance towards his or her own knowledge, and that of others. It finds a warrant for one's own knowledge in a stock of personally acquired, firsthand, experience. Thus knowledge and expertise are grounded in biography, accumulated and 'sedimented' (cf. Berger and Luckmann, 1967) over the course of the professional career. As I discussed at much greater length in my account of medical education (Atkinson, 1981a), personal experience is rhetorically contrasted with the knowledge that is enshrined in textbooks (cf. Becker et al., 1961):

> even though it substitutes for scientifically verified knowledge, it [experience] can be used to legitimate a choice of procedures for a patient's treatment and can even be used to rule out use of some procedures that have been scientifically established. (Becker et al., 1961: 225)

To the extent that personal knowledge and experience are used to contrast with 'science' or 'research' each provides a framework for interpretation. Such frameworks may be used in different ways in specific social situations: they may be used contrastively, as suggested above, but they may also be used in a complementary fashion, reinforcing one another. This analytic perspective will be pursued in greater detail in the next chapter, where the *voices* of medical discourse are explored. Here attention will be restricted to a more detailed examination of expressions of faith, certainty, uncertainty and the like.

The following gives an extended example of the narrative and rhetorical expression of degrees of certainty and trust. It is used to introduce further exemplification of these aspects of medical discourse. It is taken from a clinical conference, at which one of the clinical fellows was presenting a series of cases. It provides further illustration of the narrative construction of the case, which, as will be seen, is accomplished by a complex and delicate discourse. The presentation required the clinician not merely to recount a series of facts and findings, but also to report the views of others, and to weave them into an account that conveys their relative *plausibility*. The clinician's degree of faith in what is reported is inscribed in the narrative itself. This in turn has implications for the response of the audience of fellow clinicians. The junior physician who implicitly believed everything at face value, with no apparent sense of the relative firmness of the evidence, would not offer himself or herself as a credible witness or advocate.

> *F:*   Julio Fiores is a twenty-five-year-old we were asked to see because of recurrent thromboses? His past medical history is positive for a fall to the right and *injury* to the right groin, the details of which are not really clear. It's also positive for the fact that in December of last year he was admitted with

a right ileofemoral thrombosis and he underwent a graft to that area. The course was complicated by *two* episodes of DVT on heparin. The path. specimen they removed from the artery was described as showing intimal fibromuscular hyperplasia, which when I asked the pathologists about this they claim that the only association that they find with it is trauma but thought it was similar to the lesion that you find in the kidney with renovascular hypertension. He was seen at that time by Keith Chamberlain [another haematologist] and they were concerned that there might be some sort of a hypercoagulable state, and they arranged for outpatient followup at which time he had an antithrombin three level which was done which was normal and then he was lost to followup. The patient was *dis*charged on coumarin and was being followed in *vas*cular clinic. In August the coumarin was discontinued and he was placed on aspirin and P( ), and reading their notes there was a suggestion that this caused a deterioration in the leg in the sense that it became more oedematous and perhaps the pulses in the leg were less palpable. It was sort of a *gradual* finding and when he came in for his clinic appointment in September the feeling was that something was definitely going on in the leg. And so he was admitted to hospital with a presumptive diagnosis of (ULAP) DVT. He was heparinised em*pi*rically and a venogram done on day one was negative. At that point they discontinued the heparin, however after three to four days they start to feel as though clinically the leg is becoming worse, and they took him to arteriography, where they demonstrated that he had an arterial thrombus in his ileofemoral. Since then he's had multiple (treatments) for his circulation including one round of urokinase *locally* delivered to the leg. He's had endarterectomy and a thrombectomy times two, he's been on Rheoma-crodex and eventually he was taken back for repeat graft but perhaps there was a technical problem with the first graft. At the *last* operation, which was the tenth of October, they saw extensive clot in the ileofemoral system and also noted that the vessels distal to that showed severe spasm. And at *that* point *we* were asked to see him with a question again of a hypercoagulable state. At *that* point he was being treated with heparin, when he was also on Niphetapenc, nitropaste to the leg and Ventolin. Basically when we first saw him . . . there was a great *gap* in terms of his order sheets and med sheets, a lot of them were *lost* and there's various trips back to and from the OR the RICU and so forth and our feeling is that perhaps he had never been thera*peutic* on heparin 'cos his PTT had only been above fifty-five or sixty on *two* days . . . of the time that he was on heparin. So we suggested that he be kept on heparin, and . . . that we keep an eye on whether he became hard to heparinize in any way. And to make a long story short, one of the things which occurred on heparin, and this is still a little bit confusing as the exact sequence, is he developed thrombocytopenia. And at that point we were concerned that he might have heparin-induced thrombocytopenia and/or thrombosis secondary to heparin. So we suggested that they discontinue the heparin. I went over things in great detail with Dawson the chief surgical resident, who appeared to remember a lot of the *data* from the lab sheets and med sheets that were *lost*. What we thought *might* be possible is that all the way along heparin has been perhaps potentiating his syndrome. If you accept the fact that heparin is *bad* for him you can sort of go back through his history, and at every step of the way see where the institution of heparin appeared to make him a little bit worse. I'm not completely sure that his whole coagulopathy is going to be a combination of *heparin* coupled with initial blow to femoral area starting everything off. And I think he still needs to be worked up for causes of a hypercoagulable state and I'm in the middle of making a flow sheet so I can show that to Dawson and make sure that we're not talking ourselves into something that isn't actually true.

There are several noteworthy features of the particular case narrative. First, there is the marking of past and present evidence for its relative credibility. On the one hand, many aspects of the history are reported in an unmarked fashion. They are reported as unproblematic and uncontested. For instance:

> The patient was discharged . . .
> . . . the coumarin was discontinued . . .
> . . . he was admitted to the hospital . . .
> . . . they discontinued the heparin . . .

and so on. Many of these unmarked statements are tied directly to temporal markers and benchmarks in the unfolding narrative:

> In August . . .
> At that point . . .
> At that point he was being treated . . .

These unmarked, factual statements and their associated temporal markers are thus used by the young clinician to establish a narrative framework. It provides, metaphorically speaking, a scaffolding or armature of uncontested events and decisions. They establish with relative certainty a chronology of events and decisions that form a basic structure for the case account and – more importantly – a backdrop for more problematic aspects of the account. Part of that framework of unmarked and unproblematic issues is a series of medical interventions and reported decisions. For instance:

> . . . he was admitted with a slight ileofemoral thrombosis and he underwent a graft to that area . . .
> He was seen at that time . . . and they arranged for out patient follow-up . . .
> The patient was *dis*charged . . . and was being followed . . .

It is, however, noticeable that against this background of unmarked statements about the patient's career there is a more complex series of statements that indicate very different orientations towards the events and the information that are reported. For instance:

> . . . the path. specimen . . . was described as showing . . . which when I asked the pathologists . . . they claim . . .
> He was seen at that time . . . and they were concerned that there might be some sort of . . .
> . . . sending their notes there was a suggestion . . . in the sense that . . . and perhaps the pulses in the leg . . .
> It was a sort of gradual finding . . .
> . . . the finding was that something was definitely going on in the leg.
> . . . they start to feel as though clinically . . .
> . . . *we* were asked to see him with a question again . . .
> . . . and our feeling is that perhaps . . .
> . . . we were concerned that he might have . . .
> . . . we thought *might* be possible is that . . .
> I'm not completely sure that. . .

These various utterances are marked in various ways to suggest that the evidence they report on is not certain, or that the interpretation of that information is unsure, tentative or contested.

Here, therefore, we find the presence of 'evidentials' in the rhetoric of medical presentations. The general analytic issue of *evidentiality* in discourse analysis or pragmatics concerns the linguistic coding of epistemology. In its broadest sense it is concerned with the ways in which speakers (or writers) display their attitude towards, their belief in, or claims concerning facts, knowledge, opinions, inferences and the like.

> Languages typically provide a repertoire of devices for conveying these attitudes toward knowledge. Often enough, speakers present things as unquestioningly true; for example: 'Its raining'. On other occasions English speakers for example, may use an adverb to show something about the reliability of what they say, the probability of its truth: 'It's probably raining' or 'Maybe it's raining'. Inference from some kind of evidence may be expressed with a modal auxiliary: 'it must be raining'. Or the specific kind of evidence on which an inference is based may be indicated with a separate verb: 'It sounds like it's raining'. The view that a piece of knowledge does not match the protoypical meaning of a verbal category may be shown formulaically: 'It's sort of raining'. Or an adverb may suggest that some knowledge is different from what might have been expected: 'Actually, it's raining'. (Chafe, 1986: viii)

As Chafe indicates, English – unlike some languages – does not have strict lexical or morphological encoding of evidentiality, but provides a wide repertoire of resources for its representation.

It is clear, therefore, that the case presentation reproduced above is replete with indicators of evidentiality. These are used by the young physician to construct various contrasts and hierarchies of credibility in the evidence incorporated into the case narrative. That narrative itself is no mere chronicle of events and facts. It includes threads of responsibility, culpability and judgement. The use of evidentiality creates a story which, first, brings the reported events under the single unifying rubric of a case or a history, and, secondly, creates different domains of credibility and zones of competence. The teller of the case examined here does not treat all the evidence as equally sound and definitive. On the contrary, her report is developed through an exposition and exploration of evidence marked as problematic.

It is noticeable too that the first part of the narrative culminates at one identifiable cusp or crux. It is signalled by:

> And at *that* point *we* were asked to see him . . .

This is one of the key temporal markers in the narrative's chronology. It is emphasized by an almost immediate repetition:

> At *that* point he was being treated . . .

This point in the story marks an important transition in the history and the narrator's orientation to it. The first half of the story is one of progressive muddle and catastrophe, to a point where a possible reinterpretation of events and a plausible explanation begins to emerge. We do not exactly have a denouement to this story, for it is presented in terms of growing complexity and perplexity. But there is an important antithesis built into the narrative of the patient's history – before 'we' were called in to see the patient and after. The first builds on a concatenation of unexplained complications; the second on a series of possible explanations, culminating in the preparation of a flow-chart for the chief surgeon.

In gross terms, therefore, this account is replete with aspects of uncertainty, derived from various sources. It has – in common with many such accounts (Atkinson, 1992a) – aspects of a mystery story: problems that defy definitive explanation and resolution. It is important, however, to note how precisely the physician *locates* the sources and nature of doubt, equivocation and the like. It is, of course, embedded in an account – complex in itself – of the medical division of labour. This itself is expressed rhetorically, drawing on devices of *contrastive rhetoric* (Hargreaves, 1981). Such narrative contrasts may compare 'us' and 'them' (or 'here' and 'there'); and this account has several implied contrast structures. It is, of course, noticeable that in the first half of the account, before the consultation that brought in the haematologists, the account refers entirely to what 'they' thought and felt. The structure of plausibility is established: what 'they' did, thought and recorded is established with a certain judicious distancing from the narrator. The chronicle of events is reported as 'their' acts (which are reported factually) and 'their' judgements (which are evidentially marked).

After the consult, the narrator's interpretations and suggestions remain evidentially marked. It is not the case that their uncertainty is replaced by our certainty. Rather, the haematologist's tentatively proposed and marked proposals, for example,

> . . . at that point we were concerned that he might have heparin-induced thrombocytopenia and/or thrombosis secondary to heparin . . .

are proposed as judicious candidate solutions to the problems and puzzles that were posed in the first half of the narrative. The technical division of labour is reflected in the distribution of trust and evidentials. We have the descriptions of what they (the surgeons) did, saw, described and felt. We have what the pathologists 'claim'. We have what the chief surgical resident 'appeared to remember'. At the end of the day, the clinical fellow in haematology concludes in a tentative manner:

> I'm not completely sure that his whole coagulopathy is going to be . . . and I think he still needs to be worked up . . .

Each actor or group of actors, including the narrator herself, is thus placed in relation to this complex and potentially confusing story. The narrative itself thus constructs various zones of credibility – coding information and interpretation for their relative trustworthiness.

The discursive treatment of uncertainty includes the device known as *hedging* (Prince et al., 1982). Hedging refers to the use of words or phrases 'whose job it is to make things fuzzier' (Lakoff, 1972). Analysing a corpus of interactions in a paediatric intensive care unit, Prince et al. suggest that hedges of various kinds can be identified at the rate of 150 to 450 per hour, or more than one every fifteen seconds. Prince et al. identify a small number of major types of hedge in physician encounters. First is a general class of 'approximators', which are used to modify medical terms and descriptions in order to render them less precise than their unmarked version would be. These are of two types. 'Adaptors' are used to indicate that there is a degree of mismatch or flexibility between a 'prototypical' description and the observed or reported conditions. 'Rounders' are used to indicate a *range* of values, or a degree of approximation. The other major category, described as 'shields', mark the speaker's degree of commitment to the report. Again, two types are identified. First, there are 'plausibility shields'. They indicate that the speaker is less than fully committed as to the credibility of a report. Alternatively, there are 'attribution shields', which are used to indicate that knowledge and beliefs have been derived – by hearsay or by report – from others. These may be used to qualify the credence to be placed on the account.

Prince et al. provide examples of each category of hedge. They suggest that 'certain types are a linguistic reflection of speaker-uncertainty, or, more precisely, of a marked commitment on the part of the speaker to the truth of the proposition that s/he is conveying' (1982: 96). It is unfortunate that Prince and his co-authors again chose to assimilate all these discourse features to the general category of physician 'uncertainty'. In doing so they rather blunt the analytic edge of their typology. Rather than exploit the greater precision afforded by discriminating between the types and functions of 'hedging', they collapse them into the all-too-familiar and crude category. Further, they provide examples from physicians' discourse for each of their types. They do little to suggest just how these strategies are used in the context of case discussions. Yet, as we have seen from the extended example reproduced above, expressions of credibility and plausibility, of approximations and attributions, are embedded in narratives such as case histories within which they may be used to construct complex domains or hierarchies of trust and responsibility. A serious consideration of the pragmatics of 'hedging' therefore requires a more systematic examination of the pragmatics of physicians' collegial talk.

The complex marking of evidentiality and the deployment of so-called hedges reflects Anspach's observations on her data on case presentations. Anspach contrasts physicians' treatment of patient accounts and physician accounts:

> When presenting a clinical history obtained from a patient, the physician has two choices. One is to present events and symptoms reported by the patient as facts, just as physical findings and laboratory results are presented. This is done occasionally . . . Alternatively and more commonly, the history is treated as a subjective narrative consisting of statements and reports. (Anspach, 1988: 368)

By contrast:

> . . . physicians are inclined to present information obtained from the physician as though it were factual, while treating information from the patient as accounts. (Anspach, 1988: 368)

As the example presented above demonstrates, however, the marking of credibility and the use of 'evidentials' is (or at least, may be) more complex than just a distinction between patient and physician. There is clearly ample opportunity here for fine distinctions between medical practitioners in the attribution of plausibility. The presenting physician's narrative may thus inscribe varying degrees of trust, certainty and uncertainty into the case history itself.

The following extended example provides another case presentation in the course of which a complex medical problem (or series of problems) is recounted in a narrative that distinguishes and marks several domains of medical credibility and responsibility. The case presentation also demonstrates some important discourse features that bear on the narrative production of disease and medical work. The young doctor has just presented a brief summary follow-up of a female patient who was being treated – apparently with some success – for an acute leukaemia.

> F: This is to be contrasted with Mr Austin Grant who is *not* doing so well. He is as you remember our seventy-three-year-old patient *also* with APML, who had a year's history of anaemia quote unquote treated with *iron* by a local doctor and came into this hospital after two weeks of fatigue and dyspnoea, and he was found to be pancytopenic. He had a bone marrow which was a dry tap but the touch prep showed a lot of blasts which looked like they had granules in them and the bone marrow biopsy was felt by Carol Green to be most consistent with acute promyelocytic leukaemia. He was treated with ( ) and Daunorubicin and ( ) for seven days and Dauno for *three*. And he started day one on the seventh of October. He also was started on heparin because his fibrin splits bumped up from one to five twelve, and he did well until Friday night when all of a sudden he developed a temperature spike and over the weekend had a rapid deterioration notable for the following events: fevers, hypocalcaemia, a problem with moving his *limbs*, he was totally unable to lift his arm and legs off the bed, hypotension, increased respiratory rate, a cough, a creatinine that went up to the threes, an inferior wall MI by ECG and afib. It *appears* that the initial deterioration was due to staph (oral) sepsis and five out of six cultures have subsequently grown out *positive* for staph. Howe*ver* . . . when he was initially empirically covered for his fever spike he was really on *poor* staph coverage at that time there was some question about *abdominal* pain which is really not panned out and for that reason he was started on (Cefoxin) and Gentamicin so for almost three days his staph coverage was clearly suboptimal and that probably led to the hypotension, and a lot of other complications. To take them sort of one by one, the *renal* people feel that his renal deterioration is on the basis of hypotension secondary to sepsis, he *did* have a slightly elevated creatinine *initially* which they haven't really add*ressed* um he also had renal scan to rule out renal abscess as being a focus for his infection and that has been negative . . . He has developed a total inability to lift his arms and legs off the bed. Initial concerns were raised about possibly an epidural abscess or thrombotic event and eventually it seemed like the most likely thing was that he was suffering from acute hypocalcaemia with possibly some hypomagnesaemia. We were a little bit uncomfortable with attributing all his neurological problems to this and asked them to consult the neurologists, which they haven't really agreed to do until today, thinking that it was all a myopathy from the hypocalcaemia. However, this *morning* his arms are

better and his calcium is back to normal and his *magnesium*, which had not been available throughout the weekend, *is* normal. So I *think* a myopathy from hypocalcaemia consequent on inflammatory myopathy is still *possible* but I'd be worried about some other thing going on and the neurologists seeing him.

Here we can note how the story of Mr Grant is assembled and produced. It is one which includes a number of frames and episodes. First, it incorporates a summary of the patient's prior history which itself indicates a medical error. The diagnosis of anaemia by a local doctor is marked by the clinical fellow's use of 'quote unquote' markers. It alerts the audience of specialists to the fact that the problem was originally inappropriately classified and managed. (It is by no means uncommon for haematological problems to be so identified and treated with supplementary iron, only for the haematologists themselves to define this as an error on the part of the primary care physician or non-haematological specialist.) This problem is partially resolved when investigation reveals pancytopenia (reduction in blood cell production) which in turn precipitates a bone marrow biopsy. The clinical pathologist's diagnosis then initiates chemotherapy.

There is, however, a *complicating* phase to the narrative. The story as told by the fellow proceeds by means of a series of complications and puzzles. Indeed, the purpose of the presentation is to present a 'mystery' story: the nature and causes of the patient's sudden change, with fevers, hypocalcaemia and the difficulty in moving his limbs. The narrative unfolds the problems that emerge. The original diagnosis and treatment are not in doubt, but there are further processes that are less well understood. The bacterial infection and its treatment, the deterioration in the patient's kidneys, and the possible neurological problem are all presented as part of the narrative sequence. The narrative itself imposes the chronological order onto the reported facts and events. It does not yet provide for a single interpretative framework: the mystery story lacks a resolution. The case narrative again inscribes a division of medical labour. We have already seen the 'local doctors', responsible in the past for what is now regarded as an error. By contrast Carol Greene, the clinical pathologist, is invoked to substantiate the diagnosis of APML. There is also an implied criticism of the primary care team. The initial treatment of the temperature spike provided poor coverage for staphylococcal infection. Plus there is a hint that a reported symptom of abdominal pain was inadequately investigated. Two further consulting specialisms are invoked – the renal specialists, whose opinion on the deterioration in the kidneys is reported on, and the neurologists, who are to be consulted, although again it should be noted that 'they' (the primary team) are reported as having been reluctant and tardy in initiating that particular consultation, which had been suggested by the haematology fellow.

In this case presentation, then, we can see once more that although the patient's problems are presented in terms of the generically 'depersonalized' medical mode, the medical domain itself is far from undifferentiated. On the contrary, the narrative invokes a *dramatis personae* of medical agents. While the story pulls the various actors and events into a single temporal framework, and provides a unifying perspective from the standpoint of the haematologist, it carefully ascribes views and responsibilities and distributes them among the various characters.

This, then, is a story without an ending. It sets up a mystery. It invites candidate solutions from the audience. It recounts a series of puzzles, and the advice given or solicited from other medical personnel. It is again noticeable that the narrative is itself characterized by the marking of evidence. We have already seen that the local doctor was dismissed by having his or her diagnosis strongly marked and bracketed with the 'quote unquote' device, thus rendering it entirely lacking in credibility. This contrasts with the evidence of the current hospital admission. 'He was found to be pancytopenic' establishes a firm contrast with the mistaken diagnosis of the past.

Interestingly, however, the medical work of the current admission is itself evidentially marked in various ways. For instance:

> the touch prep showed a lot of blasts which looked like they had granules in them and the bone marrow biopsy was felt by Carol Greene to be most consistent with acute promyelocytic leukaemia.

Here the clinical fellow quite carefully acknowledges that appearance and interpretation are involved in the diagnosis. Likewise the use of the phrases 'most consistent with' and 'was felt by' are indicative of a judicious assessment of the available evidence (even though the bone marrow aspirate was not ideal). It is worth noting in passing that this *personal* attribution, naming the clinical pathologist, is an apparent deviation from the depersonalizing of biomedical discourse. This particular pathologist, however, was invoked by name far more than the majority of other colleagues. She it was whose interpretations of biopsies and other tissues were regularly treated as 'oracular' by the haematologists. Her skills were highly respected. Her judicious and careful pronouncements were held to provide the last available information. Consequently, this attribution to a named individual endows the interpretation with particular status – for all that its character as an opinion is marked in the discourse.

Similar marking is found elsewhere:

> . . . it appears that the initial deterioration . . .
> . . . there was some question about *abdominal* pain . . .
> . . . his staph coverage was clearly suboptimal and that probably led to the hypotension . . .
> . . . the *renal* people feel that . . .
> Initial concerns were raised about possible . . . and eventually it seems like the most likely thing was . . .
> . . . we were a little bit uncomfortable with attributing . . .
> . . . I *think* a myopathy from hypocalcaemia consequent on inflammatory myopathy is still *possible* but I'd be worried about other things going on . . .

In other words it is again clear that the clinical fellow here makes careful discrimination in terms of the sources and relative credibility of information.

The fellow's own orientations are likewise encoded, in that they are graded and expressed with various nuances of commitment, strength and character ('we were a little bit uncomfortable'; 'I *think* . . . is still *possible* . . . I'd be worried . . .'). Here again, then, we can detect a complex and carefully managed narrative that distributes opinions among different agents. The plausibility of evidence and the narrator's commitment are coded in the marking of evidentiality throughout the account.

Conclusion

In this chapter I have tried to demonstrate how the structuring of medical discourse and medical narratives can be coded, often in complex and subtle ways, to convey a variety of orientations towards facts and opinions about the case. Not all knowledge is treated as having equal value. It has different sources, has different weight attached to it, and may be regarded as more or less warranted. These orientations to knowledge cannot be reduced to generalized categories of certainty and uncertainty in medical discourse. Degrees of certainty may be expressed, and they are embedded in the discursive and organizational context of the case-talk. In expressing his or her attitude towards facts and opinions, the clinician also inscribes aspects of the moral and technical division of labour among medical specialists. The contrastive rhetoric between the past and the present, between the speaker and other practitioners, delicately expresses attributions of responsibility, credit or blame. It interweaves the chronicle of the patient's career and current admission with the reported or implied competence of specific doctors (cf. Delvecchio-Good, 1985). The sociology of medicine needs to pay very careful attention to just how medical knowledge is expressed in these and other work settings. Medical work and medical talk are closely interwoven, and a micro-sociology of medical knowledge should be grounded in the formal analysis of such discourse. In the next chapter I develop such an analysis further, by examining the multiple *voices* to be heard in such medical talk. That is, the contrasting orientations to medical reality that are captured in the accounts and narratives of specialists in the clinic.

7

Voices of Medicine

This chapter continues to develop the themes introduced in the previous one. It furthers the analysis of physicians' attitudes or orientations to domains and warrants for medical knowledge. It explores the grounds for authority and expertise that are inscribed in physicians' presentations and discussions of their cases.

The analysis draws initially on accounts of doctor–*patient* interaction that seek to capture the micro-politics of medical encounters, grounded in detailed discourse analysis. The purpose here is not to recapitulate all of that micro-political analysis. Rather, I intend to use a number of sensitizing concepts and apply them to spoken interaction between medical practitioners.

In particular, I draw on Mishler's treatment of doctor–patient interaction and his characterization of the *voices* of the encounter (Mishler, 1984; see also Clark and Mishler, 1992). It will be argued that Mishler's account, though limited in itself, can be extended and developed to illuminate micro-social features of physicians' talk. Mishler's original analysis is based on the detailed examination of extended extracts from a restricted corpus of recordings – the strategy that has been employed to some extent in this study. His data consist of taped consultations in which a patient's history is elicited. They appear to be – and are so characterized by Mishler himself – fairly routine, unproblematic consultations. While by no means representative of the full range of medical settings, Mishler's data are typical in that the majority of sociological observers have – as we have seen – focused their attention on one-to-one, routine doctor–patient interactions.

Mishler provides an unremarkable initial characterization of the basic structure of his corpus of consultations. He draws attention to the recurrent (and familiar) presence of a three-part discourse structure. This cycle of talk-exchange consists of the doctor's *elicitation*, the patient's *response*, the doctor's *assessment* of the response, followed by a further elicitation, and so on. The recurrent nature of this elementary discourse structure provides for the chaining of utterances into prolonged (or, at least, potentially expandable) strings of questions and answers. The overall economy of this *speech exchange system* is asymmetrical: types of utterance are distributed unequally between the two parties. This type of discourse has, of course, been identified in medical encounters by other observers, as well as in other contexts – most notably in school classrooms and other instructional settings, where long stretches of instructional talk characteristically consist of elicitation–response–evaluation chains (for example, Mehan, 1979).

In his characterization of the routine medical interviews, however, Mishler adds a less familiar analytic perspective. Borrowing the concept from Silverman and Torode (1980), he introduces the idea of the *voice*. He identifies the voice of medicine and the voice of the lifeworld. He thus moves away from a purely formal treatment of speech exchange, and introduces a more hermeneutic or phenomenological turn. In this usage, 'voice' does not correspond simply with notions like perspective or culture. Mishler is not simply saying that there is a difference between lay and medical understanding. Equally, the idea of a voice does not equate with a speaker. One speaker may articulate more than one voice; different speakers may share the same voice. Torode (1984) had originally developed the use of voice in relation to the social order of school classrooms, and it translates well into the treatment of medical exchanges.

Different voices distinguish contrasting orientations to the world and to the moral order. Voices articulate differing presuppositions concerning language and reality. They have different implications for avowals or attributions of agency and responsibility. Each voice realizes a particular relationship between the speaker and the world. Mishler's contrast between the voice of medicine and the voice of the lifeworld refers not just to the subject-matter of discourse, but also to its discursive organization. Mishler's first characterization of the medical interview suggests that it is dominated by the voice of medicine. The exchange appears to be controlled by the physician's use of questioning routines. By means of this control mechanism, the voice of medicine maintains ascendancy. While patients occasionally articulate the voice of the lifeworld (grounded in their personal experiences and preoccupations), for the most part it is overlooked by the voice of medicine. In this model, the interview is a struggle for dominance, the voice of the lifeworld occasionally breaking through, or interrupting, the voice of medicine.

Mishler goes on, however, to question the adequacy of this initial interpretation. He reverses the emphasis. He suggests that the patient's utterances can be understood in terms of a personal narrative of illness experience which is repeatedly 'interrupted' by the impersonal and decontextualized voice of contemporary biomedicine. The patient communicates the voice of the lifeworld *and* of medicine. This formal analysis of the discourse of medical interaction is thus linked to an interpretative, phenomenological perspective, drawing on Schutz's conceptualization of 'provinces of meanings' and 'structures of relevance'.

Mishler's interruption analysis, it must be emphasized, is very different from the analysis of phenomena like interruptions or overlaps studied in medical encounters by authors like West (1984). The voices may interrupt each other without the speakers actually breaking into and overlapping each others' utterances. Analytically, the two issues are distinct, although in practice the two phenomena may coincide.

There is, however, a basic limitation to Mishler's formulation of the voice of the lifeworld and the voice of medicine. It remains too simple, too readily dichotomized. Mishler tends to imply that it is only the voice of the lifeworld that is grounded in biographical experience, and couched in a narrative format. By contrast, he implies that the voice of medicine is decontextualized: that there is a more or less uniform orientation towards contemporary biomedicine. In other words, Mishler's characterization of the medical encounter is predicated on the identification of a single, dominant voice of medicine. It is all too easy to follow the Schutzian model to produce a radical contrast between everyday, narrative experience on the one hand, and expert knowledge, couched primarily in scientific propositions on the other.

It is all too plausible to construct such a model, because – as was argued earlier in this book – social scientists have focused obsessively on the doctor–patient dyad. Each partner may thus be held to be a microcosm of two sets of contrasting interests, orientations and stocks of knowledge. Of course, the social world of the lay patient may be divided further – in terms of class, gender, ethnicity or language. By contrast, it is easy to treat the physician as standing for a much more homogeneous domain of medicine *per se*. Sociological recognition of segmentation and cleavage within the profession notwithstanding, it is thus possible to attribute to medicine a more or less homogeneous orientation to its own knowledge and practices. This reflects the anthropological-cum-sociological construction of biomedicine as a cultural system.

It will be argued here that, on the contrary, medicine is characterized, in Mishler's terms, by several voices. They coexist, and are sometimes in competition. To some degree we have already taken on board a gross version of this. The distinctions between *personal experience* and *text-book science*, captured in notions like the 'clinical mentality', hint at the possibility of competing voices in medical discourse. It will be seen that these voices are part and parcel of the formal arrangements of collegial discourse in medicine.

As we have seen, medical discourse has its own narrative formats. Here we shall go on to consider some of the complexities of narrative accounting, based on the lifeworld experience of the individual physician. We shall see that the junior doctor may be interrogated – his or her voice of narrative *interrupted* – by the supervisory senior colleague. Just as the primary care physician quizzes the patient over the presenting complaint, so the attending or consultant physician cross-questions his or her subordinate over what the junior has seen, done, elicited or read. Just as Mishler's lay patient constructs a biographically grounded account of his or her perceptions, feelings, theories and happenings, so the resident or student doctor constructs his or her narratives, piecing together fragments of evidence from various sources. In turn the senior physician may de-contextualize aspects of the narrative – lifting aspects out of the here-and-now concerns of the junior doctor, and transforming them into general principles and problems of medical knowledge and practice.

Then again, there are further contrasting voices, variously articulated by senior and junior colleagues. The junior doctor (sometimes the student) articulates the voice of the eye-witness – reporting and vouching for what has been seen and done. Here, then, the doctor stands in a personal relation to the knowledge. By contrast, the senior physician – the attending or consultant – may adopt a different, but also personal, attitude towards medical knowledge. This is expressed in *the voice of experience*. It voices not the here-and-now experience of the concrete particulars of the case to hand. It is, rather, a voice of accumulated experience, a biographical warrant for knowledge and opinion. This too may be expressed in narrative formats. But the narratives of personal experience are often explicitly constructed as personal reminiscences. The voice of experience comes closest to an everyday notion of story-telling – sometimes expressed as stories about doctoring. The narratives are used to articulate personal knowledge, preferences, understanding and so on.

Yet another 'voice' may be glossed as *the voice of science*. That is, an articulation of knowledge that is warranted by an appeal to research such as published scientific papers. This voice of science is not especially associated with any one category of medical personnel. As will become apparent, however, it may interrupt with the voice of experience. It may be one of two alternating modes of authority: experience and science. As the senior physician articulates experience, he or she may oppose the scientific appeal of the junior colleague.

Within the clinical round or the round-table discussion of a case, therefore, there may appear complex interweavings and interruptions of different voices. To put it another way, there are different frames in play – characterized by different attitudes towards knowledge and expertise. These are differentially distributed between the parties to the medical encounter. They draw on different discursive formats and are marked differently.

An understanding of collegial talk in medical settings, therefore, must include a careful mapping of these contrasting voices and orientations. This is not just a matter of the formal description of the pragmatics of medical discourse. It is fundamental to a micro-sociology of medical knowledge. Indeed, it bears directly on issues of authority and expertise, and – no less fundamentally – on the micro-politics of medical work. These contrasts in voice or orientation do have real consequences: their mutual support or mutual interruptions have implications for the practical outcome of physicians' deliberations. They are among the carriers of medical culture. They reproduce the technical and social division of labour, and the stratification of expert knowledge within and between medical specialties.

We have already seen that there is a potentially complex accounting process in the construction of a case in its presentation. The narrator – such as the medical student or junior hospital doctor – draws on and reports information that itself derives from diverse sources, and may be implicitly granted differential value. In presenting the case, the student or doctor reconstructs a narrative. I have already argued that cases are themselves narrative accomplishments. In the course of their narrative reconstructions, however, the presenters of cases may find themselves cross-questioned by their peers and superiors. In other words, the presenter narrates a story which contextualizes the various reports and findings (symptoms and signs) into a coherent chronological and cognitive frame of reference. The medical superior, interrogating the narrator, may *fragment* the story, decontextualizing the various elements of the story, and subjecting them to critical scrutiny.

The following extract provides one example. The student is presenting a fairly formal account of a patient:

St: . . . Eight weeks prior to admission he had a right mandibular fracture while playing football and he tells of infection of the soft tissue which apparently resolved on fixation and drainage and erythromycin, and the fixation was removed three weeks prior to admission with good occlusive result. However on November *second* the patient presented to the Emergency Ward with a swelling and a obvious recurrence of infection. He was admitted for treatment with (IRD) with general anaesthesia and incidentally his platelets were found to be decreased. His diabetes mellitus has been for five years . . . for which he's getting forty-five ( ) per day. And he was hospitalized in 5 '79. At the *same* time at the same [Hospital] admission he also was already (in serious) alcohol abuse and developed acute hepatitis, with an SGOT to two thousand five hundred and he was hepatitis B surface antigen *negative* at *this* time. In January '84 has had another [Hospital] admission for diabetes mellitus and again he has abnormal (LFTs) but this time he is HB antigen *positive*. Since several months he's decreasing his alcohol abuse, and since one week prior to admission he has no drink at all. He also used IV cocaine in the past and the last time was five months ago.

At: Has he used anything else IV?

St: Um

At: Recently?

St: No

At: So he's been reformed for a few months you mean?

St: Hm?

At: He has been reformed for a few months?

St: Well, I suppose

At: He has not been doing anything bad for the past few months?

St: Well apparently he is going on um

F: He's had no more than a six pack in an evening in the last few months

St: (Yeah)

St2: I thought he'd been broke

At: No medication, *nothing*

St: No medication

. . .

St: On physical exam, he's afebrile, no petechiae on the skin, no jaundice, no meningeal signs, no lymphadenopathy. He has some petechiae on the gums. He has petechiae on the *gums*? No petechiae on the conjunctivae. He has um

At: [*To the clinical fellow*] No, the way he is going I don't know whether I am supposed to see them or I am not supposed to see them

F: We were asked to evaluate him for thrombocytopenia
At: Oh okay. Sure. He has *no* petechiae
St: Yes, only at the gums
At: Oh, there only. Okay
St: Okay. Lungs were clear. Heart normal. His abdominal exam, his liver is
At: = Below the costal margin?
St: Yeah about six centimetres
At: What's the span?
St: Mm?
At: What is the liver span?
St: That is about fifteen centimetres
At: Okay
St: He has a palpable spleen
At: He has a palpable spleen too
St: = Yes. So that's basically it.
At: = He has evidence of splenomegaly
St: Right. That's basically his exam.
At: No adenopathy
St: No adenopathy
At: No lower extremity petechiae
St: No
At: Any history of ( ) bleeding? You didn't tell me that.
St: A (few) he denied all
At: = No nose bleeds
St: No nose bleeds
At: No frequent bruises
St: I asked for any spots anywhere on his body or for any bleeding and he denied
there was
F: And in fact we know when he was here in January '84 when he was known to
be surface antigen and B antigen *positive*.
At: Mm
F: His platelet count was one hundred and fifty-seven thousand
At: = In January
F: = In January of '84. *And* 7 of '84, July of '84 on a routine visit to a
maxillo-facial *surgery* a CVC was sent and a platelet count was estimated at
normal
At: So it's really recent
F: Yeah
St: Mmhm
At: Since July
St: Mhm. His
At: = Can you say what the splenomegaly is? No?
F: Well we = I think the last time I saw a note I looked and he was examined in
January when he came in with the hepatitis and had a palpable liver
At: Mm. And the spleen?
F: I didn't see them mention a spleen then
St: No
F: No, I think they did *not* palpate a spleen then. Now *I* felt it but I'd like you
At: That's most unusual so early. Okay
St: His electrolytes are normal. Creatinine point seven, blood sugars two
hundred and fifty, bilirubin one point zero, alkali phosphates is eighty
At: eight oh?
F: Eighty, yeah
St: ye-yeah

Apart from an occasional contribution from a second medical student, there are three parties to this exchange. The medical student presents the case in a routinely formalized way. This is couched in a standard format. Hence, the medical student presents the kind of case narrative that has been identified already. This is a reconstruction of the patient's career, which covers a long time span, several hospital admissions, and a number of different medical problems and episodes.

It is noticeable how the recitation of the case is interrupted by the attending physician. When the student's narration reaches the mention of intravenous (IV) cocaine use, the attending breaks in and disrupts the narrative flow. He checks whether the patient reports any other intravenous substance use, and follows up by checking on the patient's recent behaviour in the recent past. It is noticeable that at this point the form of the discourse changes. The narrative format is replaced by a question-and-answer sequence, in which the attending physician cross-questions the student about the case. It must be emphasized that the attending has not taken a history or examined the patient himself. He is, therefore, assembling the case history from the information presented and elicited by the medical student, and (subsequently) by the clinical fellow.

Several of the sequences in the exchange between the attending and the student have a classic three-part structure, in which the attending seeks to elicit information by a question, the student responds and the senior physician acknowledges and evaluates that response.

St: . . . His abdominal exam, his liver is
At: Below the costal margin?
St: About six centimetres
At: What's the span?
St: Mm?
At: What is the liver span?
St: That is about fifteen centimetres
At: Okay

The attending physician also uses the question-and-answer recitation format to elicit information not contained in the student's original presentation. The student indicates in two successive turns that the presentation of the physical examination has been completed: 'So that's basically it'; 'That's basically his exam'. But the attending pursues the physical exam findings with further probing questions, to which the student responds:

At: No adenopathy
St: No adenopathy
At: No lower extremity petechiae
St: No
At: Any history of (   ) bleeding? You didn't tell me that.
St: A (few) he denied all
At: = No nose bleeds
St: No nose bleeds

One should note in passing the student's characteristic use of 'deny' in reporting the patient's own account. Also, at that point the student is projecting a longer turn in the case presentation mode. The attending, however, cuts it short with an immediate prompt, checking on 'nose bleeds'.

From time to time in the ensuing exchanges, the student regains the floor as fragmentary case presentation elements are resumed. The projection of lab results provides occasion for a resumption of the monologic format. Here again, however, the attending interrupts in order to check the values. Moreover, the student's account is further interrupted by the clinical fellow, who does have firsthand knowledge of the case. The fellow intercedes to repair aspects of the student's report of lab results. The following is a clear example of such a sequence:

> *St*:   His platelets were sixty-nine on November two
> *At*:   Was his haematocrit assessed?
> *St*:   Yes, okay. Haematocrit is forty-seven point six, MCDs ninety-five, red blood cells five point zero, white blood cells nine point seven, platelets sixty-nine on November two and forty-seven on November three
> *F*:   No, *sixty*-seven

From time to time, therefore, the clinical fellow interjects, repairs the report, and resumes the narrative. Between them the attending and the fellow interrupt the narrative of the student's case presentation. There are thus complex patterns of discourse as the three parties to the encounter variously hold the floor and interrupt one another. It is instructive to compare this overview of the case conference or round with a characterization of doctor–patient encounters. As I have already suggested, Mishler's analysis of 'voices' is instructive, and will be drawn on more fully as the analysis proceeds.

First, it is noticeable that in many of the sequences of daily haematological rounds, there is a clear homology between doctor–doctor interaction and doctor–patient interaction. Concerning the latter, numerous sociologists and sociolinguists have drawn attention to the *asymmetry* in the exchange of speech. Formulations of the phenomena vary, but one way or another there is a widely held view that characteristic interactional patterns in the consultation reflect the unequal distribution of power and resources. It is argued, therefore, that the physician may control the interaction through his or her ascribed rights to interrogate the patient, and to manage the stream of spoken interaction by the exercise of various discourse strategies. The initiation and maintenance of question-and-answer is one mechanism whereby the physician's control may be exerted in the ordinary consultation:

> Clinical interviews are structured in ways that limit patients' opportunities to tell the stories of their illnesses. Although patients initiate the encounters and their problems are the central topics, physicians control the process, following a medical agenda to accomplish the primary tasks of diagnosis and treatment. (Clark and Mishler, 1992: 346)

Mishler has elaborated on the rather simple model of turn-taking found in many studies by his use of 'voice'. This suggests that the interplay of the consultation can be understood as that between two contrasting orientations. Mishler summarizes his perspective thus:

> The basic three-part unit of such discourse and the ways in which these units are linked together has been described, as well as the functions served by this structure – the physician's control of organization and meaning. I referred to this patterned relationship between structure and function as the 'voice of medicine', and suggested that it expressed the normative order of medicine and clinical practice. This voice provides a baseline against which to compare other medical interviews that depart in some way from normal practice . . .

> Some preliminary comparisons have already been made. In each of these unremarkable interviews the patient interrupted the flow of the discourse by introducing the 'voice of the lifeworld'.

Mishler goes on to reverse this initial emphasis, arguing that one can productively regard the voice of medicine as interrupting the voice of the lifeworld.

Each 'voice' implies a different orientation or attitude (in Schutz's sense) to the subject matter of the encounter.

> I am proposing an interpretation of the medical interview as a situation of conflict between two ways of constructing meaning. Moreover, I am also proposing that the physician's effort to impose a technocratic consciousness to dominate the voice of the lifeworld by the voice of medicine, seriously impairs and distorts essential requirements for mutual dialogue and human interaction. (Mishler, 1984: 127)

Here then is an analytic perspective that tries to relate the organization of discourse to problems of relevance and frameworks of knowledge.

In his most recent contribution, Mishler's work explores further the voice of the lifeworld, concentrating on its narrative organization.

> From their responsiveness to questions, it is evident that patients tend to cooperate with physicians pursuing the medical tasks of diagnosis and treatment. However, recurrent conflict between the respective 'voices' and patients' persistent efforts to go beyond what is asked for suggest that patients have an additional aim that falls outside the boundaries of the typical, narrow medical agenda. This confronts patients with a different task, namely to tell their stories of their problems in ways that make sense to them while cooperating with the physician. (Clark and Mishler, 1992: 346)

In other words, in the voice of the lifeworld, personal troubles are constructed through stories while the voice of medicine – articulating the domain assumptions of biomedical knowledge and practice – repeatedly interjects, interrupting the narrative, decontextualizing 'information' from its biographical context and recontextualizing it into the frameworks of medical orthodoxy.

Formally speaking, therefore, there is a parallel between the consultation and the daily round. The student or junior physician presents in narrative mode. While recounting the case he or she has the floor. But the narrative account may be interrupted by the senior physician, who may interrogate the junior in much the same way as the primary care physician interrogates the patient. In both cases, question-and-answer formats are used to elicit and to structure 'information': the discourse structure itself inscribes the asymmetry in status and power of the respective parties.

Of course, in the instances, we have looked at already, there is no radical contrast between those 'voices' (in Mishler's sense). Demonstrably, both junior and senior physician are expressing the voice of medicine. The narrative of the student or junior is not at all like the stories that patients might seek to tell. Case presentations are couched in the register of clinical medicine. Their formats are clearly prescribed by professional medical conventions. Their *content* rarely strays beyond the strict confines of medically defined knowledge and vocabulary. On the other hand, there is clearly room for the voice of medicine to be realized in different formats, and for different voices to coexist in the medical domain. The possibility arises therefore, that there are many – or at least several – voices of medicine. Moreover, a first examination of this issue raises the intriguing possibility that those different voices might themselves be in conflict; or if not in conflict exactly, at least 'interrupt' one another. In other words, collegial discourse in medical settings might display contrasting orientations to medical work, knowledge and talk. Those orientations might – as in Mishler's analysis – reflect different assumptions about knowledge and the material world.

One of the most striking characteristics of speech exchange in daily rounds is the deployment of personal narratives and reminiscences on the part of *senior* physicians. Attending physicians seem to claim, tacitly, the right to tell personal stories and to relate medical knowledge back to their biographical experiences. These stories and personal experiences contrast with the narratives of case presentations. They represent two different modalities of medical knowledge. The stories of the senior physicians also interrupt the de-personalized accounts that are shared by seniors, juniors and students.

Consider, for instance, the following excerpt from a morning round or conference. The attending, the fellow and the student have been discussing the action of the drug heparin. The student asks a question:

St: Does heparin have a pretty short half life, doesn't it? So
F: Yeah, but there is a certain [*clears throat*] there's a certain amount I think that *does* get bound to the platelet and the endothelium and sticks around. In most cases *stopping* it or starting aspirin, and there's been a suggestion the reason why protamine hasn't and it's been sort of *twofold*. One they're not sure exactly what they're neutralizing, and *two*, they feel that they may *exacerbate* the problem with the protamine. Since you have somebody who's *clotting* and to give them *pro*tamine, you know as Dr de Kalb says, you don't *titrate* it right, who knows how to *titrate* it, then you might actually make things *worse*.
At: So you got time for a quick, quick anecdote about um
F: Sure
At: I used to live in California at UCLA before I came to Beacon, this was years ago and my *chief* was Warren Ross Church, who was a very well known haematologist, and he used to take care of all the movie stars, and you know

F: Mfm

At: = and he would get *called*. And there was an *actress*, her name was Clara Raine, I don't know whether you every heard of her. One day I heard on the radio that she'd had a *stroke* and she was in hospital. And then *that* day Warren Church was called to see her along with everybody else.

F: Mm

At: And when *he* got called *I'd* get called, 'cos I had to go to do the *work*. So, I went to the hospital, and he wanted me to do a *clot*ting time – that's what we did in those days and a couple of other tests – and I'd brought along my water bath and everything 'cos I wanted to do it at thirty-seven degrees. There she was, she was un*conscious* and there was blood in the spinal fluid. I drew blood from her and I started doing a *clot*ting time and you know sort of (inverting) it in there, the blood wouldn't clot.

F: Mhuh

At: And I stood there for forty-five minutes and an hour and it just wouldn't *clot*. So I had some of my *own* blood taken and we mixed *my* blood with *her* blood and then *my* blood wouldn't clot. So she had some sort of, certainly, anticoagulant, and it really was severe, because when I diluted her blood it *still* had anticoagulant.

F: Mm

At: I *then* found out that she'd been going to an internist in Beverly Hills who was giving people *heparin* in large doses to prevent atherosclerosis or something, there was some *theory* he had and he had a lot of patients coming in and he'd given her a, you know he wasn't contr*olling* it, and they omitted this in the history. And er I got out the protamine and I tried to *tit*rate it used a little bit in vitro before giving it to her and calculated a *dose*, and we gave it to her and then I was supposed to come back the next day for rep*eat* tests and as I was driving down Sunset Boulevard I had my radio on and I heard she'd died.

St: Mm

At: But this was a case of heparin toxicity that, you know there was *no* history of it but I should say I think I did *two* sets of tests on her and the heparin was nearly *gone* the second time. You asked the half life. It has a rapid half life, but (that) popped into my head as she was telling about that, but er

F: Mhhm

St: So that was when you were a resident or?

At: = No it was at . . . I think I was just starting out as a research fellow. I don't know what I was, I can't remember

F: Hhuhuhhuh

At: Anyway. That'll be a good *topic* for a conference. Yeah

F: Hhuh

St: And so he had to have an amputation?

This stretch of talk arose out of the presentation and discussion of a patient with a sequence of problems associated with a heparin-induced state. To some extent, therefore, his medical troubles – which had culminated in an amputation – were iatrogenic in origin. At the point where the extract begins, the participants are discussing the nature of heparin itself and various approaches to its use. (That sequence itself has some interesting features and is discussed elsewhere.) The fellow responds to the student's question about the half-life of heparin by enunciating some of the principles and problems in using protamine to neutralize heparin. The fellow's account includes characteristic markers of *complexity* or *uncertainty*:

... there's a certain amount I think . . .
. . . there's been a suggestion . . . and it's been sort of . . .
. . . they're not sure exactly . . . they feel that they may . . .

This brief exposition of the tentative or provisional state of current knowledge is turned into a concluding moral or homily:

... you don't *titrate* it right, who knows how to *titrate* it, then you might actually make things *worse*.

At the point the fellow offers this modest advice, the attending physician explicitly claims the floor in order to produce a personal reminiscence. This story is notable for two reasons. First, it has intrinsic interest, given that it is about the death of a well-known movie star (and my pseudonym does indeed hide the identity of a well-known actress from the past). Secondly, it provides a vivid and memorable account of an iatrogenic problem related to the use of heparin. The story has a particular effect, which I suggest is generic to anecdotes such as this. The senior physician provides general advice and observations, pertaining to the medical matter in hand, which are based on his or her past experiences. The justification for the story as 'evidence' does not derive from the warrant of textbooks, journals or other sources of biomedical science. It derives primarily from a biographical frame of reference. The warrant that is implicitly claimed is that of *personal experience*, and the mode of presentation is transparently that of a story. Here, then, we find a narrative mode that is different from the narrative of the case presentation. The former is explicitly based on reminiscence and the narrator is clearly implicated in the story. This is the clearest divergence from the impersonal mode of medical discourse described by Anspach (1988) that I have also identified in the haematology data.

There is no doubt that this is a voice of medicine. The physician's account is quite recognizably grounded in the presuppositions and procedures of orthodox biomedicine. None the less, this is not quite the same voice as that which is reflected in standard case presentations, summaries and discussions. We can call it *the voice of personal experience*.

The following provides another clear example of this mode of personal narrative. The participants are discussing the action of the spleen, and the attending physician is drawing at the blackboard:

At: But I think that when the spleen really gets *going* and er some of the cells don't quite *make* it you may end up with a piece taken off something.
F: Mhmmm
At: = like so, a piece like *that* eventually it will be a spherocyte
F: Mhm
At: I'm sure that that's what it is. I remember a case that *I* saw a couple of years ago that really bears on this point about . . . Maybe I told you about this girl already but let me tell it again for the benefit of the students. This was a young *college* girl who who was home for Christmas, from I think it was Smith College, and she was perfectly *well*. She was at a party with her *family* on New Year's Eve and was *well*. The next day didn't feel very good. Everybody was joking that she'd had too much to drink and everything, but she *didn't* have too much to drink, and she became acutely ill during the day

and was brought into the hospital that night, and I saw her. And she had a very severe Coombs positive haemolytic anaemia with *fifty* per cent retics or something like that. And her white cells were hypersegmented. And for some reason we did a bone marrow, I don't know why. It was *very* megaloblastic. And I suspect that this thing was building up for a few days and then got severe, but in *those* few *days* it probably exhausted the folate reserves right there in the *bone* marrow. It's a very early sign of marrow overactivity, or dem*ands* on the marrow . . . That's what you have here. You may or may not find a low folate. The folate *will* be low if this keeps up. The folate is *low* in the bone marrow.

F: Mm
At: Well, that's interesting.

Here, then, the particular issue of medical knowledge – a clinical possibility illustrated from a single case – is located directly within a framework of *reminiscence*. This voice is not merely one of narrative reconstruction. In addition, this voice identifies medical knowledge and experience uniquely with the narrator. While not a voice of the lifeworld (in Mishler's sense), this is a voice that inscribes personal knowledge as the property of the teller. The recounting of personal experience by a senior clinician is by no means the only voice of *seniority* that can be identified in the data. Of equal importance is a voice of advice and maxims. This contrasts with the voice of journal and textbook medicine, in that it conveys a personalizing voice. It differs from the decontextualized knowledge of a generalized biomedicine. It conveys the personal advice of the clinician, and is frequently addressed directly to his or her junior colleagues, in that it formulates what 'you' ought to do. Equally, it may be expressed in terms of 'what I would do' in such circumstances.

The following case conference extract illustrates the deployment of such 'advice' from the attending physician:

F: Here this is what it was. He was treated on the second and his nadir was reached three days ago on about the eleventh, er ten days out there was approximately ten days out
At: Great. Excellent
F: So
At: Oh that's good
F: And the last time we treated him was with a thousand milligrammes
At: Mhm
F: Of Cytoxan thirty milligrams of Adria and one day I think of a hundred and twenty of VP sixteen
At: Mhm mhm
F: So um
At: I think we should go up on the Adria
F: Right, that's what I thought – keep the Cytoxan where it is? Or do you wanna
At: You could probably go up in both
F: Twelve hundred?
At: Yeah
F: And fifty
At: Twelve hundred and forty-five
F: = forty-four

At: Hahahh
F: Witchcraft
F: And the VP sixteen for only a day?
At: = You could you probably give him two days and see how he does
F: Yeah I think we should try to give him. And what I thought is since he's recovering now if he continues to recover, probably by the end of the week which would be about two, a little over two and a half weeks.
At: = Mhm
F: = by Thursday, Friday we can repeat the
At: =Mhm
F: = cycle while he's still here it would be wonderful
At: Ye-yeah I wouldn't give it more often than three weeks
F: Okay. He was treated on the second so
At: = I wouldn't try and push it up. I think you'll, you might get into a little trouble because.
F: Okay even though they're concurrent?
At: Yeah, I'd be a little dubious about going faster
F: Okay, so three weeks would be twenty-one days right?
At: Yes
F: From the second so the twenty-third
At: = so, the twenty-third
At: So we're talking about mid next week
At: Mhm
F: Okay

In the following example, the senior physician aligns a personalized view of appropriate treatment with a historical perspective on what 'we' in the specialty have had available. This is not the only example in the data in which the senior physician relates his or her preferred knowledge to such a historical frame of reference. It is noteworthy that the fellow begins with a statement of the patient's treatment having been 'typical', while attending physician contrasts that claim with a more personal warrant.

F: The other I guess the other issue was, well the course was for you know the typical four days
At: Four days
F: = for every six weeks? Is that? mm
At: Well
F: Four days?
At: I think optimally you should give it more often than that
F: Mm
At: But I think you can usually get away with that. We'll get on in a minute to the optimal treatment regimens in different myelomas. Let's talk about normal treatment to begin with. I think that in her case I'd probably have done the same thing – I'd probably go with that kind of regimen. And the reason is that I'd like to get a little response before I go in with more multiple drugs, just in terms of her being intravenous.
F: Mhm. As opposed to being high dose
At: Um I wouldn't like
F: = intravenous Cytoxan
At: *No* what I'm talking about. Well let's just talk about it now
F: Okay
At: I think historically, Melphalan–Prednisone, well historically before that looking at single agents for myeloma we had nothing before the alkylating drugs came in. So like in the fifties people began to use alkylating agents and

getting some response in myeloma. Then Prednisone was found to potentiate the effect and traditionally therefore it's become an alkylating agent and Prednisone. Then the only really significant thing before you get into controversial territory was the addition of Vincristine and just studies comparing Melphalan-Prednisone *with* Vincristine does show that there is an improved – slightly improved – response rate and slightly improved survival by the addition of Vincristine. So I think unless there's a contraindication to Vincristine that has now replaced Melphalan–Prednisone as the standard form of initial treatment.

F: The three drugs, mhm
At: Mm right. Now the controversy comes as to whether you can improve on that by giving more drugs
St: Four drug regimen
At: Giving four drugs instead of three or other drugs and screening for single agents we haven't really come up with anything that potentially would really make a big difference. For example the response rate to Adriamycin is no greater than the response rate of alkylating agents. It's not that like in many diseases. You're adding a more aggressive drug and you can really go more places. But in fact Adriamycin is not that great a drug compared to the alkylating agents, nor is platinum, nor is anything else. However studies have come out and SWOG – the South West Oncology Group – has been very active in myeloma, and they have come out with some more aggressive regimens that they are now touting as the standard treatment for myelomas compared to the MEP regimens. And we're talking about four drugs now, we're talking about for example VMCP which would be the same regimen but with the addition of Cytoxan as the fourth drug.

The following example of a senior clinician's maxim arises out of a discussion of one of the patients diagnosed as having aplastic anaemia. The fellow and the attending have have just begun responsibility for the service's consults, and are – as it were – catching up on cases like this. The attending physician has been cross-questioning the fellow about the case and its management.

At: . . . Should have got his chest *CAT* scanned, did he have one? Looking for a thymoma?
F: I don't know what his actual workup was. It's an interesting thought. I would hope, I mean I would presume that they went through the differential . . . Would you routinely do a CT scan, yeah? For something like this? I guess that you would
At: Without question. Without question. Because you can't pick those up *without* a CAT scan and . . . you know *one* of several things that enter into the differential when, you know when you have someone who comes in with pancytopenia. [*To student*] Sophie, if you could pre*dict* at this stage one fact or piece of information that Hale's given us which has allowed this man to be alive with his diagnosis there now six or eight weeks after we've met him, what could be the one bit of information that Hale's given us that makes sense to why he's hanging in there the way he has?

Here, then, the senior clinician typically translates his turn into the opening move for an instructional exchange with the medical student. Before that, however, one can see how he articulates axiomatic advice or *maxim knowledge* about what 'you' should do in situations like the present one. It is noticeable too that this statement is marked as a categorical one ('without question'). The more junior colleague's tentative query about whether a scan should routinely be undertaken is responded to with an unequivocal response on the part of the senior colleague. (A review of the various presentations and discussions of this particular patient's history and diagnosis suggest that a scan in search of a possible thymoma had not previously been ordered as part of the workup of his aplastic anaemia. It is hard to be certain about that: there is never a single, definitive statement of the 'case'.)

The following extract is taken from a different account of the same patient, between the same attending and a different fellow. Here they are joined by another resident physician (R) from the medical service, who was at that time participating in various haematology meetings and conferences.

R: But is this guy haemolysing?
At: = What it is is that many times following aplastic anaemia you can have PNH. *PNH* can produce aplastic anaemia and then either one of these can go on to leukaemia. So there is some kind of a link between these three things and er certainly.
R: But you don't have to actually see haemolysis, right? At the time of a clinically significant haemolysis you don't always see it, do you?
At: In the regular PNH patient you always see a haemolytic component, *especially* after exercise . . . If you *tie* their legs with a tourniquet and put them on the bike, as they did once at the [Hospital], you will see haemolysis (down) from the increased lactic acidosis . . .

In the presentation of maxims and advice, therefore, a voice of medicine is heard that contrasts with other voices. It and the personalizing voices of reminiscence also contrast with the *voice of journal science*. While reproduced orally, this realizes the biomedical knowledge of decontextualized biomedical science. Here the clinician warrants his or her knowledge by more or less direct reference to research. I refer to it as the voice of journal science, even though specific publications may not be cited, in order to recall Ludwik Fleck's usage, as I shall explore below (Fleck, 1935).

In the following sequence, for example, we can identify the invocation of research and journal science, coupled with personal advice and maxims from the attending physician. The discussion is between the attending, a fellow and a student:

At: Yeah. And the other figure I remember I think also came out of that study. Oh no, it's a different study, maybe this was the (Karl) study. They looked at the data every possible way, they must have a computer buff there, but they took all cases of lymphoma, B cell lymphoma, that they had and saw the incidence of monoclonal gamopathy in those patients and I think it was about six or seven per cent. So it's actually quite a low per cent, but very reproducible.
St: Mhm
At: Um and I think the converse was also true: of all monoclonal gamopathies about six per cent were lymphomas. So I think that's why I remember that number of six per cent
   . . .
At: . . . then just to talk about the light chain variants a minute . . . I don't know if you've had a chance to look at anything on that over the weekend. The paper that I remembered, I hadn't got a copy

St: = Mmm

At: = of but I brought along the American Journal. This is a good paper because it fits her light chain kappa

F: Oh light chain kappa what is that?

At: *This* was approached from a different point of view. This started out by saying that normally in myeloma > I mean it alluded to this < renal dysfunction is caused by light chains being excreted in the urine interacting with the tubules.

F: Mhn

. . .

At: And the debate about light – some light chains being more toxic than others. Alright, well that's very interesting except that what about people who present with renal failure and proteinuria? How many of those turn out to have myeloma? And that's the approach that these people took, and I guess that these were renal people.

St: Hm

At: Um pathology and hypertension nephrology unit. So they what they did was they took patients who *presented* with renal failure and proteinuria and I think they had about had over a thousand biopsies that they had done and thirteen of these thousand-some biopsies or eleven patients who were not only not diabetic but had also presented in this way, they did biopsies on and they found [*they look at the figures in the journal offprint*] they found eleven patients out of this thousand-some who had light chain nephropathy as their initial presentation.

F: And how did they make the diagnosis? Based on staining?

At: Yes

F: 'Cos she needs to have that done

At: This was a pathological analysis, and they took the biopsies and they stained them. They looked at them then looked at immunohistochemistry and made a couple of other stains.

. . .

At: So you know, it's not *rare* rare, it's uncommon. And they looked at the clinical features of these eleven patients that they'd pulled out and let's see [*consults the journal offprint*]. So a lot of them presented with symptoms of renal failure, renal involvement, > pretty much all had renal involvement < but other systems involvement, if you look at plasmacytosis greater than thirty per cent, only four out of eleven had that to go along with the diagnosis of myeloma. This table was also quite useful 'cos it lists the eleven *patients* and talks about what the IEPs showed and some of them were *normal*. Serum IEPs were normal.

. . .

At: Some of them turned out on retrospective to have a lot of – I would say about fif–er thir–er > what did I say < thirty per cent of them, or four out of eleven, had plasmacytosis of a significant degree, greater than thirty per cent to make a diagnosis. But some did and some did *not* have IEP findings to go along with that. But all of them had these deposits that stained in the kidney with kappa

St: Okay

At: = And lambda chain

St: Hhm

At: So it *can* present this way . . . It's *rare* but it's an entity

F: = Right

At: = that you should be looking for. If someone has renal failure and proteinuria you should probably stain with the kappa and lambda chains

F: Consider the IEP.

At: And *then* consider an IEP. So it's something that you can be caught out on because it's rare but now having now come across it you shouldn't.

The following extract from a morning round illustrates the intersection of voices – of personal knowledge and journal science. It is noteworthy that the senior physician, the attending, articulates and – to some extent – adjudicates between the respective warrants for knowledge. The discussion was occasioned by the death of a patient whom the haematologists had been following. He had hairy cell leukaemia, but there were other aspects of his case that had been giving cause for concern. The discussion – between the attending physician, a resident in Medicine, a fellow and a student – centres on the possible role of the medication the patient had been receiving.

F: As a matter of fact we were all worried about his bleeding time prolongation. We got platelet aggregation studies and a rist [and Coopers] *pending* and he was on Amalcar initially because I guess they thought he had a ruptured *Berry* and we, you know, we talked about whether *that* could, you know. The case reports have, we're actually gonna look that up today, high dose Amalcar. He became suddenly dyspnoeic, looked like he may have had a pulmonary embolus. He also had a gallstone

At: The other day

F: So·

R: Well what's the issue? I mean, here's a prolonged bleeding time. You're worried about it and it looks like he *may* have had a pulmonary embolus but . . . he did *not* bleed. The *question* is what did he do? Was he primary? He had a *cardiac*, 'cos he did have epicarditis and had a valve perforation or something like *that* or it was a primary process with dyspnoea and *hopefully* the Alamcar. The Amalcar got started last week, so it was six or seven days. [*To attending*] What is your experience?

At: I have never, never *seen* any problems or . . . *Certainly* there *are* reports. I don't *think* we have ever seen one in *this* place.

St: Mm

R: It's certainly routinely done for patients on subarachnoid haemorrhage

At: Well, even on double blind study there seems to be no doubt that that diminishes the amount of bleeding

R: I forget the incidence that the literature on significant enhancement

At: Of?

R: Of thrombic phenomena

At: Right, from Amalcar

R: Yeah I mean it's in the order of like five to ten per cent.

At: I am *unaware* of that high incidence. There are reports, but if it *has* become a statistic I was unaware of it

. . .

At: I am not saying you're wrong . . . *I* was unaware of it. Every time I have *looked*

R: What do you think about the data

At: = On re-bleeding on Amalcar? It's not really ever been shown to . . . There was one *large* study that was published over the past five years where before that again it was a routine thing, and then within the past five years there was one study that was published that *distinctly* established that this was, *this* diminished. And pulmonary embolism as far as *I* know is from Amalcar is not the common thing, it's CVAs and there are other thrombotic problems . . . I don't see why not, why you could not get a pulmonary embolism

R: = Mm
At: And lots of people could *use* it. The only problem with what would happen if
        you used it over a prolonged period of *time*. If you look at the places where
        they use it often. Upstairs in the SICU they use it very often and it's
R: = It's supposed to be contraindicated in haematuria. Right? A lot of people
        say right because the
At: = The only contraindication in haematuria *again* is from reports of
        haemophiliacs, where when they have a lot of bleeding . . .

Here again, then, we can see how seniority is reflected in the voices of
medicine. The more junior physician – the resident – is of course seeking the
attending physician's views quite explicitly. Indeed, there are contextual
grounds for suspecting that the resident's inquiries were not altogether
disinterested. They appeared to be part of a procedural display of
well-informed enthusiasm. He seemed to be managing a self-presentation as
a keen junior colleague. Be that as it may, the spoken discourse is
noteworthy for the various knowledge-bases and their respective warrants
that the doctors invoke. Of particular interest is the relationship between a
journal science mode, in which reference is made to case reports, double-
blind clinical trials and published statistics. This is contrasted with the senior
physician's personal knowledge, supported with references to his biographical warrant: what *he* has seen, and what *he* is aware of. It is not exactly the
case that one mode of knowledge is privileged over the other. The attending
physician does not quite contradict the junior colleague's reported claims.
On the other hand, the personal experience of the older and more senior
man is certainly not superseded or overriden by the knowledge of journal
science. Indeed, it is a feature of such clinical discourse that different
orientations or (in Schutz's terms) attitudes may co-exist. The example
presented above also illustrates the expression of *local* knowledge and
traditions in the warranting of knowledge. The attending physician makes
explicit reference to what has been seen 'in this place' and practice in the
neighbouring Surgical Intensive Care Unit (SICU). This is one of the
constituent features in the discursive production of experience in medical
knowledge and practice. It is a mode of knowledge that is locally
contextualized, grounded in the traditions and practices of particular places
and clinical teams. Such a warrant for knowledge is related directly to the
oral transmission of knowledge intergenerationally within a firm.

Conclusion

In collegial interactions such as these, therefore, we can see in operation
alternative, even competing, modes of knowledge. Medical knowledge and
practice are warranted on different grounds. The scientific basis of medicine
is frequently invoked by the haematologists, but it is by no means the only
source of legitimacy. Various sources of personal knowledge are also
invoked. In contrast to the decontextualized and impersonal modes of
journal science there exist various forms of personal knowledge. Some of

those are expressed in narrative ways, especially in the personal anecdotes of recollection and biographically grounded experience. These are almost exclusively the prerogative of senior physicians. Of course, by virtue of their seniority and extended professional careers, they have more such knowledge to draw on, but that is not the whole story. The nature of seniority itself is partly constituted by physicians' rights to tell such stories. The differential distribution of authority within the clinical team in turn implies the unequal distribution of such discursive rights and resources.

The same is true of the use of maxims. A good deal of practical knowledge in clinical medicine is transmitted through aphorisms, proverbial formulations and similar forms (cf. Bursztajn and Hamm, 1979). Here again we can see the discursive expression of authority. Maxim-knowledge reflects seniority and also draws on essentially personal authority for its expression.

This analysis of the voices of medicine took Mishler's contribution as a point of departure. Its outcome has been to call into question his treatment of the voice of medicine. By shifting the sociological gaze away from the dyad of doctor and patient one can see that medical discourse does not articulate a single lifeworld. There are cleavages and fault-lines running through the culture of medicine. The tensions between alternating frames of reference emerge repeatedly in processes of knowledge production and reproduction. In tracing those differences my analysis also owes something to Fleck, who distinguished between different modes of scientific knowledge. He distinguished between *journal* science, *textbook* science, *vade-mecum* science and popular science. He suggested that there are regular processes of knowledge transformation as it passes (as it were) from one site of knowledge representation to another. As one moves from journals, through textbooks and vade-mecums, or handbooks, to popular works, so knowledge becomes increasingly categorical, increasingly *apodictic* in its expression (see also Kahn, 1983). There Fleck was dealing primarily with textual representations of scientific knowledge. If we trace some of the frameworks of spoken knowledge production, then we can see how medical opinion can also become increasingly apodictic as one moves from journal science to the primarily personal warrants of experience. Apodictic knowledge is quintessentially transmitted through maxims and through the lessons of anecdote and recollection.

8

Conclusion

My goal in this book has not been the production of a general ethnography of a medical setting; nor has it been a general essay on the sociology of work and medical knowledge. Rather, I have tried to use the data from haematology to address a number of related themes in the sociology of medical knowledge. I do not recapitulate them here. They are intended to contribute to the micro-sociology of medical knowledge. That is, an understanding of how knowledge is produced and reproduced in particular local settings. Knowledge is approached as the outcome of everyday work, and much of that work is enacted through talk shared among medical colleagues.

It is not, I think, just the idiosyncratic focus of this book that leads me to be struck by the extent to which patients provide occasions for talk in the clinic. As I have tried to capture in this book, the discourse of medicine stretches far more widely than the current coverage of the social sciences might imply. Sociologists, anthropologists and linguists have become unduly preoccupied with the clinical encounter between the patient and the medical practitioner. That face-to-face encounter is undoubtedly important, and its significance is enhanced when it is treated as a synecdoche for the cultural politics of health care in contemporary society. The clinical encounter, from that perspective, can partly stand for the institutional frameworks within which are enacted the hidden injuries of class, race and gender.

Nevertheless, the consultation between patient and practitioner is but one locus of medical discourse. It does not capture the complex organization of modern medicine. Indeed, an obsessive focus on the one-to-one clinical consultation makes the tone of so much medical sociology and anthropology seem almost nostalgic for a simpler age of medical work. As I have tried to emphasize, the complexity of modern medicine seems all too often to elude sociological and anthropological observers. The clinical gaze of bedside medicine has been supplemented (but not supplanted) by the laboratory gaze and the distinctive technologies of modern medicine (Reiser, 1978), while medical work itself is increasingly located in organizations of considerable complexity. Responsibility for patient management is thus distributed among a quite bewildering array of specialisms and sub-specialisms. It becomes increasingly important for a sociology of the clinic to pay some attention, therefore, to the distribution of knowledge and expertise within this complex social and technical division of labour. The vantage point of research in a consulting discipline which itself draws on the work of the laboratory has helped to bring such issues to the foreground.

Medical discourse, then, goes far beyond the dyad of patient and practitioner. Indeed, much of it is socially and physically divorced from the patient. I make no apology for the virtual absence from this book of patients as social actors in their own right. It serves to highlight how patients and their cases are assembled elsewhere, in professional talk that constitutes them as the objects of description and action. In the course of this book we get occasional, sometimes tantalizing, glimpses of some of the haematologists' 'consults'. The full corpus of data, in fact, allows one to trace the career of particular cases from round to round, from presentation to presentation, over several weeks. It is, however, appropriate that we should, as it were, see the patients askance and from a distance. Of course, the haematologists saw their patients and so did I in their company. Yet I want to convey not just a characteristic of this one group of haematologists, but a general feature of modern medicine. That is, the dislocation of the case from the patient's bedside and indeed from the patient's physical presence. The sick person is resolved into fragments of corporeal and other traces. He or she is repeatedly transmuted into objects of scrutiny and discourse 'elsewhere'. It is that process, or aspects of it, that I have tried to evoke.

It is, then, against such a background that I have documented aspects of the liturgy of the clinic. In employing that phrase I have sought deliberately to capitalize on the connotations of the liturgical. I do so in order to emphasize two related things: the extent to which medicine is accomplished and celebrated through ritualized forms, and the element of performance that runs through so much medical culture, even in its most advanced and technologized manifestations. Medicine retains its ceremonial forms within the most bureaucratized of organizational settings. The grand round, the teaching round, the clinical lecture, the mortality review and other settings all contribute to the spectacular enactment of medical culture. Some such ceremonies are highly theatrical, and remind one of the spectacle of, say, the Padua anatomy theatre or the theatricality of clinical lectures by figures like Charcot. Others are more mundane, more profane, but still retain the characteristic forms of observance.

The liturgy of the round or the conference is a collection of culturally prescribed devices whereby medical work is accomplished in stable and predictable ways. The presentation of the case at a conference or review, for instance, normally conforms to ritualized formats. The resulting narration of the case is one powerful way in which it is assembled *as* a case. It is a device whereby the diverse types and sources of knowledge, and actions derived from different time-frames, are brought together under the auspices of a single discursive organization and made available for the collective gaze of medical colleagues. One may metaphorically substitute the narrative for the body of the patient as the object of clinical scrutiny.

The liturgical reconstruction of the case in the course of rounds is also a potent device for the reproduction of medical knowledge. Throughout the extracts of data reproduced in the preceding chapters, we have seen medical students who are learning to perceive and to narrate in approved ways. The discussion of a case may well provoke disagreement and dissent. It is equally, however, a mechanism whereby the forms of knowing are affirmed and reproduced. In that sense, therefore, the liturgy of the clinic mobilizes the participation and cultural acquiescence of its participants.

We have seen also how the liturgy of the clinic embodies the varieties of knowledge that co-exist within the modern clinic. Professional knowledge, whether we label it as biomedicine or not, is far from homogeneous. The clinical mentality endorses various types and sources of valid knowledge. Clinical knowledge and action are warranted in contrasting ways. It is part of the strength of clinical medicine that it can accommodate such variety. It is, therefore, rash and inadequate to treat the discourse of medicine as monolithic. The discourse of rounds and conferences is inhabited, as I have tried to indicate, by different voices. Those voices, as they are described metaphorically, reflect contrasting orientations to medical knowledge. An adequate representation of medical work and medical culture must take full account of the co-existence of these alternating frames of reference. The personal knowledge of the clinician and the depersonalized knowledge of journal science may be expressed in harmony or they may compete for legitimacy, used as contested warrants for diagnosis and actions.

Clinical discourse – by which I mean actual uses of language, not a vague formulation of culture – is thus revealed as complex and variegated. Through its rhetorical forms are articulated the division of labour and the distribution of authority among practitioners. It provides powerful resources for the expression of orientations towards knowledge and opinion. I have tried to show, for instance, how the discourse of clinical discussions is subtly coded for the expression of certainty and doubt.

The nature and functions of uncertainty in clinical practice have been investigated from various sociological and anthropological perspectives. Uncertainty has been repeatedly represented as a pervasive feature of medical culture and clinical decision-making. Here I have explored how opinion is expressed in medical discourse to display attitudes of tentativeness, confidence or dogmatism. Again, I have tried to show that these are not simple matters. The attention to evidentials is not intended to contribute to formal linguistics in this area. Rather, it is used to demonstrate the complexity of clinical culture and talk. Neither uncertainty, nor over-confidence, nor dogmatism are all-encompassing features of medical knowledge. Equally, medical knowledge is defined exclusively by neither indeterminacy nor technicality. These analysts' terms reflect practitioners' occasioned attitudes towards knowledge and action. They are context-dependent and matters of local accomplishment. Global characterizations of medical or biomedical culture in such terms are liable to fall wide of the mark, therefore. Equally, attempts to deal with uncertainty by means of decision-making models and algorithms, or to incorporate micro-economic models into medical reasoning are likely to founder precisely because of their failure to recognize the complexities of practical work and thought. As I have tried to illustrate, these issues need to be grasped through a linguistically informed phenomenology. Analyses of how physicians reason among themselves must take full account of the practical acts of talk and thought that embody decision-making processes.

It has been implicit throughout this book, and explicit at places, that many contemporary treatments of decision-making in clinical contexts are flawed in one way or another. Too many neglect the organizational contexts within which medical work is conducted. By that I mean not just that they are too simple, for simplification is a virtue if used to create ideal types and models. I mean that they mistake the nature of such acts fundamentally. They too readily miss the organizational and discursive production of knowledge and action. Too many advocates of decision-making models also assume that professional actions are to be explained primarily in terms of mental acts, and bounded events of deciding. In the first place, the haematologists operate more like the reflective practitioner, as described by Schon (1983). That is, their expert knowledge is expressed through practical activities, and is often the emergent property of interaction between colleagues, or of processes over time. It is far from clear that one is dealing with unitary acts, mental or otherwise, rather than social processes. The liturgy of the clinic enshrines procedures of collegial talk through which past acts, current opinions and projected actions are endorsed, challenged, justified and negotiated. The processes of knowledge production and opinion formation are dispersed in time, space and personnel. It is more useful to understand how these practices occur in naturally arising settings than to devise models and expert systems with the aim of supplanting them.

I do not mean to conclude with the impression that I am preoccupied solely with the adequate representation of decision-making *per se*. I have addressed that specific analytic issue as a way of pointing up the complexity and the variety of shared talk in these clinical settings. The joint production of medical knowledge and opinion is a topic that repays close scrutiny. It provides important insight into the day-to-day accomplishment of contemporary medicine. We still lack a systematic and cumulative sociology of medical knowledge that will stand comparison with the sociology of scientific knowledge. We need ever closer collaboration between the respective scholarly networks, and more studies of medical knowledge production that will complement the corpus of laboratory studies of scientific work.

Appendix: Use of Transcription Conventions

As I have explained in the text, the tape-recordings of rounds, conferences and other interactions were transcribed delicately, using the full range of typographical conventions that are now standard for the purposes of conversation analysis. Such transcripts are intended to capture a variety of the features of spoken action, such as pauses (timed), false starts and interruptions, stress, relative amplitude, audible intakes of breath or exhalations, noticeable lengthening of sounds and syllables. In preparing data extracts for publication and commentary here I have deliberately simplified the transcripts. The interaction has, therefore, been rendered in a more readable fashion. This has involved the removal of some of the slight hesitations, repetitions, incomplete words and other common aspects of speech that are inessential to the kind of commentary I have offered here.

I have retained some of the normal conventions, and they are listed and explained here.

(word)	parentheses round a word or words indicate uncertainty about the transcription
( )	empty parentheses indicate failure to transcribe a word or part of an utterance
[ ]	brackets indicate onset and end of simultaneous talk
=	equals sign indicates 'latching' of utterances with no intervening silence
,.?	punctuation indicates intonation contours, not grammatical categories
wor–	word cut off abruptly
word	italics indicate emphasis
WORD	upper case indicates increased loudness
<word>	noticeable slowing of speech tempo
>word<	noticeable increase in speech tempo
. . .	omission of portion of transcript

References

Amann, K. and Knorr-Cetina, K. (1990) 'The fixation of (visual) evidence', in M. Lynch and S. Woolgar (eds), *Representation in Scientific Practice*. Cambridge, Mass.: MIT Press. pp. 85–121.

Anspach, R. (1987) 'Prognostic conflict in life-and-death decisions: the organization as an ecology of knowledge', *Journal of Health and Social Behavior*, 28: 215–31.

Anspach, R. (1988) 'Notes on the sociology of medical discourse: the language of case presentation', *Journal of Health and Social Behavior*, 29: 357–75.

Arksey, H. (1994) 'Expert and lay participation in the construction of medical knowledge', *Sociology of Health and Illness*, 16: 448–68.

Arluke, A. (1980) 'Roundsmanship: inherent control on a medical teaching ward', *Social Science and Medicine*, 14A: 297–302.

Armstrong, D. (1983) *Political Anatomy of the Body: Medical Knowledge in Britain in the Twentieth Century*. Cambridge: Cambridge University Press.

Armstrong, D. (1990) 'Use of the genealogical method in the exploration of chronic illness: a research note', *Social Science and Medicine*, 30: 1225–7.

Arney, W. R. (1982) *Power and the Profession of Obstetrics*. Chicago: University of Chicago Press.

Atkinson, J. M. (1982) 'Understanding formality: notes on the categorization and production of "formal" interaction', *British Journal of Sociology*, 33: 86–117.

Atkinson, J. M. and Drew, P. (1979) *Order in Court: The Organisation of Verbal Interaction in Judicial Settings*. London: Macmillan.

Atkinson, P. (1976) 'The clinical experience: an ethnography of medical education'. Unpublished PhD thesis, University of Edinburgh.

Atkinson, P. (1977) 'The reproduction of medical knowledge', in C. Heath, R. Dingwall, M. Reid and M. Stacey (eds), *Health Care and Health Knowledge*. London: Croom Helm. pp. 85–106.

Atkinson, P. (1981a) *The Clinical Experience: The Construction and Reconstruction of Medical Reality*. Farnborough: Gower.

Atkinson, P. (1981b) 'Time and cool patients', in P. Atkinson and C. Heath (eds), *Medical Work: Realities and Routines*. Farnborough: Gower. pp. 41–54.

Atkinson, P. (1984) 'Training for certainty', *Social Science and Medicine*, 19: 949–56.

Atkinson, P. (1985) 'Talk and identity: some convergences in micro-sociology', in S. N. Eisenstadt and H. J. Helle (eds), *Perspectives on Sociological Theory Volume 2: Micro-Sociological Theory*. Beverly Hills, Calif.: Sage. pp. 117–32.

Atkinson, P. (1988) 'Discourse, descriptions and diagnoses', in M. Lock and D. Gordon (eds), *Biomedicine Examined*. Dordrecht: Kluwer.

Atkinson, P. (1989) 'Voices from the past', *Sociology of Health and Illness*, 11: 78–82.

Atkinson, P. (1990) *The Ethnographic Imagination: Textual Constructions of Reality*. London: Routledge.

Atkinson, P. (1992a) 'The ethnography of a medical setting: reading, writing and rhetoric', *Qualitative Health Research*, 2: 451–74.

Atkinson, P. (1992b) *Understanding Ethnographic Texts*. Newbury Park, Calif.: Sage.

Atkinson, P. (1994) 'Rhetoric as skill', in M. Bloor and P. Taraborrelli (eds), *Qualitative Research in Health and Medicine*. Aldershot: Avebury. pp. 110–30.

Banks, C. G. (1992) '"Culture" in culture-bound syndromes: the case of anorexia nervosa', *Social Science and Medicine*, 34: 867–84.

Barnes, B. (1977) *Interests and the Growth of Knowledge*. London: Routledge and Kegan Paul.

Barrett, R. J. (1993) 'Clinical writing and the documentary construction of schizophrenia', *Culture, Medicine and Psychiatry*, 12: 265–99.

Bartley, M. (1990) 'Do we need a strong programme in medical sociology?', *Sociology of Health and Illness*, 12: 371–90.

Bates, M. S. (1990) 'A critical perspective on coronary artery disease and coronary bypass surgery', *Social Science and Medicine*, 30: 249–60.

Baumann, A. O., Deber, R. B. and Thompson, G. G. (1991) 'Overconfidence among physicians and nurses: the "micro-certainty, macro-uncertainty" phenomenon', *Social Science and Medicine*, 32: 167–74.

Becker, H. S., Geer, B., Hughes, E. C. and Strauss, A. L. (1961) *Boys in White: Student Culture in Medical School*. Chicago: University of Chicago Press.

Berg, M. (1992) 'The construction of medical disposals: medical sociology and medical problem solving in clinical practice', *Sociology of Health and Illness*, 14: 151–80.

Berger, P. L. and Luckmann, T. (1967) *The Social Construction of Reality*. London: Allen Lane.

Bloor, D. (1976) *Knowledge and Social Imagery*. London: Routledge and Kegan Paul.

Bloor, M. (1976a) 'Professional autonomy and client exclusion: a study in ENT clinics', in M. Wadsworth and D. Robinson (eds), *Studies in Everyday Medical Life*. London: Martin Robertson, pp. 52–68.

Bloor, M. (1976b) 'Bishop Berkeley and the adeno-tonsillectomy enigma', *Sociology*, 10: 43–61.

Bloor, M. (1978) 'On the routinised nature of work in people-processing agencies: the case of adenotonsillectomy assessments in ENT out-patient clinics', in A. Davies (ed.), *Relationships Between Doctors and Patients*. Farnborough: Gower.

Blumhagen, D. (1980) 'Hyper-tension: a folk illness with a medical name', *Culture, Medicine and Psychiatry*, 4: 197–227.

Bond, J. and Bond, S. (1986) *Sociology and Health Care*. Edinburgh: Churchill Livingstone.

Bosk, C. L. (1979) *Forgive and Remember: Managing Medical Failure*. Chicago: University of Chicago Press.

Bracegirdle, B. (1978) *A History of Microtechnique*. Ithaca, NY: Cornell University Press.

Broadhead, R. S. (1983) *The Private Lives and Professional Identity of Medical Students*. New Brunswick: Transaction Books.

Bronzino, J. D., Smith, V. H. and Wade, M. L. (1990) *Medical Technology and Society: An Interdisciplinary Perspective*. Cambridge, Mass.: MIT Press.

Brown, P. (1993) 'Psychiatric intake as a mystery story', *Cul;ture, Medicine and Psychiatry*, 17: 255–80.

Brown, P. and Funk, S .C. (1986) 'Tardive dyskinesia: barriers to the professional recognition of an iatrogenic disease', *Journal of Health and Social Behaviour*, 27: 116–32.

Bucher, R. and Strauss, A. L. (1961) 'Professions in process', *American Journal of Sociology*, 66: 325–54.

Burkett, G. and Knafl, K. (1976) 'Judgement and decision-making in a medical specialty', *Sociology of Work and Occupations*, 1: 82–109.

Bursztajn, H. and Hamm, R. M. (1979) 'Medical maxims: two views of science', *Yale Journal of Biology and Medicine*, 52: 483–6.

Bursztajn, H. J., Feinbloom, R. I., Hamm, R. M. and Brodsky, A. (1990) *Medical Choices, Medical Chances: How Patients, Families, and Physicians Can Cope with Uncertainty*. New York: Routledge.

Bury, M. R. (1982) 'Chronic illness as biographical disruption', *Sociology of Health and Illness*, 5: 158–95.

Bury, M. R. (1986) 'Social constructionism and the development of medical sociology', *Sociology of Health and Illness*, 8: 137–69.

Bury, M. R. (1987) 'Social constructionism and medical sociology: a rejoinder to Nicolson and McLaughlin', *Sociology of Health and Illness*, 9: 439–41.

Calnan, M. (1984) 'Uncertainty: is it a problem in the doctor–patient relationship?', *Sociology of Health and Illness*, 6: 74–85.

Chafe, W. (1986) 'Introduction', in W. Chafe and J. Nichols (eds), *Evidentiality: The Linguistic Coding of Epistemology*. Norwood, NJ: Ablex.

Clark, J. A. and Mishler, E. G. (1992) 'Attending to patients' stories: referencing the clinical task', *Sociology of Health and Illness*, 14: 344–72.

Clarke, A. E. and Fujimura, J. H. (eds) (1992) *The Right Tools for the Job: At Work in Twentieth-Century Life Sciences*. Princeton: Princeton University Press.

Collins, H. M. (1984) 'Concepts and practice of participatory fieldwork', in C. Bell and H. Roberts (eds), *Social Researching*. London: Routledge and Kegan Paul.

Collins, H. M. (1990a) *Artificial Experts: Social Knowledge and Intelligent Machines*. Cambridge, Mass.: MIT Press.

Collins H. M. (1990b) 'Expert systems and the science of knowledge', in W. E. Bijker, T. P. Hughes and T. Pinch (eds), *The Social Construction of Technological Systems*. Cambridge, Mass.: MIT Press. pp. 329–48.

Conn, H. J. (1961) *Biological Stains: A Handbook on the Nature and Uses of the Dyes Used in the Biological Laboratory*, 7th edn. Baltimore: Williams and Wilkins.

Cortazzi, M. (1993) *Narrative Analysis*. London: Falmer.

Daly, J. (1989) 'Innocent murmurs: echocardiography and the diagnosis of cardiac normality', *Sociology of Health and Illness*, 11: 99–116.

Davenport, H. W. (1987) *Doctor Dock: Teaching and Learning Medicine at the Turn of the Century*. New Brunswick: Rutgers University Press.

Davis, K. (1988) *Power Under the Microscope*. Dordrecht: Floris Publications.

Delvecchio-Good, M.-J. (1985) 'Discourses on physician competence', in R. A. Hahn and A. D. Gaines (eds), *Physicians of Western Medicine: Anthropological Approaches to Theory and Practice*. Dordrecht: Reidel.

Denig, P., Haaijer-Ruskamp, F. M., Wesseling, H. and Versluis, A. (1993) 'Towards understanding treatment preferences of hospital physicians', *Social Science and Medicine*, 36: 915–24.

Dingwall, R. (1977) *Aspects of Illness*. London: Martin Robertson.

Douglas, M. (1970) *Natural Symbols*. London: Barrie and Rockliff.

Dowie, J. and Elstein, A. (1988) (eds) *Professional Judgment: A Reader in Clinical Decision Making*. Cambridge: Cambridge University Press.

Dubois, B. L. (1987) '"Something on the order of around forty to forty-five": imprecise numerical expressions in biomedical slide talks', *Language in Society*, 16: 527–41.

Elstein, A. S., Shulman, L. S. and Sprafka, S. A. (1978) *Medical Problem Solving: An Analysis of Clinical Reasoning*. Cambridge, Mass.: Harvard University Press.

Fenn, R. K. (1982) *Liturgies and Trials: The Secularization of Religious Language*. Oxford: Basil Blackwell.

Ferrante, J. (1988) 'Biomedical versus cultural constructions of abnormality: the case of idiopathic hirsutism in the United States', *Culture, Medicine and Psychiatry*, 12: 219–38.

Fisher, S. (1984) 'Doctor–patient communication: a social and micro-political performance', *Sociology of Health and Illness*, 6: 1–29.

Fisher, S. and Todd, A. D. (eds) (1983) *The Social Organization of Doctor–Patient Communication*. Washington, DC: Center for Applied Linguistics.

Fleck, L. (1927) 'Some specific features of the medical way of thinking', in R. S. Cohen and T. Schnelle (eds) (1986), *Cognition and Fact: Materials on Ludwik Fleck*. Dordrecht: Reidel.

Fleck, L. (1935) *Genesis and Development of a Scientific Fact*. First pub. Basle: Bruno Schwabe. English translation pub. 1979. Chicago: University of Chicago Press.

Foucault, M. (1973) *The Birth of the Clinic*. London: Tavistock.

Fox, N. J. (1992) *The Social Meaning of Surgery*. Milton Keynes: Open University Press.

Fox, R. (1957) 'Training for uncertainty', in R. K. Merton, G. Reader and P. L. Kendall (eds), *The Student Physician*. Cambridge, Mass.: Harvard University Press.

Fox, R. (1959) *Experiment Perilous: Physicians and Patients Facing the Unknown*. Glencoe, Ill.: Free Press.

Fox, R. (1980) 'The evolution of medical uncertainty', *Millbank Memorial Fund Quarterly*, 58: 1–49.

Fox, R. and Swazey, J. P. (1974) *The Courage to Fail: A Social View of Organ Transplants and Dialysis*. Chicago: University of Chicago Press.

Frankel, R. (1984) 'From sentence to sequence: understanding the medical encounter through micro-interactional analysis', *Discourse Processes*, 7: 135–70.

Freidson E. (1970) *Profession of Medicine*. New York: Dodd Mead.

Freidson, E. (1976) *Doctoring Together*. New York: Elsevier.

Fujimura, J. H. and Chou, D. Y. (1994) 'Dissent in science: styles of scientific practice and the controversy over the cause of AIDS', *Social Science and Medicine*, 38: 1017–36.

Gaines, A. D. (1992) 'From DSM-I to III-R; voices of self, mastery and the other: a cultural constructivist reading of U.S. psychiatric classification', *Social Science and Medicine*, 35: 3–24.

Gaines, A. D. and Hahn, R. A. (1985) 'Among the physicians: encounter, exchange and transformation', in R. A. Hahn, and A. D. Gaines (eds), *Physicians of Western Medicine: Anthropological Approaches to Theory and Practice*. Dordrecht: Reidel. pp. 3–22.

Gale, J. and Marsden, P. (1983) *Medical Diagnosis: From Student to Clinician*. Oxford: Oxford University Press.

Garfinkel, H. (1967) *Studies in Ethnomethodology*. Englewood Cliffs, NJ: Prentice-Hall.

Garro, Linda C. (1994) 'Narrative representations of chronic illness experience: cultural models of illness, mind, and body in stories concerning the temperomandibular joint (TMJ)', *Social Science and Medicine*, 38(6): 775–88.

George, V. and Dundes, A. (1978) 'The gomer: a figure of American hospital folk speech, *Journal of American Folklore*, 91: 568–81.

Gilman, S. L. (1988) *Disease and Representation: Images of Illness from Madness to AIDS*. Ithaca, NY: Cornell University Press.

Glaser, B. and Strauss, A. L. (1964) 'Awareness contexts and social interaction', *American Sociological Review*, 29: 669–79.

Good, B. J. (1994) *Medicine, Rationality, and Experience: An Anthropological Perspective*. Cambridge: Cambridge University Press.

Gubrium, J. F. (1986) *Old Timers and Alzheimer's: The Descriptive Organisation of Senility*. Greenwich, Conn.: JAI Press.

Hahn, R. A. (1985) 'Culture-bound syndromes unbound', *Social Science and Medicine*, 21: 165–71.

Hak, T. (1994) 'The interactional form of professional dominance', *Sociology of Health and Illness*, 16: 469–88.

Hall, W. and Morrow, L. (1988) ' "Repetition strain injury": an Australian epidemic of upper limb pain', *Social Science and Medicine*, 27: 645–9.

Hargreaves, A. (1981) 'Contrastive rhetoric and extremist talk: teachers, hegemony and the educationist context', in L. Barton and S. Walker (eds), *Schools, Teachers and Teaching*. Lewes: Falmer.

Helman, C. (1985) 'Disease and pseudo-disease: a case history of pseudo-angina', in R. A. Hahn and A. D. Gaines (eds), *Physician of Western Medicine: Anthropological Approaches to Theory and Practice*. Dordrecht: Reidel. pp. 293–331.

Helman, C. G. (1987) 'Heart disease and the cultural construction of time: the type A behaviour pattern as a Western culture-bound syndrome', *Social Science and Medicine*, 25: 969–79.

Hopkins, A. (1989) 'The social construction of Repetition Strain Injury', *Australia and New Zealand Journal of Sociology*, 25: 239–59.

Hunt, L. M. (1985) 'Relativism in the diagnosis of hypoglycemia', *Social Science and Medicine*, 20: 1289–94.

Hunter, K. M. (1991) *Doctors' Stories: The Narrative Structure of Medical Knowledge*. Princeton, NJ: Princeton University Press.

Jamous, H. and Peloille, B. (1970) 'Professions or self-perpetuating systems? Changes in the French university-hospital system', in J. A. Jackson (ed.), *Professions and Professionalization*. Cambridge: Cambridge University Press.

Jeffery, R. (1979) 'Normal rubbish: deviant patients in casualty departments', *Sociology of Health and Illness*, 1: 90–107.

Johnson, T. J. (1972) *Professions and Power*. London: Macmillan.

Kahn, J. Y. (1983) *Modes of Medical Instruction: A Semiotic Comparison of Textbooks of Medicine and Popular Home Medical Books*. Berlin: Mouton.

Karp, I. (1985) 'Deconstructing culture-bound syndromes', *Social Science and Medicine*, 21: 221–8.

Katz, P. (1985) 'How surgeons make decisions', in R. A. Hahn, and A. D. Gaines (eds), *Physicians of Western Medicine: Anthropological Approaches to Theory and Practice*. Dordrecht: Reidel. pp. 155–75.

King, D. (1987) 'Social construction and medical knowledge: the case of transexualism', *Sociology of Health and Illness*, 9: 351–77.

Kleinman, A. (1980) *Patients and Healers in the Context of Culture*. Berkeley: University of California Press.

Kleinman, A. (1988) *The Illness Narratives: Suffering, Healing and the Human Condition*. New York: Basic Books.

Knafl, K. and Burkett, G. (1975) 'Professional socialization in a surgical specialty: acquiring medical judgement', *Social Science and Medicine*, 9: 397–404.

Knorr-Cetina, K. D. (1983) 'The ethnographic study of scientific work: towards a constructivist interpretation of science', in K. D. Knorr-Cetina and M. Mulkay (eds), *Science Observed*. London: Sage.

Kuipers, J. C. (1989) ' "Medical discourse" in anthropological context: views of language and power', *Medical Anthropology Quarterly*, 3: 99–123.

Labov, W. (1972) 'The transformation of experience in narrative syntax', in W. Labov, *Language in the Inner City*. Philadelphia: University of Pennsylvania Press. pp. 352–96.

Labov, W. and Waletsky, J. (1967) 'Narrative analysis: oral versions of personal experience', in J. Helm (ed.), *Essays on the Verbal and Visual Arts*. Seattle: American Ethnological Society. pp. 12–44.

Lakoff, G. (1972) 'Hedges: a study in meaning criteria and the logic of fuzzy concepts', in P. Peranteau, J. Levi and G. Phares (eds), *Papers from the Eighth Regional Meeting*. Chicago Linguistics Society.

Latour, B. and Woolgar, S. (1986) *Laboratory Life: The Social Construction of Scientific Facts*, 2nd edn. Princeton, NJ: Princeton University Press.

Lave, J. (1988) *Cognition in Practice: Mind, Mathematics and Culture in Everyday Life*. Cambridge: Cambridge University Press.

Lave, J. and Wenger, E. (1991) *Situated Learning: Legitimate Peripheral Participation*. Cambridge: Cambridge University Press.

Law, J. and Lynch, M. (1990) 'Lists, field guides, and the descriptive organization of seeing: birdwatching as an exemplary observational activity', in M. Lynch and S. Woolgar (eds), *Representation in Scientific Practice*. Cambridge, Mass.: MIT Press. pp. 267–99.

Lehrer, A. (1983) *Wine and Conversation*. Bloomington: Indiana University Press.

Light, D. (1979) 'Uncertainty and control in professional training', *Journal of Health and Social Behavior*, 20: 310–22.

Light, D. (1980) *Becoming Psychiatrists*, New York: Proctor.

Lindenbaum, S. and Lock, M. (eds) (1993) *Knowledge, Power and Practice: The Anthropology of Medicine and Everyday Life*. Berkeley: University of California Press.

Lipton, J. P. and Hershaft, A. M. (1985) 'On the widespread acceptance of dubious medical findings', *Journal of Health and Social Behaviour*, 26: 336–51.

Lock, M. (1985) 'Models and practice in medicine: menopause as syndrome or life transition?' in R. A. Hahn and A. D. Gaines (eds), *Physicians of Western Medicine: Anthropological Approaches to Theory and Practice*. Dordrecht: Kluwer, pp. 115–39.

Lock, M. and Gordon, D. (eds) (1988) *Biomedicine Examined*. Dordrecht: Kluwer.

Low, S. M. (1985) 'Culturally interpreted symptoms or culture-bound syndromes: a cross-cultural review of nerves', *Social Science and Medicine*, 21: 187–96.

Lowy, L. (1988) 'Ludwik Fleck on the social construction of medical knowledge', *Sociology of Health and Illness*, 10: 133–55.

Lupton, D. (1994) *Medicine as Culture: Illness, Disease and the Body in Western Societies*. London: Sage.

Lynch, M. (1985a) 'Discipline and the material form of images: an analysis of scientific visibility', *Social Studies of Science*, 15: 37–66.

Lynch, M. (1985b) *Art and Artifact in Laboratory Science*. London: Routledge and Kegan Paul.

Lynch, M. (1990) 'The externalized retina: selection and mathematization in the visual documentation of objects in the life sciences', in M. Lynch and S. Woolgar (eds), *Representation in Scientific Practice*. Cambridge, Mass.: MIT Press. pp. 153–86.

Lynch, M. and Woolgar, S. (eds) (1990) *Representation in Scientific Practice*. Cambridge, Mass.: MIT Press.

Macintyre, S. (1978) 'Some notes on record taking and making in an antenatal clinic', *Sociological Review*, 26: 595–611.

McLean, A. (1990) 'Contradictions in the social production of clinical knowledge: the case of schizophrenia', *Social Science and Medicine*, 30: 969–85.

Mattingly, C. (1991) 'The narrative nature of clinical reasoning', *Journal of American Occupational Therapy*, 45: 988–1005.

Mehan, H. (1979) *Learning Lessons: Social Organization in the Classroom*. Cambridge, Mass.: Harvard University Press.

Merleau-Ponty, M. (1962) *Phenomenology of Perception*. London: Routledge and Kegan Paul.

Millman, M. (1976) *The Unkindest Cut: Life in the Backrooms of Medicine*. New York: William Morrow.

Mishler, E. (1984) *The Discourse of Medicine: Dialectics of Medical Interviews*. Norwood, NJ: Ablex.

Mizrahi, T. (1984) 'Coping with patients: subcultural adjustments to the conditions of work among internists-in-training', *Social Problems*, 32: 156–65.

Nettleton, S. (1992) *Power, Pain and Dentistry*. Buckingham: Open University Press.

Nicolson, M. and McLaughlin, C. (1987) 'Social constructionism and medical sociology: a reply to M. R. Bury', *Sociology of Health and Illness*, 9: 107–26.

Nicolson, M. and McLaughlin, C. (1988) 'Social constructionism and medical sociology: a study of the vascular theory of multiple sclerosis', *Sociology of Health and Illness*, 10: 234–61.

Pasveer, B. (1989) 'Knowledge of shadows: the introduction of X-ray images in medicine', *Sociology of Health and Illness*, 11: 360–81.

Pettinari, C. J. (1988) *Task, Talk and Text in the Operating Room: A Study in Medical Discourse*. Norwood, NJ: Ablex.

Pithouse, A. and Atkinson, P. (1988) 'Telling the case', in N. Coupland (ed.), *English Discourse Styles*. London: Croom Helm. pp. 183–200.

Preston, D. R. (1982) 'Ritin fowlklower daun 'rong: folklorists' failures in phonology', *Journal of American Folklore*, 95: 304–26.

Preston, D. R. (1985) 'The Li'l Abner syndrome: written representations of speech', *American Speech*, 60: 326–36.

Prince, R. (1985) 'The concept of culture-bound syndromes: anorexia nervosa and brain-fag', *Social Science and Medicine*, 21: 197–203.

Prince, E. F., Frader, J. and Bosk, C. (1982) 'On hedging in physician–physician discourse', in R. J. Di Pietro (ed.), *Linguistics and the Professions*. Norwood, NJ: Ablex.

Raffel, S. (1979) *Matters of Fact: A Sociological Inquiry*. London: Routledge and Kegan Paul.

Rees, C. (1981) 'Records and hospital routine', in P. Atkinson and C. Heath (eds), *Medical Work: Realities and Routines*. Farnborough: Gower.

Reiser, S. J. (1978) *Medicine and the Reign of Technology*. Cambridge: Cambridge University Press.

Reynolds, J. and Swartz, L. (1993) 'Professional construction of a "lay" illness: "nerves" in a rural "coloured" community in South Africa', *Social Science and Medicine*, 36: 657–63.

Richardson, L. (1990) *Writing Strategies: Reaching Diverse Audiences*. Newbury Park, Calif.: Sage.

Riessman, C. K. (1990) 'Strategic uses of narrative in the presentation of self and illness: a research note', *Social Science and Medicine*, 30: 1195–1200.

Robinson, I. (1990) 'Personal narratives, social careers and medical course: analysing life trajectories in autobiographies of people with multiple sclerosis', *Social Science and Medicine*, 30: 1173–86.

Rodin, M. (1992) 'The social construction of premenstrual syndrome', *Social Science and Medicine*, 35: 49–56.

Roth, J. (1974) 'Professionalism: the sociologist's decoy', *Sociology of Work and Occupations*, 1: 6–23.

Ruben, A. J., O'Neill, C. W. and Ardon, R. C. (1984) *Susto: A Folk Illness*. Berkeley: University of California Press.

Sacks, H. (1992) *Lectures on Conversation, Volume 2* (ed. G. Jefferson). Oxford: Blackwell.

Schon, D. A. (1983) *The Reflective Practitioner: How Professionals Think in Action*. New York: Basic Books.

Schutz, A. (1964) *Collected Papers, Vol. 2*. The Hague, Nijhoff.

Schutz, A. (1967) *The Phenomenology of the Social World*. Evanston, Ill.: Northwestern University Press.

Schutz, A. (1970) *Reflections on the Problem of Relevance* (ed. R. M. Zaner). New Haven, Conn.: Yale University Press.

Schutz, A. and Luckmann, T. (1974) *The Structures of the Life-World*. London: Heinemann.

Scully, D. (1980) *Men Who Control Women's Health: The Miseducation of Obstetrician-Gynecologists*. Boston, Mass.: Houghton Mifflin.

Shuval, J. T. (1980) *Entering Medicine: The Dynamics of Transition*. Oxford: Pergamon.

Silverman, D. (1987) *Communication and Medical Practice: Social Relations in the Clinic*. London: Sage.

Silverman, D. and Torode, B. (1980) *The Material Word*. London: Routledge and Kegan Paul.

Slomka, J. (1992) 'The negotiation of death: clinical decision making at the end of life', *Social Science and Medicine*, 35: 251–9.

Stafford, B. M. (1991) *Body Criticism: Imaging the Unseen in Enlightenment Art and Medicine*. Cambridge, Mass.: MIT Press.

Stefan, M. D. and McManus, I. C. (1989) 'The concept of disease: its evolution in medical students', *Social Science and Medicine*, 29: 791–2.

Strauss, A., Fagerhaugh, S., Suczek, B. and Wicner, C. (1985) *Social Organization of Medical Work*. Chicago: University of Chicago Press.

Strong, P. M. (1984) 'The academic encirclement of medicine?', *Sociology of Health and Illness*, 6: 339–58.

Tannen, D. (1984) *Conversational Style: Analyzing Talk Among Friends*. Norwood, NJ: Ablex.

Tannen, D. (1985) 'Relative focus on involvement in oral and written discourse', in D. R. Olson, N. Torrance and A. Hildyard (eds), *Literacy, Language and Learning: The Nature and Consequences of Reading and Writing*. Cambridge: Cambridge University Press.

ten Have, P. (1989) 'The consultation as a genre' in B. Torode (ed.), *Text and Talk as Social Practice*. Dordrecht: Floris Publications. pp. 115–35.

Torode, B. (1984) *The Extra-Ordinary in Ordinary Language*. Konteksten No. 5. Rotterdam: Instituut Preventieve en Sociale Psychiatrie, Erasmus University.

Turner, B. S. (1984) *The Body and Society*. Oxford: Basil Blackwell.

Turner, B. S. (1987) *Medical Power and Social Knowledge*. London: Sage.

Turner, B. S. (1992) *Regulating Bodies: Essays in Medical Sociology*. London: Routledge.

Waitzkin, H. (1989) 'A critical theory of medical discourse: ideology, social control, and the processing of social context in medical encounters', *Journal of Health and Social Behaviour*, 30: 220–39.

Waitzkin, H. (1991) *The Politics of Medical Encounters: How Patients and Doctors Deal with Social Problems*. New Haven, Conn.: Yale University Press.

Waitzkin, H. and Stoeckle, J. (1978) 'Information control and the micropolitics of health care: summary of an ongoing research project', *Social Science and Medicine*, 10: 263–76.

Weiss, M. (1993) 'Bedside manners: paradoxes of physician behaviour in grand rounds', *Culture, Medicine and Psychiatry*, 17: 235–53.

West, C. (1984) *Routine Complications*. Bloomington: Indiana University Press.

Williams, G. (1984) 'The genesis of chronic illness: narrative reconstruction', *Sociology of Health and Illness*, 6: 175–200.

Woolhandler, S. and Himmelstein, D. V. (1989) 'Ideology in medical science: class in the clinic', *Social Science and Medicine*, 28: 1205–9.

Wright, P. and Treacher, A. (eds) (1982) *The Problem of Medical Knowledge: Examining the Social Construction of Medicine*. Edinburgh: Edinburgh University Press.

Young, M. F. D. (ed.) (1971) *Knowledge and Control*. London: Collier-Macmillan.

Yoxen, E. (1982) 'Constructing genetic diseases', in P. Wright and A. Treacher (eds), *The Problem of Medical Knowledge: Examining the Social Construction of Medicine*. Edinburgh: Edinburgh University Press. pp. 144–61.

Yoxen, E. (1990) 'Seeing with sound: a study of the development of medical images', in W. E. Bijker, T. P. Hughes and T. Pinch (eds), *The Social Construction of Technological Systems*. Cambridge, Mass.: MIT Press. pp. 281–303.

Zerubavel, E. (1979) *Patterns of Time in Hospital Life: A Sociological Perspective*. Chicago: University of Chicago Press.

Index